THE
MANDE BLACKSMITHS

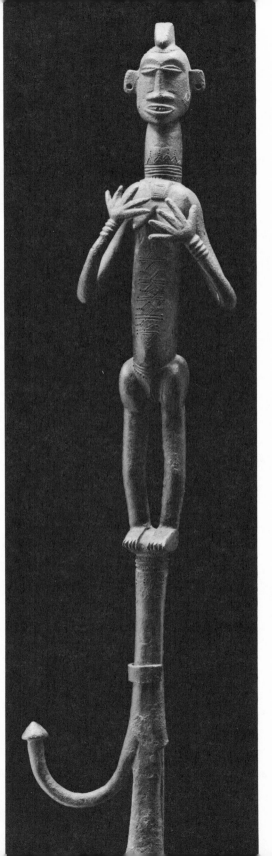

Traditional Arts of Africa

Editors
Paula Ben-Amos
Roy Sieber
Robert Farris Thompson

Bamana forged iron figure and staff (h. 20 1/4 in.). Collection of Paul and Ruth Tishman. Photograph by Jerry L. Thompson, courtesy of the Metropolitan Museum of Art.

THE
MANDE BLACKSMITHS

Knowledge, Power, and Art
in West Africa

PATRICK R. McNAUGHTON

INDIANA
UNIVERSITY
PRESS
Bloomington and Indianapolis

First Midland Book Edition 1993

This book was brought to publication with the assistance of a grant from the Andrew W. Mellon Foundation.

Manufactured in the United States of America

Library of Congress Cataloging-in-Publication Data

McNaughton, Patrick R.
The Mande blacksmiths.

(Traditional arts of Africa)
Bibliography: p.
Includes index.
1. Mandingo (African people)   2. Blacksmiths—Mali.
3. Sculpture, Mandingo (African people)   4. Witchcraft—
Mali.   I. Title.   II. Series.
DT551.45.M36M38   1988   306'.089963   86-46347

ISBN 0-253-33683-X

ISBN 0-253-20798-3

2   3   4   5   6   97   96   95   94   93

Plates I–VIII, in color in the original clothbound edition, are reproduced here in black and white.

For Jesse McNaughton

CONTENTS

Preface   xiii

Note on Orthography   xxii

Acknowledgments   xxiii

I.   BLACKSMITHS IN MANDE SOCIETY   1

   The Mande Social System   1

   The *Nyamakala* Special Professionals   5

   Nyamakala and the Smiths' Ambiguous Status   7

II.   THE MANDE SMITHS AS CRAFTSMEN   22

   Techniques   23

   Products   32

   Articulation   37

III.   SMITHS AND THE SHAPE OF CIVILIZED SPACE   40

   The Principles of Medicine and Sorcery   42

   A Hierarchy of Practitioners   46

   Rainmaking   50

   Divination   51

   Doctoring   56

   Amulets and Secret Devices   58

   Social Instrumentality   64

   Circumcision   66

   The Relative Roles of Blacksmiths and Hunters   71

IV. THE BLACKSMITHS' SCULPTURE   101

The Character of Sculpture and the Other
   Roles of Smiths   102

The Smiths' Iron Art   111
   Tamaw: Spear Blades   112
   Fitinew: Iron Lamps   114
   Nègèmusow and *Nègèsotigiw:* Iron Women and
      Iron Horse Masters   120
   Kòmòkunw: The Power Masks of the Mande Smiths   129

V. THE MANDE SMITHS AS MEN OF MEANS   146

The Problem of Explanations   146

The Unity of Enterprise   149

The Resolution of Movement   152

The Contradiction of Position   156

The Responsibility of Artists   161

Notes   201
Bibliography   217
Index   237

Plates, Maps, and Illustrations

All photographs are by the author unless otherwise indicated. Maps by John Hollingsworth. Drawings by Sandra Clothier.

THESE PLATES FOLLOW PAGE XXIV

   I. Two new door locks.
  II. Senior smith and apprentices at their forge.
 III. Hunters' association performance.
 IV. Door lock and door.
  V. Traditional iron lamp.
 VI. Traditional iron lamp.
 VII. Iron staff with a figure of a woman.
VIII. Masked member of a youth association branch.

MAPS

Map 1. Center of the Mande diaspora   xviii
Map 2. The Mande diaspora   xx

ILLUSTRATIONS

Sedu Traore working at his forge.   xii
Numbers 1 to 41 follow page 72.
Numbers 42 to 77 follow page 164.

1. Blacksmith's forge.
2. Blacksmith's forge.
3. Abandoned bellows.
4. Two smith's apprentices.
5. Sedu Traore carving knife handles.
6. Sedu Traore carving a stool.
7. Sedu Traore carving the end of a knife handle.
8. Sedu Traore removing adze marks from a knife handle.

9. Four adzes in the rafters of Sedu Traore's forge.
10. Sedu Traore making the hafting hole in a hoe handle.
11. Detail of a pestle.
12. Some of Sedu Traore's tools.
13. Sedu Traore forming the haft of a knife blade.
14. Cross-section of an iron mine.
15. Variations of shaft-type iron smelting furnaces.
16. Variations of dome-type smelting furnaces.
17. Hoe and blades.
18. Variations of hoes and blades.
19. Calabash for carrying seeds.
20. Assortment of cutting tools.
21. Hoe-shaped implement for carrying earth.
22. Women grinding millet.
23. Carved wooden door lock.
24. Wooden door and door lock.
25. Water trough for cattle.
26. Indoor granaries.
27. Figural heddle pulley. Photo: Jeffrey A. Wolin.
28. Gun made by Cekòrò Traore.
29. Cekòrò Traore at work.
30. Detail of the gun depicted in Ill. 29.
31. Knife with janus head. Photo: Jeffrey A. Wolin.
32. House door.
33. Bird dance masquerade.
34. Cowry shell divination.
35. Divination by stone throwing.
36. Sand used for divination in Sedu Traore's forge.
37. Sand divination.
38. Vegetable materials used for herbal medicines.
39. Antitheft amulet in Sedu Traore's forge.
40. *Boli* shaped like a person. Photo: Henry 1910.
41. Assortment of amulets. Photo: Jeffrey A. Wolin.
42. Carved "little animal head." Photo: Jeffrey A. Wolin.
43. Carved *kore* mask. Photo: Jeffrey A. Wolin.
44. Carved *kore* mask. Photo: Henry 1910.
45. Carved *kònò* mask. Photo: Henry 1910.
46. Carved headdress for bird masquerade.
47. Sidi Ballo performing his bird masquerade.
48. Forged antelope headdress. Photo: Jeffrey A. Wolin.
49. Carved twin figure. Photo: Henry 1910.
50. Carved mother and child. Photo: The Metropolitan Museum of Art.
51. Small forged figure. Photo: Jeffrey A. Wolin.
52. Forged figure with horns, animal hair, and hide. Photo: Jeffrey A. Wolin.
53. Forged portrait of a wilderness spirit. Photo: Jeffrey A. Wolin.

54. Spear blade variations.
55. Mold for making iron lamp cups.
56. Simple one-cup iron lamp.
57. Single-cup lamp with an elaborately forged shaft. Photo: Jeffrey A. Wolin.
58. Two simple lamps.
59. Beautifully forged lamp. Photo: Koninklijk Museum.
60. Forged lamp with feet. Photo: Jeffrey A. Wolin.
61. Symbols in cloth and writing.
62. Iron staff. Photo: Koninklijk Museum.
63. Figural portion of an iron staff. Photo: Steve Sprague.
64. Forged figural staff. Photo: Jerry L. Thompson.
65. Forged figural staff.
66. Forged equestrian figure and staff. Photo: The Metropolitan Museum of Art.
67. Forged equestrian figure and staff. Photo: Service Photographique des Musées Nationaux.
68. Equestrian figure from a forged staff. Photo: Jeffrey A. Wolin.
69. *Kònò* mask and *boli*. Photo: Henry 1910.
70. Carved horn used in *kòmò* and *jo* associations. Photo: Jeffrey A. Wolin.
71. Forged horn used by *kòmò* association. Photo: Jeffrey A. Wolin.
72. *Kòmò* mask. Photo: Afrika Museum.
73. *Kòmò* mask. Photo: Michael Cavanagh & Kevin Montague.
74. *Kòmò* whisk. Photo: Ken Strothman & Harvey Osterhoudt.
75. *Kòmò* whisk. Photo: Ken Strothman & Harvey Osterhoudt.
76. *Kòmò* mask. Photo: Lowie Museum.
77. Two youth association members dancing at a bird masquerade performance.

Sedu Traore working at his forge, 1973.

Preface

Blacksmiths in sub-Saharan Africa occupy confusing social spaces, as if they lived in two conflicting dimensions. They are at once glorified and shunned, feared and despised, afforded special privileges and bounded by special interdictions. To western observers, the status of smiths in African societies seems enigmatic, and most authors, from the earliest colonial officers and missionaries to contemporary scholars, have felt hard pressed to make sense of it. A statement of the dilemma is provided by anthropologist Laura Makarius:

> The status of the blacksmith in tribal societies poses one of the most puzzling problems of anthropology. By a strange paradox, this noted craftsman, whose bold and meritorious services are indispensable to his community, has been relegated to a position outside the place of society, almost as an "untouchable." Regarded as the possessor of great magical powers, held at the same time in veneration and contempt, entrusted with duties unrelated to his craft or to his inferior social status, that make of him performer of circumcision rites, healer, exorcist, peace-maker, arbiter, counselor, or head of a cult, his figure in what may be called the "blacksmith complex," presents a mass of contradictions.[1]

In the vast savanna lands of the Western Sudan among the large group of societies that speak Mande languages, there is a third dimension to this problem: here, the Mande blacksmiths are also important artists, making most of their culture's wood and iron sculpture. This art, along with the other things they do, gives smiths important roles in everyone else's professional, social, and spiritual lives, thereby putting them in a surprisingly prominent position, given their enigmatic status.

How can artists fill so many other roles, and how do these other roles influence their art? This book seeks a preliminary answer to these questions. Exploring the principal roles of the Mande smiths, it shows that their work as artists is enhanced, in a sense even made possible, by their activities as technicians, healers, sorcerers, and mediators. At the same time it demonstrates that all the work they do is aimed at shaping the environments and the individuals around them, while their social status both enhances their work and is the result of it.

Officers and missionaries of the colonial era were the first to write at length about Mande culture. Early in this century, Father Joseph Henry described the sculpture types. Over the next few decades, Maurice Delafosse, Louis Tauxier, Charles Monteil, and Henri Labouret provided useful materials on the culture. Around mid-century the French anthropologists Marcel Griaule, Germaine Dieterlen, Salonge de Ganay, Viviana Pâques, and Zacharie Ligers examined various aspects of the culture and cosmology, while Carl Kjersmeier and F. H. Lem assembled fine collections of sculpture. More recently, Mary Jo Arnoldi, Charles Bird, Sarah Brett-Smith, James T. Brink, George E. Brooks, Gerald Anthony Cashion, Kate Ezra, Barbara E. Frank, Bernhard Gardi, Kathryn L. Green, Pascal James Imperato, John William Johnson, Martha B. Kendall, Peter Weil, and Dominique Zahan have made valuable contributions to the literature. Since the early decades of this century, west African scholars, including Youssouf Cissé, Bokar N'Diaye, Massa Makan Diabaté, Mamby Sidibé, and Moussa Travélé, have also published materials that greatly enrich our understanding of Mande culture. Still, the corpus of Mande sculpture is large, and its contexts are complex. It will take many more scholars and many more studies before we may claim a systematic understanding of the culture.

I went to the Republic of Mali as a Ford Foreign Area Research Fellow in 1972–1973 and returned for the summer of 1978, with hopes of learning about traditional blacksmiths. I knew what the literature told us: that the Mande smiths were also sculptors and that they possessed much notoriety as sorcerers. I had also read that they were casted and in some measure looked down upon. In actual fact, I knew little about these artists and their roles in society, because only a small percentage of the scholarly literature addressed them directly. By extension, then, I realized that I also knew little about the motivations and intentions of their art.

The majority of my time that first year was spent in small towns between Bamako and Bougouni, just east of the Niger River (Map 1). I also made some brief excursions: north to the area around the town of Banamba; east to the areas around Ségou, Markala, and San; south through Sikasso; and west on the roads to Sibi and Kita. In 1978 I visited San, but spent most of my time in the Mande Plateau near Bamako.

In the early months I traveled from one town to another, asking youngsters and elders where I might find blacksmiths. In every town I was introduced to at least one and sometimes several. I watched them work and asked them questions. I saw many of them on a regular basis, and some, including Dramane Dunbiya, Magan Fane, and Sedu Traore, I visited quite often. I also saw a good deal of Seydou Camara. He was born a smith and maintained a forge in his hometown in the Wasoulou region of southern Mali, but he had found that he loved music and so gave up smithing to become one of Mali's most renowned hunters' bards. He was extremely knowledgeable about the institution of smithing, and he provided me with a great deal of information. His nephew, Bourama Soumaoro, was also very knowledgeable, and, though I saw less of him, he too helped me greatly.

Ultimately, I found myself in a casual way apprenticed to the blacksmith Sedu Traore, and, while maintaining my contacts with the others, I worked with Sedu constantly. Sedu was from the southernmost region of the Bèlèdougou area north of Bamako. His father, in later life, had built a small blacksmiths' hamlet at the top of the Mande Plateau, which afforded a magnificent view of the great plains astride the Niger River. But I met Sedu in a town south of Bamako, where we spent most of our time together. I began to work intensely with him just before he became busy in the planting season with tool making and repairing, and, since his sons were all grown up and on their own, he let me spend many hours developing my technique on the bellows. Occasionally, Sedu had me try my hand at wood carving. More occasionally, I sat behind his anvil with a hammer in my hand, trying to make red-hot iron move the way Sedu did. The results of these enterprises were dismal but instructive; they made clear the depth of skill and acumen good sculpting requires of its practitioners.

Clients often came to Sedu, to have old tools repaired or new tools made. But they also came with requests for soothsaying, amulet-making, medical diagnoses and treatment, and general advice on all kinds of problems. I watched and listened and learned a great deal. When we were alone, working wood or iron, we talked for hours about every aspect of blacksmithing, from sculpting to sorcery. Sedu explained the importance of knowledge to every aspect of his trade. He related to me the experiences of his youth and what they had meant to his development as a smith. He discussed the usefulness of travel for the acquisition of wisdom, the importance of attaining genuine expertise, and the equal importance of maintaining a good name. He often discussed the rudiments of herbal and occult lore and the ethics that smiths should apply in their manipulation. He explained the tensions that develop regularly in communities as individuals negotiate their lives, families negotiate their communty positions, and communities address an array of problems from the socialization of their youth to the inhibition of antisocial forces in the human and spiritual environments. He made the role of smiths in all these problems quite clear to me, and other smiths I talked to corroborated his account.

Sedu was generally fond of company, and so we visited a lot and were visited in turn. Dramane Dunbiya, the senior smith in Sedu's town, was a frequent companion with a wealth of information. So were several other community smiths with whom Sedu associated. A commonality of interests binds smiths together, and they tend to maintain extensive networks of friendship and communication. Therefore, Sedu and I traveled often and rather widely. I had a car, and we took full advantage of it to visit his fellow smiths in distant towns as well as his clients, his hunting companions, and other friends. He knew people everywhere, and I was pleased to be his chauffeur, because in these gregarious contexts I learned a great deal about smiths, their clients, and their cosmos.

When my informal apprenticeship began, Sedu marked me with a small white bead he hung around my neck. He passed a piece of string through it, which he knotted as he chanted. The bead was a special blacksmiths' device, used to announce membership in the profession and to protect the wearer from the unpleasant occult activities of others. For me it became a passport and an agent of transformation. Everywhere I went, both with and without Sedu Traore, people knew its meaning and accepted me on different terms from those they had applied before. Just once I used the bead avariciously. Back in Bamako at the main cloth market I had long been negotiating with a recalcitrant vendor over the price of a fine piece of cloth. He wanted to charge me the tourist price and I would not pay it. Finally one day I noticed a middle-aged woman watching us from an adjacent table, and I concluded that she was my vendor's boss. I marched straight over to her and, pointing to my bead, indicated that I was not a tourist. The fine piece of cloth instantly became mine.

The bead initiated a fundamental change in what people perceived me to be. Mande smithing is steeped in beliefs about the manipulation of nature's most powerful forces. The act of working iron and the myriad other acts that blacksmiths undertake embed them in a dangerous atmosphere of energies that we would define as occult or supernatural. My bead became the first link in a chain of protection from these forces. Gradually, Sedu gave me more amulets and some of his own tools; through these devices, Sedu and his colleagues believed, I gradually acquired the energies needed by someone who expected to spend much time in the intimate company of blacksmiths and their forges. I was not born a smith. But they made me resemble one closely enough to do my work.

The dimension of power that blacksmiths inhabit is matched by an equally important dimension of secrecy. The profession floats on a sea of secret expertise that outsiders have no right to learn about. My developing status as an informal apprentice began to make up in large measure for my foreign nature. Yet, I made plain from the start that I was doing research, with the goal of writing up whatever they would permit me to share with Westerners wanting to learn about Mande smiths. It was made equally plain to me that I would learn only what I was worthy of and only what they believed would do no harm. In fact, I learned what any beginning Mande apprentice might learn: the Mande principles of secrecy but not the secrets. Sedu, the other smiths of his community, and the elders who governed it were extremely careful about what I could be told, but they told enough for me to build a sound picture of their world.

I also made a point of interviewing Mande citizens who were not blacksmiths, both before and after I wore the bead that Sedu gave me. As a result, I acquired an idea of how the general Mande populace perceives the smiths. Nevertheless, my perceptions, as presented in this book, are aligned more closely with those of the blacksmiths than with those of the general population.

Most of my research assistants and colleagues were not smiths, and I enjoyed many hours of talk with them. They were quite different from one another, and quite different from the smiths. Chiekna Sangare was a teacher in Mali's public school system. Possessed of an open mind and a great curiosity, he had nevertheless known very little about blacksmiths until he began spending time in their forges with me. Abdulaye Sylla worked with the Ministry of Education as a curator at the National Museum in Bamako. He was quite knowledgeable about art and took a great interest in efforts to preserve and explain it. Dugutigi Traore was a farmer who came to Bamako with the hope of discovering another line of work. I met him through my friend Adbulaye Sissoko and decided it might be helpful to work with him for a while and watch his responses to smiths. Sissoko was himself born a smith, but he made a living welding and repairing all types of vehicles. He also owned several trucks that carried trade goods to Mauritania and elsewhere. He was an amateur inventor, and at one point he built and ran a restaurant-nightclub on the banks of the Niger River. Although I never really worked with him, we spent much time together and he provided me with many insights. Sekuba Camara was also born a smith; he was the son of the hunters' bard Seydou. Rather than practice smithing, however, or taking up the hunter's harp like his father, Sekuba was a student aspiring to teach or to work for the Ministry of Education. Having been raised in the Wasoulou as a smith, he knew a great deal about the many enterprises of smiths. In the summer of 1978, when I returned to Mali for a second visit, I spent much of the time with Sekuba, transcribing, translating, and interpreting blacksmith songs sung by his father.

Finally, there was Kalilou Tera, who was finishing his degree at Mali's Ecole normale supérieure when I encountered him working with Charles Bird at Indiana University in the summer of 1977. We had many discussions that summer and then worked together in Mali during the summer of 1978. I found his depth and clarity of understanding to be invaluable. He was the son of a well-known ascetic Muslim and the grandson of an equally well-known marabout. But he believed in the value of Mande traditional religion and wanted to know as much as possible about Mande beliefs and practices. All his life he had talked with elders. He had acquired as a result a sense of Mande civilization as supple and complex as the culture itself.

The terms *Mande, Manding,* and *Mandingue* have all been used, inconsistently, to identify the civilization that now encompasses the western third of Africa's great northern savanna and large sections of the coastal forests. *Mande* is the term used in George Peter Murdock's classification of African cultures, and it is used generally in linguistic classifications including those by Joseph Greenberg, William Welmers, and Derek Fivaz and Patricia Scott, to identify a branch of the Niger-Congo language family.[2] The spelling of *Mande* also represents most completely the accepted or received pronunciation of the word by the majority of Mande language speakers. Manding and Mandingue are derived from pronunciations used in the western regions of the diaspora, in areas the Mande colonized as they expanded their Mali Empire.[3]

In its narrowest indigenous sense the term *Mande* identifies a geographic homeland. Its boundaries are subject to a broad latitude of interpretations,

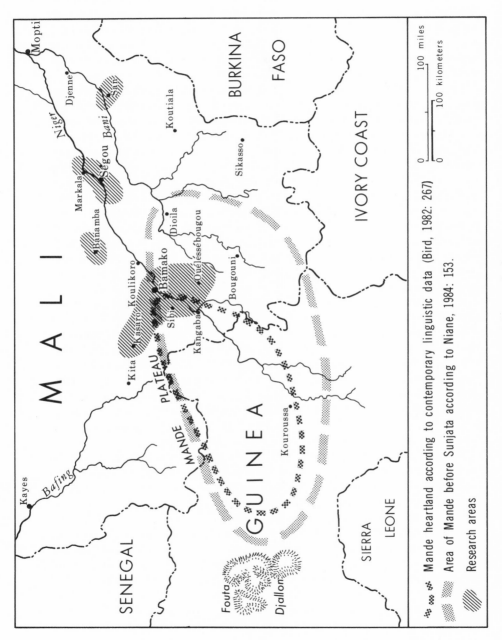

MAP 1. Center of the Mande diaspora.

which vary with regional beliefs and politics. A reasonable generalization describes it as a small area south of Bamako, west of Ouèlèssèbougou, north of Kouroussa, and east of the Bafing River (Map 1). From this core the Mali Empire is said to have coalesced and spread, making it the wellspring of the Mande diaspora. This area is also alleged to be the initial setting for the dramatic events that compose the Mande creation myths collected by Marcel Griaule's group of French anthropologists.[4]

In its broader indigenous sense, *Mande* refers to all the lands now occupied principally by Mande language speakers. From the core these lands extend east into Burkina Faso, west into Senegal and The Gambia, and south into Guinea, Sierra Leone, Liberia, Ivory Coast, and western Ghana (Map 2). They include a number of ethnic groups, with the Bamana (or Bambara), Maninka (or Malinké), and Dyula constituting their linguistic and cultural nucleus. The Maninka built the vast medieval Mali Empire, which endured from the thirteenth to the seventeenth centuries and greatly influenced the course of history in west Africa. The Bamana founded two great states, Ségou and Kaarta, which thrived from the seventeenth to the nineteenth centuries. The Dyula established phenomenal long-distance commerce networks, thereby expanding both the Mande frontier and its complex economy.

Linguistically, culturally, and geographically close to this nucleus are the other savanna groups: the Somono and Bozo, who make their living fishing and plying the Niger and Bani Rivers, and the Wasuluka, a division of the Maninka, who live in southern Mali and northern Guinea. Other savanna groups include the Kagoro, Khasonke, Marka, and Soninke. Then come the southern forest groups, such as the Kuranko, Kono, Vai, Susu, and Yalunka.

I worked in an area where the Bamana and Maninka come together and often overlap, east and west of the Niger River and out on the Mande Plateau. Sedu Traore and his relatives are Bamana, and so in fact were a great many of the smiths who talked to me. Yet many others were Maninka, and I also came to know a few smiths who had moved north from the Wasoulou. This experience reflects the kind of internal melding the Mande frequently display. They value their Mande identity above membership in the specific ethnic groups that compose the Mande at any given time. Clans seem to be the important units, constituting and reconstituting themselves into larger political-ethnic entities, sometimes for some practical reason, sometimes just as a matter of happenstance.

These ramifications of a complex and often dramatic history help explain the tremendous regional variation so typical of Mande peoples. The Bamana who live in the Bèlèdougou region, for example, are quite different from those who live south of the Bani River, or around Ségou or San. The number of Bamana, Dyula, and Maninka dialects alone makes this quite clear.[5] But there are also significant differences in aspects of culture, such as the secret initiation associations[6] and other elements of spiritual and social practice. The degree to which Islam is present from area to area and even from community to community varies immensely, for example, and not just in num-

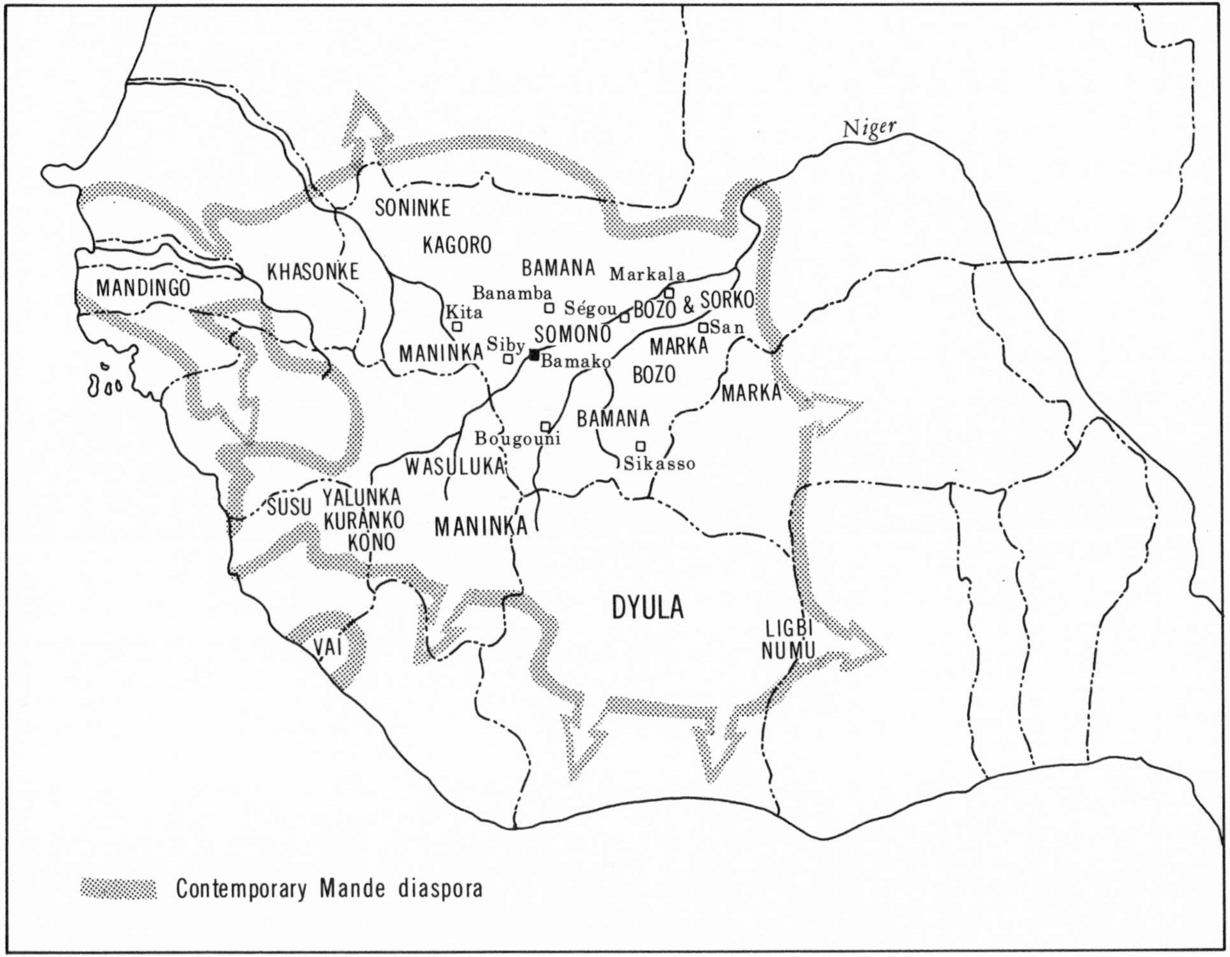

Niger

SONINKE

KAGORO

KHASONKE

MANDINGO

ꝺၒၥ

BAMANA   Markala

Banamba

Kita

MANINKA

Siby

Bamako

SOMONO

Ségou   BOZO & SORKO

□San

MARKA

BOZO

Bougouni

BAMANA

□Sikasso

WASULUKA

MANINKA

SUSU YALUNKA
      KURANKO
      KONO

VAI

MARKA

DYULA

LIGBI
NUMU

MAP 2. The Mande diaspora.

▨▨▨ Contemporary Mande diaspora

bers of followers but also in the ways they worship. Many Mande say they are Muslims, when in actual fact they partake of a complicated array of religious beliefs and practices, some grounded in Islam, others grounded in devotions of strictly indigenous genesis.

The Mande, like people everywhere, have reshaped their culture with each generation, and they have done so with great variation across the whole of their everchanging diaspora. Thus, I must qualify the title of this book by emphasizing that it focuses most immediately on Bamana, Maninka, and Wasuluka smiths in the heart of the diaspora.

The ideas that give meaning and form to blacksmith activities, however, are deeply seated in Mande culture. They include traditional divisions of labor, concepts of sorcery and occult energy, beliefs about the world of spirits, and the characteristics of traditional knowledge. To be sure, there is variation here, too. But there is also a strong underlying unity. For that reason, in a general way my findings apply beyond the geographic region where I did most of my work. The data I acquired on trips outside that region and the materials shared with me by my research assistants corroborate this.

Beyond the Mande, the data presented here may shed some light on the enterprise of smithing in other areas of the continent. Near Lake Victoria in eastern Africa, in northern Nigeria and Niger, and near the ancient trade center of Djenne in Mali, we know that iron-working traditions extend well back in time, to periods many centuries before Christ.[7] In many sub-Saharan cultures blacksmiths have long played complex, prominent, and enigmatic roles. I will be most pleased if this book contributes to an understanding of the art of smithing elsewhere in Africa.

Note on Orthography

I have followed the orthography for Bamana words as set forth in *Lexique Bambara,* by the Ministère de l'Education Nationale, 1968. For songs performed in Maninka I have used the spellings of Kalilou Tera and Sekuba Camara. The names of individual Malian authors or artists that have appeared in print using other orthographies have not been altered. To avoid confusion, place names are spelled as they appear on the maps of L'Institut Géographique National, Paris. Mande forms the plural of nouns by adding the letter "w" to the end. In this text I use singular or plural according to the grammatical context.

Acknowledgments

It is a pleasure to thank the people and the institutions who helped me with this work. First there are the blacksmiths. I thank with deep gratitude Magan Fane, Dramane Dunbiya, Seydou Camara, Kodari Fane, Cekoro Traore, Mamadu Sumaoro, Baba Kumare, Faji Bagayoko, Kalifa Kone, Jema Fane, Gwama Kone, Samba Dunbiya, Kasba Bagayoko, Famusa Kumare, Musa Diabate, Ceba Bagayoko, Fana Bagayoko, Satigi Dafara, Sedu Dunbiya, Gona Konte, Jara Kulibali, Kuteli Dunbiya, Sedu Balo, Magan and Zan Kumare, Ce Fane, Bamanake Fane, Lansina Koulibali, twenty-one Kante smiths from Ferentumu, Fajala Badayoko, Sekuba Kante, and the many other smiths who saw fit to spend their time with me. These men were always kind and informative. I hope this book reflects something of their characters. Most especially I thank Sedu Traore, whose knowledge and expertise, patience and sense of humanity animate these pages as thoroughly as anything I may have contributed.

I also want to thank my Malian research colleagues and friends, Abdulaye Sylla, Dugutigi Traore, Bourama Soumaoro, Mamadou Kante, Adama Timbo, Joe the Mechanic and Mamadu Sangare. My friend Sissoko helped me in many ways that he will never know. Above all, I acknowledge my great debt to Chiekna Sangare, Sekuba Camara, and Kalilou Tera.

At home I have benefited frequently from the good counsel of friends and colleagues: Mary Jo Arnoldi, Sylvia Boone, René Bravmann, James T. Brink, Gerald Cashion, Kate Ezra, Perkins Foss, Barbara E. Frank, Anita Glaze, John Hutchison, Pascal James Imperato, John William Johnson, Martha Kendall, John and Faith Lewis, and Eleanor Saunders. They were all most generous with their ideas and suggestions. Warren d'Azevedo, Ivan Karp, Janet Rabinowitch, Roy Sieber, and Robert Farris Thompson read drafts of the manuscript and gave much time and very sound advice. Finally there is Charles Bird, who knows the Mande world with uncanny subtlety and has shared his knowledge with a degree of generosity one rarely encounters. To Charles I extend my deepest thanks.

Chris Buth Furness and Jane Waldbaum have earned my gratitude for their patient editing. Karen Astulfi, Flow Mayday, Fatemah Salahudin, Monica Verona, and Mary Voell typed various stages of the manuscript. John Hollingsworth made the maps, Sandra Clothier made the drawings, and Andy Lovineski made prints of the Henry photographs. Jeffrey A. Wolin photographed many of the objects. I want to thank them all heartily, along with my Indiana University Press editor, Ken Goodall.

The generosity of the Ford Foreign Area Research Council sent me originally to Africa. Subsequently, the Social Science Research Council awarded me a postdoctoral grant that allowed me to return. Yale University's African Studies Program provided supplementary funds that facilitated my first research trip. The University of Wisconsin-Milwaukee and Indiana University helped further the later work with travel funds and summer research fellowships. Finally, the National Endowment for the Humanities granted me a summer stipend to work on another project, the results of which have found their way into this one.

I extend my heartfelt thanks to the government of the Republic of Mali, and most especially to the Institut des Sciences Humaines, in the Ministère de l'Education Nationale. During my first trip Mamadou Sarr headed the institute. During my second trip Alpha Konare was its director. Both these men and their staffs were exceedingly generous with their time and support. They helped enlarge the sense of hospitality one can feel in Mali and they encouraged my research every step of the way.

Finally, I must extend my greatest thanks to Diane Pelrine. She edited and reedited the work, offered outstanding critique and numerous suggestions, typed much of the final version, and offered her support whenever it was needed.

I.
Two new Bamana door locks made in a small town near Ouelessebougou,
1973.

II.
Senior smith and apprentices working at their streetside forge in the city of
San, 1978.

III.
Several hunters' association branches performing together during the annual celebrations of the founding of the city of San, 1978.

IV.
Bamana door lock and door with carved breasts, about fifty years old, in a small town between Bamako and Bogouni, 1978.

V.
Lamp, topped with forged iron head of a cow, illuminates traditional wrestling matches in a large eastern Bamana town, 1978.

VI.
One of six lamps used to illuminate traditional wrestling matches in a large eastern Bamana town, 1978.

VII.
Bamana iron staff topped with a figure of a woman. Collection of Charles Bird and Martha Kendall.

VIII.
Young member of a youth association branch in a small town on the Mande Plateau, 1978. He is dancing a mask form borrowed from the *ntomo* association.

ONE

BLACKSMITHS
IN MANDE SOCIETY

Blacksmiths occupy a propitious position in Mande social organization. They are grouped with a few other specialized professional clans in a category that acknowledges their unique abilities and sets them apart from the rest of society. Their distinctiveness protects their professional interests, and, in some fascinating ways, it also protects other citizens from the potential the smiths possess of becoming too powerful. This distinctiveness is manifest, however, in a variety of ways within a set of complex social, spiritual, and political spheres, which makes an interpretation of the blacksmiths' social position difficult. Many scholars have found it baffling, and many have misinterpreted it. In this chapter we will examine Mande social organization with the goal of discovering the conceptual spaces from which smiths derive their status and practice their trades.

THE MANDE SOCIAL SYSTEM

Until the advent of colonialism in the nineteenth century, the Mande were divided into three main groups—farmers and "nobles," specialized professionals, and slaves.[1] This tripartite social structure probably developed with the founding of the Mali Empire in the thirteenth century, though groups such as slaves and smiths must have originated earlier.[2] Membership in and interaction among these groups certainly changed frequently as individuals and clans transformed their society politically and economically. And by the early decades of this century, European influences had effected an extensive change by outlawing the institution of slavery.

The Mande are principally agriculturalists, and most of them are full-time subsistence farmers. The Bamana and Maninka ethnic groups call these farmers *hòròn*.[3] Their towns are surrounded by women's garden plots and, beyond them, much larger family fields. During the planting and harvesting seasons these people spend much time in the fields. During other seasons there is time for other activities, and some farmers run part-time businesses to supplement their harvest. One family member, for example, might weave baskets or mats. Another might sell the excess produce from her garden at the local market. Yet another might decide to take up hunting; he would join a hunters' fraternity and spend little time on the farm. Some of these farmers become merchants, following the markets from community to community and leaving the farming chores to other family members. Nevertheless, farming generally remains the family's mainstay.

From these farming clans emerged the clans of traditional leaders or "nobles," including the Keitas, who ruled the Maninka Mali Empire, and the Diarraso, who ruled the Bamana state of Ségou. These groups were established by the dynamic activities of individuals, many during the time of the Mali Empire, from the thirteenth to the seventeenth centuries, and many more during the time of the Ségou and Kaarta states, from the seventeenth to the nineteenth centuries. They maintain their prominence to this day and are the subjects of the extraordinary epic poems that recount Mande history. Often these clans rose to prominence because of allegiances with great warriors and military strategists, who also came from the ranks of the farmers.

The slave group, now extinct, was comprised of slaves of two types: first-generation slaves, *jònw*, and second-generation slaves, who were known as *wolosow*, "born in the house" (*wolo* is the act of birth, *so* is the house). Their tasks varied according to their masters' needs, but in general they functioned much as servants do today.

Many persons became slaves as a result of military conquest. Others became slaves as punishment for major crimes or serious misdemeanors. Still others went into slavery to terminate insolvency. When debts accrued beyond a person's ability to pay, the debtor or another family member might become the dependent, or slave, of the creditor. A creditor could choose to keep such a slave in the creditor's own household and often did so if the slave's family was attempting to raise the amount of the debt to effect the debtor's release. Or the creditor could sell the slave to recoup the loss more quickly. Slaves could often earn their own freedom by creating a feeling of strong camaraderie with their masters or by working diligently. Sometimes slaves were well treated and worked no harder than free society members. But often, especially during times of war and empire building or when slaves became goods in the vast overland trade networks, they were badly treated.

People sometimes became slaves voluntarily, as a means of economic or social advancement. Charles Monteil, a colonial administrator and insightful observer of Mande culture, reported that during the period of the Kaarta and Ségou states, slaves in some communities led lives so comfortable that many free citizens were inspired to enter unbidden into servitude. Towns with large slave populations often had a slave association called *jòn kuru* or *jòn futu* that represented the indentured to their masters. The masters were financially responsible for the slaves' general well being, for their marriages, and for the circumcision and excision of their children. In such environments slaves sometimes rose to positions of considerable authority in the households of their masters, becoming property managers or family business administrators. They could even have slaves of their own.[4]

Blacksmiths belong to the third large population group, the specialized professionals, called *nyamakala*. This group comprises clusters of clans that own the rights to arcane spiritual and technological practices and are therefore able to offer special services to the rest of society.[5] In general they are organized by profession—smiths, bards, leather workers—but they may also be identified by special attributes or aspects of character, and sometimes they seem to be defined more by other citizens' experiences of their special qualities than by the jobs they do. They are considered different and unusual, mysterious and even strange. They consider themselves and are considered by others to belong to separate races, *siw*, who live with the Mande and are indelibly incorporated into Mande life. Thus blacksmiths describe themselves as a separate nation, and they say the same is true of the other members of the *nyamakala* group.

In the minds of most Mande, and certainly in the minds of the blacksmiths, endogamy (with its corollary, inherited membership) is a primary characteristic of the *nyamakala* group. While anyone can leave one of these special professions to become a carpenter, a modern mechanic, a government employee or anything else one likes, only children born to families that belong to these professional clans can take up the trades their parents practice. It is first of all a matter of corporate identity and of monopoly. A tremendous body of technical expertise is associated with each trade, and it must be learned over many years of apprenticeship that traditionally begin before the novice turns ten. That makes it inconvenient for outsiders who might want to enter these professions. Then there is the matter of special attributes. Nearly everyone believes that members of these special clans possess a mysterious spiritual power that underpins occult practices and makes the people possessing it potentially dangerous. These powers go well beyond the practice of the clan's special trade, but they are also considered essential to anyone who takes it up. Often members of these clans go to great lengths to nourish a belief in their power among the rest of the population. Indeed, they generally believe in it themselves. Furthermore, they say they are born with much of this power. It is part of their heritage and one of the things that makes them so different from everyone else. That too creates a profound handicap for any outsider who might want to learn a clan's special trade.

Beliefs such as these affect people's behavior through unwritten prohibitions and sanctions. Nobles and farmers cannot marry members of the special professional clans. The very idea is frightening. Some people even advise against spending too much time with smiths because, for example, proximity to all that power could be dangerous. At the same time smiths should not seek spouses or lovers outside their own blacksmiths' clans. Doing so would sap their strength and spoil their work. In the days when smiths still fired their iron-smelting furnaces, such extra-clan liaisons could cause an iron smelter to die, a victim of his own inherited power changing valences. Of course, all that is what people say; it is part of their culture's ideology. In the real Mande world such liaisons do occur, not frequently perhaps, but often enough. A blacksmith once recited these interdictions to me, then said he had once had a nonsmith lover, a fact he found in retrospect a little bit exciting.[6]

Slaves constituted a revealing exception to the practice of endogamy. If the slave of a blacksmith was considered both worthy and capable, he could be taught every aspect of the profession, though this might happen only after months or even years of working the bellows and carving simple hoe and knife handles. Such a slave could be taught the techniques of forging iron and even of smelting it. Furthermore, he could be aggrandized with the smith's own inherited power through ritual and contact with his master. Thereafter, he could be taught many of the religious practices for which blacksmiths are famous. Most significantly, he could be taught how to circumcise, a ceremony that is a blacksmith's special prerogative and which the Mande consider to be especially sensitive, dangerous, and important. Upon completing his training to the satisfaction of his master and the approval of the community, he could set himself up as an independent blacksmith, no longer a slave and with full professional status.[7]

Before the advent of European-style currency these special clans tendered their works for goods. They might receive cloth, the products of someone's small business such as baskets or mats, or they might receive produce. Smiths sometimes worked for the mere promise of payment, making or repairing a hoe for a farmer who would pay for it out of his next harvest. Such arrangements are still made today, most often in the smaller towns or when clients visit the smiths directly instead of going to market to purchase their equipment.

Some members of these special clans also farm, supplementing their income and providing themselves with a kind of insurance, just as subsistence farmers run sideline businesses. Many blacksmiths say that in the days before colonialism their clans never farmed, and no smiths ever went hungry. If the blacksmiths in a town ran out of grain, their senior member paid a visit to the town chief and before the sun rose again their granaries would be full.

The services these *nyamakala* clans provide are of fundamental importance. The economy is dramatically affected, for example, by what the blacksmiths and the other special clans do. Their roles in the practice of Mande religion cut across the entire spiritual spectrum, and the rest of the population seeks their expertise most frequently. The same could be said for their activities in the realms of politics and social life. Finally, in a culture that incorporates a great deal of its expressive and intellectual vitality in its art, these special clan groups generate a prodigious amount of it. In spite of the fact that these special professionals are considered separate races, their services are so pervasive in Mande society and so embedded in the Mande world view that they literally infuse the culture with much of its character. This is surely a fascinating turn of events for a segment of the population that is so carefully differentiated from everyone else. The *nyamakalaw* warrant a closer look.

THE *NYAMAKALA* SPECIAL PROFESSIONALS

Scholars have disagreed about which clans actually belong to the *nyamakala* category. The French anthropologist Viviana Pâques, for example, includes the professional fishing people called Somono, the hunters (*donson*), and two groups of meat vendors known as the *dyanna* and the *bouguena*,[8] while the Malian scholar Bokar N'Diaye adds the weavers' group called *maboube*.[9] Close examination, however, indicates that these people may be similar in some respects to the *nyamakala* but they are not part of that group. The Somono were originally farming clans who adopted fishing as a full-time profession and then were organized into a kind of navy by the Bamana state of Ségou.[10] Hunters have fraternities called *donson tòn* that offer new members instruction and perform arcane hunting rituals, and hunters are well known for their potent occult power. But they acquire this power instead of inheriting it, and their associations, rather than being restrictive, welcome members even from outside the Mande societies.[11] The *dyanna, bouguena,* and *maboube* are not Mande at all, but rather Fula, an ethnic group with a large population that lives alongside and sometimes in the midst of many Mande communities. They are symbolically related to the Mande *nyamakalaw* because they practice endogamy and can be referred to as separate races.[12]

For the Mande themselves, membership in the special professionals group actually varies by region. The French ethnographer Dominique Zahan includes three special groups as *nyamakalaw:* the *segi, surasegi,* and *kule.* The first two carve wooden household utensils, such as spoons and stirring sticks, but their special occupation is making saddles. The third group consists of male members who carve wooden plates for food, bowls for washing, canoe planks for boat building and, much more rarely, statues and masks,[13] and female members who repair cracked calabashes by sewing them with wicker. The first two groups, however, appear to live only in the more northern areas of the Bamana diaspora, while the last group is well known in the south too, but not as *nyamakala.* In the south the *kule* carvers and calabash repairers[14] are people born into farming clans who sought special training to assume their trades. The men in fact learn carving from blacksmiths, but they never acquire more than a rudimentary expertise. They make simple stools, doors, chests, and beds. They also learn to repair knife and hoe handles. For these southern *kulew*, carving sculpture would be unthinkable.

Sometimes Muslim holy men, called *moriw*, are considered members of this special Mande population. Here, though, there is great variety of opinion among the Mande, which points up a fact we must take care to acknowledge. Many words are used quite flexibly, sometimes out of ignorance or a lack of concern, or even a lack of interest in the work of researchers. Sometimes they are used, appropriately enough, to make points metaphorically by stretching strict definitions. Most Mande would agree if questioned closely that the holy men of Islam are not proper members of the *nyamakala* category. Yet these religious practitioners do many of the things true *nyama-kalaw* do. First of all, they are perceived as being situated right at the heart of a religious system, and various religious practices emanate from them. This is also how the *nyamakalaw* are perceived. Indeed, the two groups share several religious practices, such as soothsaying, amulet making, and ministering spiritually to victims of illness. It is even true that these Muslim practitioners often pass their livelihoods on to their sons. Thus they are referred to on occasion as *nyamakalaw*.

Leather workers, called *garankew*, are always considered *nyamakalaw*, although they are actually not Bamana or Maninka.[15] They are Soninke, northern Mande; that is, they claim Soninke origins and have distinctly Soninke names. The oldest members of this group seem to speak only Soninke, but most speak Bamana or Maninka, and are thoroughly integrated into Mande life. Their leatherworks can be subtly intricate, with lovely engraved patterns and complicated knotting techniques. They make beautiful bags and knife sheaths, but the most sensitive aspect of their work is the fabrication of leather covers for amulets. For this work they must possess occult power. The task is important, because the Mande believe that the amulets lose all their efficacy if they are not properly wrapped in covers made by experts possessed of the appropriate technical and spiritual expertise. Left unwrapped, amulets' powers are drained off or stolen by wilderness spirits.[16] Yet the professional leather workers do not have a monopoly on all the tasks they perform. Some are perfomed by bards and, more occasionally, by blacksmiths.

Bards, called *jeliw*, are the genealogists and epic poets of Mande society. They are at once historians, musicians, and political motivators. They are charged with the keeping of historical traditions and the performing of them in great epics about the leaders and heroes whose business was Mande statecraft. Their performances can last an entire night, and include immense numbers of praise songs, proverbs, axioms, and genealogies. While the great bards pride themselves on knowing history most authoritatively, they are rarely interested in its accurate public presentation. They manipulate the details of history to motivate their audiences. One of their most important tasks is to inspire the Mande citizenry, to fill people with the desire to live up to their potential so that society remains solid and vital. Many of these artists earn wide reputations among the Bamana and Maninka, and during the past few decades some bards have made recordings, toured Europe and America, and acquired worldwide followings.[17]

For the Mande, words are full of special energy, which can be dangerous if misused. Bards are believed to possess great reserves of this same power, and they are trained to manipulate it. Thus their songs become more than inspirational. They are instrumental. The power in them can inhabit an audience and literally drive it to all manner of acts. The speech of bards is also full of the power of sarcasm and has the potential for stinging social commentary. Thus the Mande hold their bards in great awe, mixed with a little fear, while the bards hold quite a bit of social, economic, and political clout. They often were and frequently still are attached to ruling families, and often too they enjoy sizable incomes.

Another *nyamakala* group is related to the bards. Its members are called *finaw* or *funew*, and they are described as praise sayers for the Prophet. They too could be attached to ruling families and are known for their capacity to embarrass. Some act like Muslim holy men. Others perform like bards. Many today have taken up farming and commerce.

Many Mande describe this group as possessing very little social stature. Some say its members are contaminated, to the point that other people will not even share a meal with them. Yet many of the group's members have risen to positions of great influence and prestige, and many are believed to be able to foresee the future, treat illness, and make amulets that enhance the lives of their followers.[18] The question of social status among the Mande is full of anomalies that trouble Western researchers but do not bother the Mande at all.

Finally, there are the blacksmiths, or *numuw*. Women in the blacksmith clans own the rights to make pottery. Men nearly monopolize wood carving and absolutely monopolize iron working. Thus they are the craftspersons par excellence, but they are also the Mande's sculptors. In addition, they too possess enormous quantities of special power, and many are trained to be diviners, amulet-makers, doctors, and priests. Along with bards they are often called upon to serve as social intermediaries, and they frequently give testimony at torts. Like the *funew*, indeed like all members of the *nyama-kala* clans, smiths have been described by researchers as despised, loathed, looked down upon, or considered of little account. Such statements are not exactly false. They are merely so simplistic that they make any real understanding of these clans impossible. We should direct our attention now toward coming to grips with these misapprehensions.

NYAMAKALA AND THE SMITHS' AMBIGUOUS STATUS

In 1939 the French published a compilation of customs and beliefs observed by administrators in the French West African colony. In it Alfred Aubert described the *nyamakalaw* as a wretched, worthless, miscreant population with absolutely no equivalent in Western society, and whose members were indelibly blemished.[19] He was expressing a sentiment held widely by the white population of the colonies. Earlier, the colonial administrator Charles Monteil, writing about the Mande Khasonke, described the special professionals as free but disreputable, a population held in low esteem.[20] Later, in 1970, Bokar N'Diaye, a Malian scholar, published a common etymology for the term *nyamakala,* noting that *kala* means stalk, as in corn stalk, while *nyama* means manure or filth.[21] While N'Diaye makes no attempt to show how the words relate to each other, the implication we are left with is that their name does not compliment the clans of special professionals.

Blacksmiths have often been singled out for these kinds of unpleasant descriptions. In 1886 the plant collector Dr. Bellamy wrote that Maninka and Bamana sorcerers were the blacksmiths, a scorned group with whom farmers and nobles would not mix.[22] Some thirty years later Monteil equated the Bamana smiths with ill-famed sorcerers, describing them as a caste looked upon with fear and scorn, and kept at a safe distance by other Mande.[23] He developed an elaborate proof, based on a lengthy description of an aged Bamana blacksmith published by Anne Raffenel, who explored the area of the old Bamana state of Kaarta in the 1840s. The smith's name was given as Niany, and he seems to have been actively involved in supernatural pursuits. Raffenel described him as a priest to ancestors and wilderness spirits, a doctor, exorcist, and intermediary. In one lengthy passage the venerable smith was observed curing a women of snakebite. In another he expelled a malicious spirit from the writhing body of a Bamana woman.[24] Monteil extrapolated from this description a negative characterization of smiths, grounded in the observation that blacksmiths, like all artisans, are viewed as practitioners of antisocial sorcery.[25]

In 1932 another colonial administrator, Oswald Durand, published an article about the industries of the Fouta Djallon region, an area that is inhabited mostly by Fula but has a large population of smiths who are either Mande or the descendents of mixed Mande-Fula marriages. Durand said these smiths were like the caste of smiths found all over French West Africa; that is, they were held in great disdain that seemed grounded more in a kind of fear than in scorn. He noted that blacksmiths were under constant suspicion of acting like sorcerers, and that to the rest of society they appeared to be priests of an unknown religion, linked to mysterious sects and possessed of supernatural powers.[26]

This is not a rosy picture of the Mande blacksmiths, and it has promoted several misconceptions. First, it suggests that smiths are virtual outcasts in their society. Second, it seems to imply, by extension, that an Indian-like caste system, complete with low-stature groups of polluted populations, is in place among the Mande. Third, it interprets sorcery, or magic, or supernatural activity as decidedly unpleasant and universally recognized as such by the Mande.

It is also not a completely accurate picture of the smiths. Its sources are all European and all associated with a colonial regime. We might surmise, therefore, that Western ideology and the pragmatics of exploitative administration conspired to picture the smiths and other *nyamakalaw* so negatively. Yet that would be too facile an explanation, simply because there is some truth to what these individuals claimed to have observed. Furthermore, it is an interpretation that was, I think, encouraged by the general Mande population, the *nyamakalaw,* and the smiths themselves. We can begin to understand this by working back from the idea of castes, through sorcery, to the Mande concept of energy.

Several contemporary scholars who have studied social organization use the term *caste* to distinguish blacksmiths and the other special professionals from the rest of Mande society. Examination of works by these scholars suggests that they had no intention of recalling India's caste system.[27] Nevertheless, they do sometimes report that the *nyamakala* groups possess low status,[28] and no matter how much they may have exaggerated or misinterpreted, they, like the colonial-era authors before them, must have acquired their opinions from somewhere.

In fact, I can add to their impressions with some of my own. In the mid-nineteenth century the explorer Raffenel reported that some towns in the old Kaarta area were ruled by smiths.[29] I found such rule to be exceptional, however, and most Mande assert that blacksmiths can never be town chiefs. Often they say so with a definite note of superiority.

I can cite another kind of example that is more revealing, because it is more confusing. When I worked with the smith Sedu Traore in 1978 he had moved back to the hamlet his father had built, because his older brother had died, his only other senior brother was ill, and Sedu was needed as leader to some twenty members of his extended family. Just over a hill is the small town of Sibiridugu, "Saturday City," whose chief was forever coming to visit Sedu in search of advice. When important problems needed the chief's attention it was understood by all that he should make no decision without first getting the opinion, and then the approval, of a senior blacksmith. This appears to be true everywhere among the Mande. So the chief came to Sedu, full of respect and the spirit of camaraderie.

But on the two occasions when I visited this chief in his own town, with no blacksmiths in attendance, he defamed Sedu by saying, "Oh, he is only a smith" in tones utterly devoid of the respect that had filled him at Sedu's house. One might conclude from this that smiths are held consistently in low esteem, and the need to seek their advice and approval is just pro forma. Yet I have also been party to other conversations in which smiths were discussed quite respectfully, and other evidence lends support to that respect.

In 1971, when Sedu lived in the large town of Senou along with several other blacksmith families, his clients often dropped by to visit, especially during the midday hours when people stop working to eat and relax. Frequently, four or five people might be sitting around Sedu's forge, with no other reason to be there except the desire to have a good chat. In fact, I found farmers enjoying the company of smiths everywhere I worked, including the Markala area near Ségou. Sometimes these visitors even ate lunch with the smith. This seems to contradict the advice some Mande give, to avoid the smiths and other *nyamakalaw* and certainly to avoid eating with them. Thus, as students of Mande culture we are stuck in the middle of ambiguity.

Actually, however, we ought to be pleased, and take the extra step our data suggest. We have ambiguity, and we also have ambivalence, just as the Mande experience it. Now we need only explain it.

We can begin by considering the "joking relationship," a Mande institution characterized by stylized insolence. The Bamana call it *senenkun* or *sinankun;* the Maninka call it *sananku-ya;* and the colonial author Henri Labouret notes that other savanna ethnic groups, such as the Fula, Wolof, and Songhai, also maintain this institution.[30] Joking relationships are social contracts that allow individuals to hurl insults at each other in a benign, often public environment where retribution takes the form of additional insults. These insulting sessions startle outsiders. For no apparent reason, two people suddenly begin to assault each other with statements that ought to lead to torts or fisticuffs. Because they are arrangements between clans, the history, reputations, and general worthiness of each participant's family or clan membership are often held up for enormous amounts of ridicule. Blacksmiths have joking relationships with many of the farming clans, and they also have them with the clans of sedentary Fula who live among the Mande. I have heard young Fula boys address senior smiths as "little brother," even though such impertinence under other circumstances would be unthinkable, given the Mande's tremendous respect for age and their mores that demand any younger person to behave almost submissively toward any older person. I have also been present when blacksmiths and Fula sat together in the evening hours, exchanging derogatory legends about one another, often to the accompaniment of uproarious laughter.

This baffling behavior masks other aspects of the relationships that are of paramount importance. Joking relationships are in fact alliances. Participants exchange services, and since they are members of different clans and likely to have different principal occupations, such exchanges can be mutually beneficial. Participants also assist each other, and will go to great lengths to provide economic aid in the form of produce or manufactured products whenever it is needed. Finally, participants very often are fast friends. I met a blacksmith and a Fula in the city of San who were inseparable, and the smith Sedu Traore had Fula friends in several towns between Ségou and Bamako.

The two sides of these joking relationships offer a perspective for considering other aspects of Mande social structure. Henri Labouret describes it marvelously in a phrase, by noting that these are alliances that unite and oppose people at the same time. He also provides another useful insight by explaining that such relationships began with individuals helping each other in contexts dramatic enough to generate profound recognition, in the form of institutionalized relationships that extended beyond the original actors to include their families and clans.[31] We can view the elements of joking relationships—debt and obligation, access to complimentary services—as Mande social morphemes which, when arranged according to a Mande social grammar, generate typical Mande social form, simultaneous attraction and rejection. Thus ambiguity and ambivalence fit nicely into the patterns of belief and practice the Mande maintain.

Ambiguity and ambivalence become even more prominent when the Mande confront sorcery. Here we enter a realm that is difficult to explore, because Western civilization is poorly equipped to consider the components of Mande sorcery on the Mande's own terms. Most of our terminology fails to reflect Mande thinking, and so misapprehensions are perpetuated almost by default. Our word *supernatural*, for example, does not describe the Mande arena in which sorcery is enacted. The Mande assert a belief in spirits and forces that most Westerners would consider a part of a supernatural realm, one they would characterize as imaginary or generated by superstition. The Mande see nothing supernatural about such spirits and forces, however. The spirits, for example, may not always be visible. They may be able to change shapes at will, to travel without recourse to our more mundane modes, to beguile people into a variety of adventures and to accomplish various other spectacular things. Nevertheless, they are considered real, and part of the natural environment, like a waterfall, a person, or a tree. A great many individuals admit they have never seen one. Some will even say they have their doubts. Yet a great many individuals also claim to have seen them, or even to have been carried off into the bush by spirits, there to be haunted, or given the gift of some special kind of knowledge. Perhaps to accommodate their views to our words we could call this realm supranatural or supraliminal, but whatever we choose to call it we must realize that the Mande themselves do not consider it supernatural.

Beyond that basic difficulty lie others. Words such as *witch, witch doctor,* or *sorcerer* are not aligned with the areas we Westerners now take most seriously, science and the Judeo-Christian religion. So, using them to identify Mande practitioners does not encourage us to reflect upon the atmosphere in which they actually practice. We should keep these limitations in mind.

An even more tenacious problem comes into play here. Many scholars still have trouble considering sorcery to be anything but evil or antisocial. That is a misconception that makes understanding Mande sorcery difficult. In Africa, harnessing special forces does not always involve malevolence. Monica Wilson, in her study of the Nyakyusa of East Africa, shows that witchcraft is valued positively or negatively according to the characters of the people using it. Certain people are believed to be born with pythons in their bellies, giving them the power to harm. Other people also have pythons in their bellies, giving them power to fight people in the first group. The former are called *abalosi*, which Wilson translates as witches. The latter are called *abanmanga*, which she translates as defenders. Their sources of power are the same, but witches act in selfishness and illegality, while defenders act morally, in accordance with the law.[32]

The Mande ascribe this same neutrality to sorcery, which is not to say that the Mande always find it pleasant. They conceive of it as special, secret expertise that focuses on the environment and the person and allows practitioners to intercede in both natural and social processes so that they may be redirected.[33] The management of the world's special forces, and the resources used to do so, are therefore neither licit nor illicit by definition, and involve no predisposition to harm or help. Even though people display profound respect for these forces, and often fear them, they recognize them simply as sources of tremendous power. The power acquires character as licit or illicit, harmful or helpful, by virtue of the intentions of the user. Jealousy, covetousness, the desire for revenge, or quests for fame or political authority frequently lead people to the illicit use of sorcery. But with equal frequency such usages are countered with licit sorcery enacted on society's behalf.

Because the power of sorcery is perceived as awesome, the Mande mitigate its potency by hedging it round with precautions and by speaking of its potential danger. It should not be toyed with; it can do far too much damage. It should not be underestimated; there is nothing more powerful. It should not be used by the weak-hearted; it can easily turn on the person not confident of controlling it. It should never be talked about unguardedly; there is power in speech that can easily be unleashed, and bits of knowledge about sorcery vocalized might well lead to chaos and destruction.

The Mande also try to hedge in sorcery by localizing its use to some degree. Virtually anyone can become a sorcerer by studying with a master. Such study is very difficult, however. It demands much time, a willingness to take many risks, and considerable expense. The *nyamakala* clan members are believed born with much of the power others have to acquire, or at least with a ready access to it, and their lengthy apprenticeships are ideally suited for learning the principles involved. Thus a great many people are happy to leave occult manipulations to the *nyamakalaw*, who are themselves most happy to offer their services and thereby enhance their incomes. Such attitudes also help the clans of special professionals maintain their trade monopolies, because in most people's minds the expertise of the *nyamakalaw*'s trades and that of their sorcery are intertwined.

So the Mande buffer sorcery, theoretically to protect incautious citizens. They also find themselves in the strange position of having to protect sorcery itself from what they perceive as the avarice of outsiders. Since the earliest phases of colonialism, foreigners have persistently asked the Mande about their occult beliefs and practices. Such questioning startles the Mande because it violates their own procedures for transferring knowledge of sorcery. No Mande would openly ask about such things; it would constitute the height of immaturity, indiscretion, and outright foolhardiness. Interested individuals first learn all they can by just listening and observing. Gradually they discover appropriate contacts and find appropriate ways to meet them.

Ultimately their growing knowledge becomes exponential. Often they become sorcerers themselves, sometimes without anyone knowing it except for other sorcerers.

The Mande consider knowledge of all kinds to be important and powerful, but the instrumental knowledge of sorcery stands at the pinnacle of potency. The great epic poems that celebrate hunters, heroes, and the founding of states all devote major portions of the texts to sorcerers' exploits. In fact, epics stress the occult strategies and preparations that prefigure major events, such as military campaigns, rather than the events themselves.[34] And, as a reflection of real life, the epics emphasize the need of leaders to have access to sorcery, as a vital component of their capacity to solve problems, address crises, subdue antagonists, and satisfy their ambitions.[35] Sorcery is part of everyone's everyday life. The vast majority of the Mande use amulets, for example, to enhance the quality of their existence and provide a kind of prophylactic insurance against catastrophe. The vast majority seek the expertise of soothsayers and traditional doctors to help them with their problems. For this vast majority sorcery provides a means for analyzing situations and a tool for responding to them, and these people can be quite open about their use of it.

But sorcery is grounded in arcane knowledge, and in real life—in contrast to legends and the epic poems—its procedures and materials are never discussed publicly. Therefore, people become extremely uncomfortable with foreign researchers who seem too interested in sorcery's inner workings. When I worked with Sedu Traore in 1971 he was interviewed by the town council of elders regularly, to be sure I was not asking for secrets.

Occasionally, as a means of controlling overzealous researchers, they are invited to join one of the sorcery institutions such as *kòmò*. There are generally two kinds of initiation, superficial and serious. Originally the superficial ones were designed for travelers likely to happen upon secret ceremonies. Such initiations protected them, by serving in a sense as passports. The motivation is different for foreigners; no significant information is offered, but the neophyte must swear never to reveal any institutional secrets.

The Mande very much resent this kind of prying, because they see it as a threat. I was often asked why Europeans and Americans were always so anxious to acquire Mande secrets, why they wanted this kind of power in addition to the political and economic clout they had held since colonial times. A typical means for dealing with such threats is to try to scare the stranger off, in the belief that absolutely horrific accounts of the occult will prove unsavory enough to provoke a shift of interest in the researcher. Unfortunately, many researchers misinterpret this as testimony of the unwholesomeness of sorcery, perceiving it as a much loathed, antisocial phenomenon. As we consider sorcery and its practitioners here, we should realize that many accounts exaggerate the negative and thereby fail to describe the true place of sorcery in the Mande scheme of things. They also fail to describe the value in its ambiguity and ambivalence.

The drama that surrounds sorcery should also be examined in the context of situations and personalities. Occult practices are prominent features of everyday life. As I have stated, most people wear amulets or keep them in their homes, and they consider these devices to be actively involved in protecting themselves or enhancing their lives. Such sorcery is not a source of great excitement; it is simply there. When the context shifts, however, to situations where sorcery has been enacted out of jealousy or covetousness or vengeance, then people grow excited indeed, believing such powerful motivations are likely to lead to horrible misfortune for those upon whom the sorcery is visited.

The kind of people who use sorcery in this way are held to be either temporarily or habitually unrestrained by the niceties of Mande mores. They are aggressive, often egocentric, and quite prepared to be extremely disruptive. Many have huge appetites for economic or political aggrandizement, just like the characters in Mande epic poetry, and many are as willful and capable as those characters. They can be secretive and conspiratorial, full of private schemes and treachery.

The Mande call this kind of aggression *fadenya*, "father childness," a term that refers to the competition for honor and resources that invariably occurs between siblings who have the same father but different mothers. The Mande value competition enormously, and most aspects of their culture— from the presentation of heroes in the epics to the traditional exegesis of family and broader social behavior patterns—encourage it. At the same time, however, it is widely acknowledged that fierce competition can be deadly or dangerous, and people must be wary of its potential to devastate.[36]

The concept of "father childness" has a counterpart called *badenya*, "mother childness," an idea grounded in the affection and loyalty asserted to exist between siblings born of the same father and mother. It denotes gentle, passive, almost naively submissive behavior, a bent of mind that rarely asserts itself or stands out in the social scheme of things.

These complementary ideas form a major axis around which much of Mande social life turns. Everyone is believed capable of either type of behavior, and people shift back and forth according to the situations they encounter. Some people, however, are predisposed toward one or the other and may act most of the time under its influence. People inclined toward "father childness" are to be feared, or at least regarded with definite caution.

Other citizens consider *nyamakala* clan members to have many of the traits associated with "father childness." Smiths, bards, and leather workers, for example, are highly secretive and extremely protective of the expertise they consider to be their rightful inheritance. They possess tremendous volumes of information not in the public domain, and no one is ever certain just how they might use it. They are also quite capable of aggressive behavior. Bards, remember, will not hesitate to insult clients in public, thereby generating much disquiet. In fact, the epic poems are full of bard and blacksmith characters that typify the "father childness" personality.

In real life blacksmiths often manifest this aggressive side of their personalities by behaving dramatically. Farmers and researchers visiting a blacksmith's forge can frequently be seen dodging the sizzling bits of mineral impurities that fly off red-hot iron with each hammer blow. The smith, however, is impervious to them, even though a quick look at his legs and feet reveals a motley collection of welts where they have landed. People often say blacksmiths do fantastic things at public festivals, such as holding red-hot iron bare-handed and working it with a hammer until it cools down. Smiths are also prone, on occasion, to fits of public ill-temper. Once when we were visiting a small town on the western border of the Ségou region, Sedu Traore encountered a meat vendor whose prices Sedu felt were a bit inflated. He harangued the fellow mercilessly, an act that left me somewhat shocked and left the meat vendor obviously wondering whether he ought to abandon his stand in favor of more tranquil surroundings. Another blacksmith I knew enjoyed intimidating innocents with his rather imposing presence. He was large and well built and he had the habit of looming over people. I once watched him order soft drinks at a roadside stand, hover for a moment, and then walk off, challenging the proprietor to muster the courage to ask him to pay. He did pay, but slowly. Thus smiths reinforce other people's opinions of them and encourage the ambivalence that insulates them.

At sorcery's base lies a phenomenon that generates its own fair share of ambivalence and disquiet among the Mande. It is perceived as the world's basic energy, the energy that animates the universe. It is the force the Mande call *nyama*, which I refer to as special energy or occult power, and which most Westerners would consider supernatural. The Mande, in contrast, are inclinded to see it as both natural and mystical, and as a source of moral reciprocity.

The missionary Father Henry said that *nyama* was hard to define; he called it force, power, and energy and then described it as a kind of fluid possessed by every living being.[37] Monteil called it a fluid common to all of nature.[38] The Malian scholar Youssouf Cissé followed the colonial administrator Maurice Delafosse in saying that it meant life or endowed with life, spirit or endowed with animated spirit. Cissé added that it was the emanation of the soul, a kind of flux or flow that executes the soul's will.[39] Labouret described it in much the same way, adding, by way of illustration, that it was the power behind human thought and will, and the force that causes rain or a lack of it.[40] Dominique Zahan described it as a force that exists in all beings and inorganic matter, and is comparable to a vibration.[41]

The Mande believe that in concentrations, especially when they are massive and uncontrolled, this force is potentially dangerous, even deadly. People can learn to control it through sorcery, however, and thereby harness it to help them carry out their activities. Thus the linguist Charles Bird describes its essence most appropriately when he calls it the energy of action.[42] *Nyama* is the necessary power source behind every movement, every task. It is a prerequisite to all action and it is emitted as a by-product of every act.

The more difficult the task, the more energy demanded and the more emitted. When the taking of life is involved, these energy levels will be particularly high. Thus, hunters must possess large stores of *nyama* and be capable of dealing with equally massive amounts when animals are killed and the life force flows from them. This is one reason why the best hunters have prowess as sorcerers. Soldiers and state builders must possess even larger stores of the energy or have access to individuals who have it and can use it, because the taking of human lives releases even greater amounts of it.

Iron working also demands a great deal of the energy of action, which is lodged in inorganic matter and is emitted as a part of enterprise. Iron smelting was an enterprise of tremendous difficulty, demanding refined expertise, arduous labor, and great amounts of time. During the process, iron ore was transformed to bloom and enormous amounts of *nyama* were given off. The same is true when iron is shaped at the forge into useful implements and art. Thus blacksmiths command and work with huge stores of the energy; it is considered part of their heritage.

Bards must also command great reservoirs of this power, in part because they work with words, and words are produced by the mouth and tongue, both of which are intensely *nyama*-laden. They, like smiths, also work with spells, the supernatural formulas that activate the energy on behalf of or against other human beings. Leather workers work with the physical manifestations of another kind of spell, the amulets constructed by priests, sorcerers, and blacksmiths for clients with particular problems to solve or particular goals to achieve. *Nyama* is the active ingredient in these devices, and so leather workers must themselves possess enough of it to defend against its potentially awesome effects. They also work with leather, which, like feathers, horn, claws, and bone, retains its life form and life force after the flesh has disintegrated.

Nyama, then, is a little like electricity unconstrained by insulated wires but rather set neatly into a vast matrix of deeply interfaced social and natural laws. But it is more than energy. When the Mande tell folk stories, recount legends, or explain things to researchers, it becomes clear that they view *nyama* as a rationale for their most fundamental behavior patterns and as an explanation for the organization of their world. Although the energy is not wholly systematic, they believe it to be distributed among earthly life forms according to principles that combine a kind of morality with a metaphoric sense of the world's grandeur and drama. Many of the wilderness' more delicate and vulnerable animals are the ones that possess the largest stores of *nyama*, which protects them from some of the hazards human beings present. Duikers, for example, the smallest antelopes in the bush, are believed to be so full of this life force that they are immensely dangerous to kill. Powerful Mande hunters therefore kill them as often as they can, to demonstrate their prowess as masters of the bush and masters of the energy of action. Indeed, each time they succeed their own power grows. Poisonous snakes also possess enormous quantities of this energy, and wilderness spirits, the *jinèw* that haunt wild spaces, are almost overwhelmingly laden with it. Thus the dangers of the bush are explained through the Mande concept of the world's energy.

This energy also provides a system of cause and effect that binds a society to its mores and exists as a barrier to catch all but the most daring, the most enterprising of its citizens. Much of the scholarly literature describes it as an awesome force to be feared and forever guarded against, and the word vengeance is frequently used to relate its effects. Monteil calls it a force that involves itself in vengeance; Father Henry says it is the envoy, the messenger of hatred and vengeance, a form of justice that travels wherever the will sends it.[43] We may add to this a statement by Germaine Dieterlen, the disciple of Marcel Griaule, that when a person dies the energy is released from the body in an extremely active form, which has the capacity to attack the person responsible for the death.[44] Henri Labouret says the *nyama* of a deceased person provides the power for that person, even though dead, to attack his enemies.[45] Youssouf Cissé states that *nyama* is good or bad according to the nature or state of the soul at the moment when it produces the energy.[46] He goes on to suggest that the most certain means of holding the *nyama* of others at bay is never to indulge in wrongful acts and always to prove oneself full of goodness, kindness, humility, passiveness, patience, and submission.[47]

Thus we have an exegesis of the forces at work in the social and natural world that encourages a cautious disposition and restraint in all areas of life. We also have an important intersection between this exegesis and the one that divides the behavior of people into modes of "father childness" and "mother childness." The folklorist John Johnson notes a process of metaphorical extension by which those ideas about affection and competition expand to become "social cohesion" and "social destruction or dislocation," and serve as markers of Mande thought about space. The safest place people can be is the sleeping quarters of their mothers. Moving out from there, space becomes progressively more dangerous as people pass through town, the women's garden plots that surround the town, the toilets and garbage heaps that ring the gardens, the farming fields that lie beyond, and, finally, the bush that surrounds the fields. The greater the distance from one's mother's home, the greater the social dislocation and potential for disaster.[48] Deep bush is the most dangerous space of all, and most Mande avoid it by sticking to the paths that civilization has cut. People perceived as aggressive, however, people who move freely into the conceptual space beyond social order, are frequent visitors to the bush, a fact other Mande interpret as proof of their potential danger. Hunters, for example, who treat nature as their private cornucopia, are held in both a certain awe and fear because of their comfort in that most uncomfortable place. Sorcerers, too, spend much time in the bush, gathering the materials of their trade. And blacksmiths, who are often sorcerers, are also quite accustomed to wild space, and were especially prone to enter it in the days before colonialism when iron ore was widely mined and smelted in furnaces located away from town. This fits with Dominique Zahan's assertion that people or groups who are isolated because of their character, age, or profession have stronger *nyama* than other people. He notes that this is true of the elders, the sorcerers, and all the artists, and he associates especially potent doses of the energy with bards and blacksmiths.[49] Thus we see the means by which the Mande link ideas about society and power with formulas that add even more intensity to the ambivalence and ambiguity associated with smiths.

One of the blacksmiths' greatest strengths resides with the spirits that live in the bush. Most people consider wilderness spirits too powerful and frightening to be pleasant. These *jinèw* can be extremely beneficial to people, but also extremely capricious and dangerous. Indeed, wilderness spirits are a major reason why most people shun the bush. But smiths and spirits are almost colleagues in the eyes of other Mande. The blacksmiths' tasks send them into wild space often, for wood and various other organic materials, and, formerly, for ore. Without alliances with the spirits that are believed virtual masters of the wilderness, success, even survival, would not be likely. The Mande consider the bush divided into zones or categories of spirit stewardship. Some spirits control certain types of ecology. Others control areas. Smiths at their most skilled negotiate treaties with a complex of spirits through ritual, and the unions thus created give the blacksmiths access to the powers of spirits for any task they care to undertake. Father Henry even observed that the most dangerous—that is, the least sociable—spirits can only be subdued by smiths or *kule* wood workers.[50] Thus the bush writ large is brought to town by individuals who themselves have a foot in each domain.

Nyama meaning energy or life force has a homonym meaning feces, trash, garbage, and, by extension, bloated, swollen, literally crawling with nature's products or processes gone out of control. This is the source for Bokar N'Diaye's etymology of *nyamakala* as manure or filth. Dominique Zahan offers a partial explanation for this linguistic conjunction when he points out that feces contain some of the life force of the animals that produce it.[51] John Johnson offers another, by noting that often a town's most powerful protective devices or "fetishes" are hidden beneath the garbage piles that surround it.[52] There is a similitude of idioms here that makes sense, given all that we have said so far. The apparent contiguity between power and filth implies the danger harbored by the power. The world's energy allowed to get out of hand could leave the world a fetid ruin. It is therefore of paramount importance that *nyama* be controlled.

Control is the idea behind another etymology for *nyamakala*. *Kala* is the word for handle, such as the handle of a hoe or a knife. The *nyamakala* clans are handles of power, points of access to the energy that animates the universe.[53] This interpretation is a useful complement to N'Diaye's, because the two together offer us the full panoply of ideas and emotions that Mande associate with their clans of special professionals.

Ideas about sorcery and the world's energy provide ideological underpinnings for the place of smiths in Mande society. There are also some pragmatic explanations. First, there is the matter of competition, a concept widely promoted in Mande social behavior. Smiths produce valuable resources and provide access through sorcery to the world's energy. This gives them tremendous power, a kind of edge other citizens can neutralize with some of the less flattering ideas and restrictions we have encountered about blacksmiths.

Zahan gives us another explanation, when he notes that the boys' initiation association called *ntomo* harbors tremendous hostility toward smiths. He finds this reasonable, because smiths are the surgeons who will circumcise the boys. That operation is frightening, and anticipated with considerable disquiet for years before it actually takes place. Its occurrence will inflict drastic social and spiritual changes on the young persons, and it will expose them temporarily to dangerous levels of *nyama*.[54]

We can add other reasons for this hostility. Many Mande believe a legendary smith named Ndomajiri created the *ntomo* association, which provides an arduous, trying, and sometimes painful program of socialization. Indeed, this boys' association is the first organized effort on the part of society to make irresponsible male children into responsible male adults. As part of that process the neophytes are at a certain point led to the bush and forced to confront what is for them at their age and stage of cultural development a most horrifying instrument. They are visited by a monstrous horizontal mask, which belongs to one of the most powerful secret Mande initiation associations, *kòmò*. It consists of enormous jaws, huge horns, and all kinds of organic matter, apparently held together by what looks like a surface of filth. This unsavory creature seems clearly to be in its own domain, wild space, and it suggests with graphic force the kinds of problems antisocial citizens are likely to encounter. In spite of its obvious social dislocation, it appears on behalf of society to encourage youth in their proper development, thereby adding confusion to fear. Since their earliest days these boys have heard about *kòmò*. They have been told that it kills sorcerers and any intemperate soul who sees it without being initiated into its cult. Gradually, as they grow older, they learn that the mask and its association articulate concepts about nature, the spirit world, sorcery, and the nature of people and society, and they come to see the mask in a wholly different light. At this first sighting, however, they understand very little about the beast. They do know, however, that the mask and the association are things of blacksmiths, the same group of people who will circumcise them and then protect them from the operation's hazards, who will provide them the tools of their trade and possibly visit sorcery upon them. It is easy to see why people view smiths with ambivalence. It is a vantage point that begins as soon as young people are old enough to see and listen, and to learn.

We cannot demonstrate the historical processes by which the blacksmiths and other special professional clans came to occupy their present places in Mande society, nor can we identify their precise origins. Some scholars have suggested that the blacksmiths of West Africa began as a single group of itinerant professionals,[55] a notion not necessarily supported by the Mande isolation of smiths as a separate race. After all, the bards and leather workers are conceived of in the same way. The blacksmiths' grasp of a highly specialized and important technology, which they shroud in thick ritual, seems to be a key feature in the perceptions other people have of them. Charles Monteil offers us some insight:

> Everywhere in the Sudan, blacksmiths are considered and, indeed, behave like magicians. The extraction of iron is surrounded by essentially magic rights in which only blacksmiths may participate.[56]

In a wonderful study of blacksmith's technology and ritual the French scholar Béatrice Appia offers us details, which focus on the complex of special relationships smiths customarily establish with wilderness spirits, so that they may work in the bush.[57] These relationships add tremendous mystique to the work of smiths, joining technology and sorcery all the more irrevocably. Several lines from a song sung during masquerade performances elegantly express the public's awe of smiths:

> When they fire the high furnace,
> One transforms another into a farming tool handle.
> When they fire the high furnace,
> One transforms another into a hoe.
> When they fire the high furnace,
> One transforms another into a pretty little mortar.
> Real smiths are the masters of sorcery.[58]

Carving hoe handles and mortars has little to do with smelting iron from its ore, and to make a hoe blade the iron must be forged after it is created in the furnace. In fact, in the area where I heard this song performed smiths have not smelted their own iron for at least a generation. Yet the song holds smelting at the fulcrum point of the blacksmith's profession. It symbolizes the beginning of complex processes by which the Mande smiths bring the fruits of metal to bear on civilization, and it symbolizes in general the blacksmiths' expertise, submerging it in the aura of sorcery, as if to explain the miracle of iron through metaphor.

The idea behind the song is paralleled by a ritual practiced in Mali's far western region of Kayes. Iron was still being smelted there in the 1970s, and at the end of the procedure a 200-pound piece was dragged steaming from the furnace. Blacksmiths poured water over it to cool it down, and townswomen came forward to lift their skirts and absorb the vapors. Others gathered the liquid after it had cascaded over the iron and drank it. They considered it charged with the *nyama* of the enterprise, controlled and rendered most beneficial by the blacksmiths.[59]

Thus, it appears that other citizens' interpretations of the smiths' technology lie at the core of the Mande characterization of blacksmiths. We shall therefore turn now to the blacksmiths' technology and examine their crafts of wood and iron working.

TWO

THE MANDE SMITHS AS CRAFTSMEN

Mande blacksmiths work in two domains. Their forges are in town (Ill. 1, 2), but they gather materials in the bush, where they used to smelt iron. In general, smiths are more mobile than other citizens; they are usually willing to resettle where business is better. A small percentage, often the younger and more adventuresome, are itinerant, but the vast majority live in towns.

Mande towns vary greatly in size. Smaller ones may only have twenty or so extended family compounds, with five to ten people living in each. The larger towns have a hundred or more family compounds and thousands of inhabitants. Even the smallest town has at least one smith family; there are just too many tools and utensils that no one else can make.[1] Most towns have at least three to five families of smiths; many have more. Sometimes the blacksmiths congregate together, forming a special quarter called a *numuso-kala*. Occasionally, smiths form their own town or hamlet, called a *numu dugu*, which generally has easy access to the nearby towns of farming clans.[2]

Small smith families will include just a husband and a wife and possibly one or two children. Large families will include a senior male smith with two or three wives and their children, his younger brothers, and their immediate families. A hamlet built for such a family by Sedu Traore's father often housed thirty smiths or more.

Generally, several male smiths in a town will work iron and wood, while at least one female member of the family will work clay. Sons and nephews of the male smiths and the daughters and nieces of the female potters are often apprentices. Sedu Traore's father trained thirteen sons, so many that most left their hometown in order not to overtax the market. Sedu, however, has trained no smiths. One of his sons became a Western-style carpenter; another decided to study the Koran.

Blacksmiths' forges are located in family compounds spread around the community, at intersections of main walking thoroughfares, or next to the clearings used as dance arenas and elders' meeting places. Often two or more smiths share a forge, or just work together by moving back and forth between the forges of each. When especially heavy labor is called for, as when an old railway tie must be reduced to hoe blades or a thick ax blade must be produced, a smith calls upon his colleagues for assistance. Every town has a "master of smiths," *numutigi*, who is generally the oldest, though not necessarily the most accomplished. He is consulted about major undertakings, and often directs joint undertakings.

Out of town, smelting furnaces used to grace the landscape with their picturesque clay forms. Now, however, they are rarely encountered, although smiths can still point out the places where they stand in ruins, or where their traces in the form of slag, the fused mineral by-product of iron smelting remain. Sometimes a single furnace stood alone. It would have been refurbished and fired once each year by one family of smiths. Sometimes several furnaces stood together, to be worked by all the smiths in a community. Morrow Campbell, a mining and metallurgy specialist working in West Africa in 1908, reported hundreds of abandoned smelting furnaces, a testimony to the past importance of iron making.[3] Candice L. Goucher, a historian, has suggested that iron-making industries used to operate in a variety of areas across the western savanna, the smelted product being a very popular item of trade.[4]

This chapter examines the techniques smiths employ and the products they make in their two spaces, town and bush. We proceed as a blacksmith's apprentice would, from the simplest tasks to the most complex.

TECHNIQUES

A young smith's apprenticeship begins sometime before the age of ten. By then he will have spent many of his free hours in his father's forge, working the bellows when he is needed and, in general, being exposed to *numu baara*, the "work of smiths." His father may have given him some old carving tools or made him a small set with which he could mimic the work of adults. The lad may have made himself a knife handle, with his father making a blade to fit it.

Once a youth becomes an apprentice, labor and learning begin in earnest. Over a period of some seven or eight years the apprentice moves from working the bellows to carving wood and then to forging iron, gradually becoming competent at each. It is very hard work, and some apprentices simply drop out. One of Sedu's brothers, for example, did not have the patience for it, and so switched fields dramatically, becoming something of a Muslim holy man.

In the beginning the labor is arduous indeed. Before the neophyte can master techniques and form, he first has to master pain. He begins at the bellows, where he spends many hours each day. Few tasks could be more boring—or, at the same time, more unpleasant, for the tedious repetition of the same simple moves quickly generates sore arms and shoulders. Just working the bellows is not pleasant, but Mande smiths do not learn to just work bellows; they learn to play them.

There are two basic types of bellows, clay and wood. Clay versions are large architectural constructions that rise from the floor of the smithy as a platform on which the worker sits (Ill. 3). Before him is a broad clay area in which two clay pots are embedded. Goat skin covers the pot tops in such a way that the worker may insert his hands into slits that open when he pulls up and close when he pushes down. Iron tubes extend forward from the sides of the pots, through a clay fire wall and down into the basin of the forge. Working the bellows forces large drafts of air through the pipes and into the forge.

Wood versions are portable (Ill. 4). Y-shaped hard wood is hollowed out so that two chambers meet at the intersection. Two iron tubes are inserted there, and when the bellows is in place the tubes pass through another type of clay fire wall and down into the heart of the forge's charcoal basin. The whole skins of two small goats are attached to the open ends of the chambers, at the top of the Y. They form large bags that are split open at the back, with small pieces of wood attached to hold the slits stiff and allow the worker to insert his hands. As he pulls back on the bag he opens his hand and the skin fills with air. As he pushes he closes his hand and the air is forced through the tubes and down into the charcoal basin.

Pushing air through either type of bellows produces a wonderful sonorous blast, which can be heard all around the forge and the immediate vicinity. The skins are pushed alternately, at first in a very even fashion that results in a kind of basic two-beat rhythm. The rapidity with which air circulates through the coals determines how quickly the coals heat up and how hot they get. Both variables are significant, and the master smith lets his apprentice know how much air is needed depending on the size and state of development of the iron piece in the forge. Too much air wastes charcoal, causing it to burn too quickly. Gradually the apprentice learns to gauge how much vigor to apply to his work, and in the process he begins to vary his basic two-beat rhythm.

The result is patterns of rhythm that resemble drum beats, except that the percussive thrust of drumming is replaced by fluid gusts of air. As a young smith grows competent, he develops a sharp, crisp precision in his rhythms, which often become astonishingly complex. Each smith has one or several favorites. The one Sedu Traore used most often is rather stately and gentle, reflecting his age. It sounded like this:

Sometimes for variety he would back into the rhythm, with this result:

Several women frequently ground millet in a mortar near Sedu's forge (Ill. 22). They alternated pounding their huge pestles into the mortar, adding hand-clapping routines and throwing the pestles up into the air when the spirit moved them. Often when they worked Sedu played his bellows rhythms in counterpoint to theirs, creating a lively atmosphere in the neighborhood.

Even though they usually play their favorites, smiths generally know many rhythms. On a trip to San in June 1978 with my research colleague Kalilou Tera, I spent a morning with a group of four smiths who shared a forge on one of the city streets. It immediately became clear that the wooden bellows worker was quite expert on the instrument, and as our enthusiasm grew, so did his repertoire and his finesse. He played for some time, drawing an appreciative audience from everyone out on the block. Then a younger smith took over, and this fellow was even better. Kalilou began calling out the names of standard drum rhythms used by the many ethnic groups that live in the region, and the smith played them all. Earlier, in 1973, I watched a very young apprentice in Bamako play rhythms on clay bellows with such speed and precision that he could have easily switched to Western trap drums and joined any band he chose.

In areas where famous blacksmiths used to live, sometimes several generations ago, young smiths of the present generation learn to play the renowned smiths' rhythms. This adds a nice historical touch to the youths' sense of profession, and it pleases their masters to no end.

In fact, learning bellows rhythms is an apprentice's first task of fundamental importance. This is even true for foreigners who become honorary apprentices. When I worked closely with Sedu in 1973, I spent many hours at his bellows. Once the town's master smith, Dramane Dunbiya, paid a visit as I was playing Sedu's standard rhythm. Dunbiya paused and then said: "Ah, now you have become a true smith."

The point is one of articulation. The most mundane, tedious task imaginable, the very first task assigned to an aspiring smith, becomes something quite wonderful and anything but boring. It acquires pleasing articulation, according to the dictates of traditional music aesthetics. Thus the value of articulation is planted early, or at least presented as something most positive and rewarding. It is a value that a good many blacksmiths will apply to their work for the rest of their lives.

Gradually, young apprentices begin to learn wood-carving techniques by making knife and hoe handles. This work is difficult too, but in a different way. Carving demands precision and patience, and a lot of eye-hand coordination. Smiths must conceptualize a form and hold it in their memory as they reduce a rough piece of wood by stages until it fits the correct image (Ill. 5). They must also learn a certain flexibility and creativity, because surprises in the wood grain, cracks, and checks can all force the carver away from his original plan. Proper selection of woods is another important acquired skill; it helps prevent many of those surprises.

Wood is collected in the bush. A smith must learn which hard and soft woods are available in his area, where to find trees that have already fallen and are weathering, and how to judge the ways in which wood is likely to check and crack. Miscalculations can result in spoiled products and wasted time. One afternoon I watched Sedu carve a stool and encounter a problem with splitting (Ill. 6). His intended design was to feature four legs joined at the bottom with crisp geometric wedge forms. But the wood he had selected was not thoroughly weathered. As the carving proceeded a split developed at the base and gew so pronounced that it ran all the way up to the stool's seat and threatened to break the whole piece in half. Sedu adjusted by changing his design, opening up the legs so that in the end only two were connected by wedges.

Mande carving centers on the adze, called *dèsèlan* or *sèmè*, a marvelous tool that can serve as ax or saw, chisel, knife, and plane (Ill. 7). A smith owns a whole set of adzes, graduated according to size, weight, and the thickness and breadth of the blade. Blades are generally hafted to handles with a tang, called *ka*, which is a long thin extension of the iron at the rear of the blade. The tang runs through a hole in the bulbous, weighty top portion of the handle. Some smiths bend the tip around, locking the blade in place. Others leave it straight, so they can take the blade out easily when it needs sharpening. The weight of an adze can be substantial, and it is always concentrated at the haft-end of the handle. The rest of the handle is long and thick enough, however, to afford the smith exquisite control of the instrument. All of the carving action is in the wrist, and when the smith bends his wrist up, a well-made adze balances there effortlessly. When the wrist is dropped, the weight at the adze's working end creates such momentum that the tool can take sizable bites out of a piece of wood with a minimum of exertion, allowing the smith to concentrate on control.

The smith begins a carving by blocking out a basic form. It happens surprisingly quickly, thanks to the lengthy apprenticeship. Then the smith uses smaller adzes to work the object into its final form. Each adze stroke leaves a trough-shaped cut with little ridges, and the piece moves through stages of being covered with finer and finer patterns of these concave marks. The carver usually works around a piece so that all of its parts develop at the same rate. By the time the work is nearly complete, the smith is using one of his lightest adzes, which, if he is good, can be controlled so expertly that it removes earlier adze marks. One hazard of adze work stems from the fibrous nature of wood. It is composed of long strands, a little like celery, and the carver must take care not to catch his blade in the grain at an angle that matches the direction the fibers flow. When that happens great lengths of wood are peeled away, and sections of a piece of work are obliterated. Learning to control adzes to avoid such mishaps is a major part of an apprentice's training, and much practice is needed before a smith acquires the necessary control.

Most smiths use a carving knife, *muru*, to apply their finishing touches. Their technique does not resemble Western whittling. Rather, they hold the cutting edge at an angle that causes the blade to glide as if it were a carpenter's plane (Ill. 8). As they pull the knife toward them, they adjust the blade angle so that they can shave off the most minute irregularities. Today, some smiths resort to a file for this work, but good smiths find the adze and knife quite adequate.

Some carved objects require special tools or techniques. Carving out the inside of a mortar, for example, demands a particularly small adze, and some smiths like to use homemade bow drills called *frin frin la* to make holes in very hard wood (Ill. 9). Hoe, ax, and knife handles must be tapped to receive the tanged blades, and for this smiths own a set of iron awls called *doliw*, which are pointed at the tip and gracefully swell toward sturdy wood handles (Ill. 10). These are placed in the forge's charcoal basin and heated until their ends glow orange-red. Then they are pushed or pounded into the wood. If the hole must be several inches long or the wood is quite hard, the awl is reheated and the process repeated several times.

Sometimes the tools or techniques recall those we associate with Western carpentry and cabinetmaking. Iron chisels with heavy wooden handles are used with hammers when holes or chambers must be made that are too small for even the smallest adzes. These chisels are used to make the cavities in the backs of door locks to accommodate the iron drop pins, and they are also used to carve holes in the very hard woods that anchor anvils in the ground. Nails are used on occasion, for making trunks, for example, and even for assembling decorative patterns of blocks on the surface of a door. Smiths make the nails themselves at their forges, and sometimes they make extra ones to sell to Western-style carpenters or boat builders.

Many objects are not considered finished until they have been decorated. Smiths say this makes them easier to sell. Knife handles or wooden door locks are often pyroengraved with the thin edge of a flat-bladed tool called a *muru gwana*, "hot knife," and large surface areas may be completely blackened by using the tool as a hot spatula to char the wood (Color Plate I). Some objects receive a more sculpted form of engraving, generally effected with the tip of a smith's carving knife. (Ill. 11).

Finally, some objects, such as door locks and other types of sculpture, are coated with herbal solutions. These are designed to protect the wood from the effects of weathering and the attacks of wood-boring insects, such as powder post beetles.[5]

Watching talented smiths work wood is deceptive, because they make it look easy. An ornate stool can be carved in an hour. A lovely door lock can be finished in half a day. Yet the skill demanded for such tasks has been patiently acquired, as anyone who undertakes an apprenticeship soon learns. Most master smiths assume a benign attitude toward their young charges. They rarely stop work in progress, preferring instead to let the lad discover his own mistakes and either rectify them as best he can or seek the senior smith's advice. That advice can be invaluable as the youth attempts to master his medium. A young blacksmith, who lived around the corner from Sedu Traore in the town of Senou once asked Sedu to come and look at a problem he was having with a pestle he was carving. Sedu advised him, and after we returned to Sedu's forge he told me the fellow had been forced to end his apprenticeship early. His family was large and there was not enough work, so his father sent him south to establish himself as best he could. He was resigned to the fact that he would never be able to carve complex objects, and he was unable to forge iron.

In both carving wood and forging iron, heavy-handled tools are directed at material to change its shape. Thus, by the time a smith has mastered wood, he will already have some of the skill needed to work hot iron. The transition, however, is enormous, because wood work and iron work have little else in common. Iron is not reduced to final form, nor is it beaten into it. Rather, it is heated to a point where it hovers at the edge of viscosity, and, in this state, well-directed hammer blows cause it to flow into whatever form a skilled smith wants. When a hammer sinks into this glowing metal, the metal moves out from under it literally in miniature waves, and the skill of smithing lies in controlling the hammer so well that these waves are pushed across an ever-changing iron surface with utter precision. The technique demands considerably more strength than wood carving does, so the earlier work on the bellows now stands the smith in good stead. But absolute control is also called for, which makes the smith's training in adze work most helpful.

Mande forges are rather consistently arranged (Ill. 4 and Frontispiece). First there are the bellows, fire wall, and charcoal basin, *ta dugu* or *fan*. To the left of the bellows worker is a water basin, *fan daga*, made from a broken calabash or anything conveniently at hand. Smiths keep their collections of pincers, *balaw*, in it, so that a cool one will always be ready to handle red-hot iron (Ill. 12). Nearby is the smith's collection of hammers, called *tòrinaw* or *fulumew* from Arabic, or *maratow* from French (Ill. 12), and further to the left is the anvil, *kulan*, embedded in a large section of very hard wood, which itself is embedded in the hard-packed earthen floor of the forge (Ill. 13).

When iron is buried in charcoal, and bellows pump air into the basin, the charcoal begins to glow yellow-orange and the iron heats by stages, changing color as it gets hotter. It passes through dark red to orange and a variety of yellows until it glows a yellow that is nearly white. From bright cherry red to nearly white the iron is in a malleable state, and it can be worked until it has cooled to a dull gun-metal gray again. The thicker the piece, the hotter the blacksmith heats it. Sometimes, if a very thick piece is being worked, into an ax blade for example, the smith may heat it to a state just beyond yellow-white, so that particles fly off of their own accord, creating an effect rather like a sparkler. For more delicate work, or when most of the basic shaping is finished and refinements are all that remain, the smith works the iron when it is cherry-red, so that it gives less beneath his hammer and can be controlled with a little more precision. For all of the stages in between, smiths' hammers are graduated by size and weight. Some are designed like adzes; the tip of the head narrows into a tang, which is hafted to a thick, strong handle. Others employ a socket-type mount, with the wood handle passing through an opening in the hammer head, like Western hammers.

To create ribs at the top ends of hoe blades or to make the tangs that hold the blades to handles, smiths use special hammers, called *faralew*. The hammers look like small paddles or very thick spatulas, with concave sides that flare at the ends. They are made entirely of iron, and, because they are designed with short handles and long hammering surfaces, they offer a more immediate kind of control than the smith's other hammers. Some are quite beautiful, and they are all considered precious. Once, when the smiths Sedu Traore and Dramane Dunbiya went with me on a trip to the Ségou region, we stopped on the way to visit one of their friends. He was a very old smith, long retired, and he showed me his *farale* hammer. He considered it a prized possession and would never consider parting with it. He, like most Mande smiths, said it was the oldest hammer type, and it seemed to symbolize his membership in the profession.

Forging iron heated in a charcoal basin is a slow process. The iron is heated, hammered, and reheated in what seems like an endlessly repeated operation. The technique offers a very special advantage, however. As the iron is repeatedly heated and beaten, mineral impurities, called *nègè fara*, "the skin of iron," fly off the surface. Thus the metal is gradually refined. In addition, with each immersion in the charcoal bed, additional carbon is absorbed into the metal's surface. Ultimately, the surface is transformed into carbon steel, becoming quite hard. The inner core, however, remains iron, and so retains its flexibility. Thus Mande wrought iron takes on the characteristics of both iron and steel. Knife and hoe blades hold sharp edges longer because they are steel. But the blades rarely break because they have a core of more pliable iron.

Given the advantages of combined iron and steel, it is interesting that Mande smiths only rarely use the metallurgical technique called quenching, the rapid plunging of red-hot iron into a basin of cold water or oil. The procedure changes the metal's grain structure, making it much harder but also much more brittle. Quenching would eliminate the advantages achieved with a carbon-forging technology, and at some point in the history of Mande iron working this disadvantage was discovered. Now smiths only quench finished ax heads, massive iron objects too thick to break very easily and very much in need of a hard, sharp cutting edge.

Unlike adzes, blacksmiths' hammers do not balance lightly in midair with the smith's wrist flexed up. The biggest hammers are so heavy they must be worked standing up with both hands, and many smiths actually grunt as they pull the monsters down toward the iron they are shaping. Even the smaller ones weigh two and one-half pounds. This weight makes hammer work a very different enterprise from adze work. The wrist is still key, but it is aided by the elbow, so that the whole forearm moves up as the wrist flexes, bringing the hammer head almost to the shoulder. When it comes back down, the forearm provides velocity while the wrist provides direction, and both parts of the anatomy must become quite strong if the smith is to be competent. Young apprentices take a long time acquiring the strength and control they need, and often enough experience great difficulty getting hot iron to flow beneath their hammers in the direction and for the distance they desire. When pieces go too far awry, master smiths reheat them and with precious few hammer strokes bring them back to shape again.

The sounds produced when hammers meet hot iron are thick and sonorous, and they carry quite a distance from the forge. Like bellows' sounds, they provide an opportunity to make music, and many smiths generate basic rhythms as they forge. Some smiths hammer in patterns, stopping after several strokes to see how the piece is moving. Each time they stop they tap the anvil lightly with their hammer. Asked why, they say it is so they can see their work. But they also say the anvil symbolizes their fathers, and so the gesture could also be a ritual of respect and continuity.[6]

When smiths work together on a thick piece of iron they hammer in careful concert that generates a simple but lively rhythm (Color Plate II). With two smiths working, the one who holds the iron with pincers uses a small hammer, which makes a "ping" when it hits the metal. The other smith generally uses the huge two-handled hammer. Starting a stroke with the hammer head above his shoulder, he pulls it down and guides it toward its mark, where it lands with a resounding "pang." A typical rhythm produced under these circumstances sounds like this:

It can be heard as two half notes followed by a whole note, in a 2/4 tempo. When four smiths work the same piece of iron, a 4/4 tempo is established, with each hammer stroke becoming a whole beat. Then the smith holding the iron may interject a vibrant chanting sequence, inserting yells of encouragement to his colleagues at each or every other half beat. In either case the man holding the iron directs the hammer strokes of his fellows with his own small hammer. Where he works, they work, and in this manner a piece is brought to completion.

Before European iron became readily available, when smiths smelted their own iron from ore, smelting was a highly regarded enterprise that called for a sophisticated technology. But mining, refining, and smelting iron ore are all painstaking, arduous processes. One smith told me the whole procedure took three weeks, but this would have varied according to the proximity of ore sources and the ore's specific characteristics. The final product, the bloom, was not quite so pure as that manufactured by modern European techniques. It contained bits of charcoal and residues of mineral impurities, or slag, not completely eliminated during the smelting operation. Subsequent forging helped expel most of these extraneous materials, but the tools ultimately fashioned of locally smelted iron were never completely free of them. This made the metal harder to shape, but it also had a helpful aspect, because the slag residues made the surface metal more brittle and able to hold a sharp edge longer.

Today, most Mande smiths collect leaf springs from French vehicles and other castaway artifacts of Europe's colonial and postcolonial presence. Imported iron is purer, and smiths often complain that it does not hold up as well as their own product, with the result that tools are frequently brought back to the forge for repairs. Imported iron is simply much easier to acquire, however, and I never heard a smith lament the loss of smelting.

Iron ore mining and smelting were widely practiced until the present older generation.[7] Reports on the processes were made by eighteenth- and nineteenth-century explorers, from the physician-traveler Mungo Park, who actually participated in a Maninka smelting operation in the late 1700s, to the colonial officer and archaeologist Louis Desplagnes, who included a photograph of Dogon smiths charging a furnace in his 1906 study of the Inland Niger Delta.[8] In the Bèlèdougou region around the town of Banamba, ore was still being smelted in the late 1960s. The same was true in the rugged and inaccessible Wasoulou region to the south and in portions of western Mali south of the city of Kayes.[9]

West Africa is quite rich in iron ore, and it has traditionally been acquired by the Mande in several ways. Sometimes ore occurs as small pebbles on the earth's surface and can simply be gathered up, as it was around Banamba. Elsewhere it occurs as large lumps of bog ore three to ten feet underground. Pits were dug to reach it, and sometimes, as for example around the southern town of Bougouni, small caverns were excavated at the base of the shafts (Ill. 14).[10]

Smelting furnaces were made in a tremendous variety of shapes and sizes, but most can be classified into types that correspond to the shaft and dome furnaces of preindustrial Europe. Mande shaft types were generally quite tall and relatively thin (Ill. 15). They ranged between six and twelve feet high, while they could be as narrow as sixteen inches across. Dome types were usually more squat (Ill. 16). They normally did not rise above seven feet and most often were much shorter. A chimney shaft emerged from a massive lower portion, which was shaped like a dome inside.

Often the interior chambers of both types extended down into the earth a foot or two. The furnaces, in fact, were made of earth, with materials such as rotting millet straw, animal dung, and pulverized termite mound mixed in to add strength and heat resistance. Usually they were fired once a year, and it seems that if well made they endured quite a number of firings. Most were designed to accommodate a number of long ceramic air tubes, or *tuyeres*, which allowed incoming air to be heated as it was guided down into the heart of the furnace. This preheated draft greatly enhanced the efficiency of the smelting operation.[11] In addition, the clay of these *tuyeres* became so hot during the firing that the lower ends melted away. This seems to have caused a natural fluxing of the ore, which also enhanced the smelting operation.[12]

As iron ore is smelted the mineral impurities become molten and flow away from the usable metal. Many Mande furnaces included channels for draining off this slag. The metal itself never became liquid but rather collected as a spongy mass that was easily removed after the furnace cooled. Charcoal was the principal combustion material. It was made of hard woods and then mixed very carefully with the ore, as a furnace was being charged for firing. Sometimes bundles of wood were set in furnace bottoms before firing to help ignite the charcoal. The length of a smelting varied according to the furnace; it ranged from ten to seventy-two hours. The quantity of iron produced from the firing of a furnace also varied. The literature suggests that large spongy masses could range from 200 to 330 pounds.[13]

Young smiths generally helped with iron smelting, hauling ore and charcoal and charging the furnace. The task was overseen, however, by a master smith with the reputation of having extensive technical knowledge. Many variables could be manipulated, from the size and shape of the interior combustion chambers to the size of the ore and the ratio of ore to charcoal. Because the operation was so grueling, failure was not appreciated, and, in spite of the variety of techniques, aspects of the technology—from combustion temperatures to chemical transformations—had to be extremely precise. Thus master smelters were highly regarded.

PRODUCTS

The earliest explorers to negotiate the Gambia River encountered blacksmiths and their products. Richard Jobson was the first, in 1623, and he noted the presence of smiths who made all of the swords, arrowheads, spearheads, and agricultural tools used by the Mandingo along the river. A century later, Francis Moore, an agent of the Royal African Company of England, lived for three years in the Gambia basin area and was taken with the locally made cutlasses.[14] A century later still, Major William Gray and Staff Surgeon Dochard undertook an extensive inland exploration of the western savanna and were impressed by the local smiths. They found the blacksmiths' products to be full of good taste and ingenuity, in spite of what they considered to be rough materials and rough tools. They observed knives, spearheads and arrowheads, bits and stirrups for horses, tweezers, turnscrews, and several other objects, along with the ever-present farming tools.[15]

Today we could make the list longer, adding nails, multipronged hooks for clearing wells of debris and recovering lost water containers, iron keys for wooden door locks, iron rasps for musicians, an occasional horse-drawn plow and Western-style crank bellows, guns, heavy axes for farmers, and very light axes for hunters. To acquire a sense of the variety in Mande smith work, we will focus our attention on several of these products.

Because agriculture is the mainstay of the Mande economy, agricultural implements are the mainstay of the blacksmiths. A line from a Mande epic poem puts it this way:

> The world would begin with farming,
> And it will end with farming.[16]

Thus blacksmiths will always be busy. In fact, as communities prepare to plant, cultivate, and harvest their crops, smiths are on everyone's mind. In late March or early April the "mango rains" arrive. Named for the fact that great gusts of wind knock mangoes out of trees, the rains are in fact meager. But they announce the coming of the wet season, and people begin their preparations. In about a month they will plant, to harvest finally in September or October. During this whole period smiths have a steady stream of customers who need new hoes made, old hoes repaired, or blades sharpened. Sedu found the time so lively that he had the habit of taking a vacation as soon as it was over, usually going off into the bush with his friends to hunt.

Smiths make a great variety of tools for farming. Most common are several types of hoe, which vary according to size, weight, and shapes of handles and blades and the angle at which the two are hafted together. The *daba* is the most widely used; it serves to some extent as an all-purpose tool for making planting mounds (Ill. 17). The *daba muso* is much larger, consisting of a complexly shaped handle and a wide blade hafted at a nearly obtuse angle (Ill. 18). It is designed to build large potato mounds. A smaller version of similar design, called *masi masi*, and the very smallest and simplest implement of this kind, the *falo*, are used to weed and maintain the mounds between planting and harvest. A very small tool with a variety of blade shapes, the *jalone* or *deni*, is used to make holes in the mounds for planting the seeds. The seeds are carried about in a little calabash, or *bara den*, which is cut, cleaned, and decorated by the smiths (Ill. 19). There are also very specialized tools, such as the *kado*, a huge blade reinforced with a series of raised ridges and hafted to a long handle for use in the cultivation of yams.

All the Mande hoes are designed to be hafted to heavy wooden handles.

The thin tang of iron inserted into the handle's head is generally just long enough to go all the way through. It is never bent around to lock the blade in place. To secure it, the farmer or the smith simply turns the hoe over so that the blade is pointing up and hits the back of the handle top against the earth. This wedges the tang in place so that the blade generally does not fall out while in use. If it breaks, however, or needs sharpening, one need only hit the handle top—on the other side this time, just beneath the blade—against a tree limb or anything hard and elevated enough to allow the blade free play. One or two sharp whacks and the blade falls out.

Like the hoes, harvesting and cutting tools also come in various types. Large axes, called *jelew*, are used to clear fields while sickles in varying sizes, *wòlòsow*, serve to clear grass. Millet and corn are harvested with a small knife, *muru*, or a specially designed tool called a millet knife, *nyo muru*. A larger knife called *muruba* or *sira baara muru* is used to cut tobacco (Ill. 20).

Smiths also make several earth-moving tools, designed for use in the manufacture of bricks and the construction of buildings, or when there is the need to move large quantities of dirt. Large picks or spades called *soliw* are used to break up earth or to loosen it for removal. The Mande use a truly enormous hoe-shaped implement much as we use a wheelbarrow. Called *njeruwe*, it looks like a cross between a hoe and a huge scoop (Ill. 21). The blade may be two feet long, and is very broad, with large side ridges. Hafted at a very acute angle, it can be carried with the wrist in a comfortable position while the blade is parallel to the ground. The handle is held with the haft in back, and when the carrier arrives at his destination he can dump his load by simply dropping his wrist.

Blacksmiths also make products for preparing the fruits of harvest. Mortars, *kolonw*, and pestles, *kolon kalaw*, are carved in great numbers and a variety of sizes (Ill. 11, 22). The Mande use them to husk grain, extract oil from karite nuts for cooking, and prepare sacrificial materials or herbal substances used in traditional medicines. Various knives and stirring implements are used in the kitchen with the clay cooking pots. Many other household objects—wooden beds, stools, doors, door locks, storage chests—are also made by blacksmiths (Ill. 23, 24). Family granaries also have smith-produced doors and locks, which are miniature versions of those found on homes. The few families able to keep a cow have carved wooden drinking troughs made by smiths (Ill. 25). Female members of smith families not only make all the cooking and storage pots but also on occasion make enormous indoor granaries, which are huge ceramic coils independently fired and linked by the kind of rabbit joinery Western carpenters use (Ill. 26).

Blacksmith products are thus key features of both home and field. But they can also be found almost everywhere else. In towns along the rivers, canoe and boat makers buy their tools from blacksmiths. So do the woodworkers who are not *nyamakala* clan members and, often, the leather workers. Professional weavers buy heddle pulleys from smiths for their looms, and some of these pulleys are splendid works of art (Ill. 27). Many people buy small wooden containers from the smiths and use them to carry everything from herbal concoctions to chewing tobacco.

The work of smiths even penetrates into the deepest bush, because it is the blacksmiths who provide the hunters with the equipment they need to survive and succeed in the bush. One of the most elegant of all the tools smiths make is the light ax called *sèmèn*, which no sensible hunter would ever be without (Ill. 9). It does double duty, being not only light enough to serve effectively as a utility ax but also heavy and well-balanced enough to serve as a club. Unlike most tools smiths make, this ax employs a socket mount. The handle is carved to a point that fits into a socket at the back of the blade. The hunter carries this tool balanced on his shoulder, and many hunters will not leave their family compounds without it.

Smiths make various other items for hunters. They include several sizes of knives and small iron tweezers for removing thorns. But by far the most important things smiths make for the bush are guns, *marafaw*, and except perhaps for smelting, these products are the most demanding technically (Ill. 28, Color Plate III).

We do not know when smiths first started making guns in the Western Sudan. European prototypes have been carried across the desert since the sixteenth century. For example, in 1582 the sultan of Morocco sent 200 soldiers armed with arquebuses to capture the salt mines at Taghaza. Three hundred years later the dynamic Dyula leader Samory used both imported and locally made guns when his army made its unsuccessful bid to defeat the French. Some sources suggest that he had 300 to 400 smiths working full time making guns and ammunition. It is said that they completed twelve guns a week, along with 200 to 300 rounds of ammunition a day. One of these smiths was even sent to take a gun-making course at the French arsenal in Saint Louis, Senegal, and, toward the end of the war, repeaters may even have been in production.[17]

The French commander Archinard, who was in charge of an artillery squadron at Bamako and wrote an informative article about the blacksmiths, examined some of Samory's guns. He found them to possess rough rifling near the muzzle end and terrible sights but very accurate breech mechanisms.[18]

Today, Mande smiths make both rifles (Ill. 29) and pistols,[19] in a range of sizes that vary according to the length and diameter of the barrel and, therefore, the power of the charge. I know of at least six rifle sizes, each with its own name.[20] They are used as single-charge weapons or as shotguns. In the latter instance they are loaded with a charge of small iron fragments from the blacksmith's forge; the fragments are held in place at the base of the barrel, *marafa bulu*, with small bits of rag.

The bullets, *kisew*, I saw made were not of the cartridge type. Rather, they were simply spheres forged from iron rods. Sedu made these bullets by heating a rod red-hot and cutting nearly all the way through it with a chisel at regular intervals. Then he broke each segment off by hitting it over the

edge of his anvil with a hammer. Next he put these little cubes in the charcoal basin, four or five at a time. Moving back and forth between the bellows
and the anvil, he removed them one at a time as they became red-hot again
and worked each until they were all roughly round. Finally, with a lighter
hammer and a softer touch, he worked them into neat little spheres.

Many smiths have a working knowledge of these guns, so that they can
take them apart and repair them when the need arises. But good Mande
guns are made by blacksmiths who specialize in the enterprise to the exclu-
sion of every other type of work. Such specialists are peppered across the
savanna. They do not live in every Mande town, but hunters know where to
find them and are perfectly willing to travel fifty miles or more to buy the
right gun from the smith of their choice.

In the eyes of other citizens, these specialists have attained a high level of
technical expertise. Indeed, Dyula groups in northern Ivory Coast honor
their rifle-making blacksmiths as the most accomplished and powerful of all
the wood and iron workers, an appropriate gesture given the recent Dyula
empire and the exploits of Samory.[21] Gunmaking blacksmiths possess the
typical array of tools, along with several more specialized items. Locally
made files, *kaka muruw*, are commonly claimed to predate the arrival of the
French and their European tool kits. Especially delicate anvils, *kulun guli-
maw*, drawn to a narrow tip in front are used to model a gun's percussion pin
and head. A knife-like tool called *nègènike muru* is sometimes used to put
threads on homemade screws. The screw is held fast in a pincer that works
like a vise, then set against the wooden top of one of the smith's hammers.
The blacksmith holds the hammer with his foot, leaving his hands free to
make the threads.

In some instances old firing mechanisms or parts from them are incorporated into new guns. In others the smiths forge all of the parts themselves.
They have no industrial aids at their disposal to ensure that the parts will fit
but instead depend on the accuracy of their sight, their memories, and their
very precise physical skills. At certain points in the fabrication process iron
pieces must be fused to one another. To weld the firing pin to the base of the
barrel, for example, smiths use an ingenious technique. They set the two
pieces together, with a fine film of white powdered flux called *burasi* applied
to both surfaces. Then they carefully coat and recoat the two joined pieces
with a clay solution that ultimately becomes a mold much like those used
across West Africa for lost wax casting. This mold is set into the charcoal
basin and covered with the coals. Then a number of smiths take turns pumping furiously on the bellows. The smith in charge keeps careful watch on the
charcoal, because it serves as his temperature index. After fifteen minutes or
more of dynamic pumping, the master smith stops the operation and examines the surface charcoal. If it continues to glow yellow and burn even when
air is no longer being forced through it, the smith judges the forge to be hot
enough to have effected the weld. During the whole operation the long gun
barrel has been sticking out of the forge, and shortly after the bellows work

begins, smoke starts pouring out of its end. This smoking barrel and the rapid bellows rhythms make the process exciting to watch.

The stocks of these guns are hollowed out, often in the most delicate fashion, to cradle the section of the barrel that holds the firing pin (Ill. 30) and to accommodate the firing mechanism and the housing for the trigger, called *kèlè tigelan*, "the war unleasher." The stocks often run to nearly the whole length of the barrel, which is lashed firmly into place at intervals with thick, tight bands of leather. Barrels themselves are made today from the steering columns of junked cars. Formerly, they may have been constructed by hammer-forging and welding long thin sections of iron around a perfectly cylindrical hard wood core.

Some of these guns are beautiful objects. Sedu Traore has a brother named Cekòrò Traore (Ill. 29), who lives in a small town well away from any of the main roads. With two blacksmith colleagues, Cekòrò specializes in the making and repairing of guns. When I first met Sedu he owned a large gun made by his cousin, but ultimately he found it a little too large and cumbersome for him. So he sold it and bought another from the cousin, the second smallest type, named *gwasaa*. This gun (Ill. 28) was elegant, being sensitively proportioned and delicately shaped. Cekòrò decorated the bottom and top of the stock with brass tacks and added an attractive metal inlay to the butt.

ARTICULATION

A beautiful gun is not surprising. It fits in with the products of many handcrafting cultures, and it certainly fits in with several things we have observed about Mande blacksmithing. But it is worthy of our attention a moment more, because it can be used to amplify an idea about articulation.

Mande smiths quite frequently remove their manufactures from the realm of pure utility by making them artful through addition. They do it most frequently with their door locks. Wooden locks with hollowed chambers for lock pins and sliding lock beams are not unique to this region of Africa. They are used by the Dogon nearby, and further east several Voltaic peoples use them. They are even known in North Africa, in basic versions consisting of a vertical rectangle of wood through which the lock beam passes. That basic form is elegantly but drastically transformed by smiths like Sedu Traore. Economy and abstraction make this possible. The lock is extended on top with the addition of a sculpted head. The thick vertical piece then becomes a torso or the body of an animal. It may swell at the sides to represent a turtle or extend at the bottom to suggest a lizard's tail.[22] Through economic additions and imaginative stylizations the locks become images. The same is true of many heddle pulleys and some knives (Ill. 27, 31); smiths change them from objects to images that interest Western curators and collectors.

Mande smiths also embellish their manufactures to make them nicer. Here too they are economical and imaginative, although their labor does not lead to figural imagery (Ill. 32). Sedu's gun falls into this category, but it is also something more. It is the product of great skill and great concern for form. It has been made beautiful not only by addition—the brass tacks—but also by articulation.

That gun is not unique, nor should we consider it typical. I have seen several that were not particularly attractive, and I have seen a few that appeared clumsy. Yet I have also seen several that showed as much concern for form as Sedu's, and this is true of many other blacksmiths' products.

I found it most striking in knives. Nearly every Mande who goes outside of town owns a knife, and many, such as hunters and blacksmiths, carry two or three in sheaths at their sides. Even sorcerers use knives, which they have prepared for special tasks by the addition of ritual and medicine. One might not take the time to concentrate on these little objects, but when one does, one finds a surprisingly large percentage to be simply beautiful forms. They can be very nicely proportioned. Great imagination may go into developing intricately shaped handles. The blades often taper or curve with elegance. And the visual interplay between handle and blade is often lovely.

The same is true of farming tools, though less frequently, since objects like hoes are literally beaten out by the dozens. Nevertheless, the blade and handle shapes can be beautiful, with sensitive curves and flares and a wonderful play between the two-dimensionality of the business ends and the three-dimensionality of the handles. Mande hoes, like knives and guns, can be richly articulated.

Do the Mande recognize this beauty? They are not particularly keen to talk about it. There is not a large, specialized vocabulary addressed to it. The literature does not contain many references to it. Under such circumstances we might invoke the old notion that African craft and art is aimed at utility alone and that aesthetics are ancillary to our inquiries. There is, however, some evidence that we should not ignore.

First, there are the objects themselves. So many are so sensitively composed that happenstance is simply out of the question. Blacksmiths spend many years refining their skills with hammer and adze, and we must expect many of them to put these skills to work aesthetically. Even if they have no elaborate aesthetic discourse and find the questions art historians ask a little absurd, they still shape their forms deliberately and find satisfaction in the results.

People's responses to forms lend support to this position. Sedu Traore was rarely neutral about a form. He was not inclined to analyze its parts, but he always made his feelings about the whole quite clear. Like smiths, members of the farming clans would also say what they liked or disliked, in discreet but concrete fashion.

Often, too, people's behavior toward objects was very revealing. Sedu had a hunter friend we visited in a large town well south of Bamako. On one of our visits I decided to wander around to photograph architecture. A middle-aged woman of imposing disposition approached to see what I was doing.

When her suspicions were confirmed, she dragged me over to her door and demanded that I photograph it (Color Plate IV). A most elaborate door lock was attached. It had been part of her wedding trousseau, and it remained something she cherished. She stated quite plainly that if I wanted to photograph nice door locks, I would find none as beautiful as hers anywhere in town.

In 1972 I met a woman at a blacksmith's forge who had come to have her hoe blade sharpened. She owned the type called *daba muso,* and it must have been ancient because it was deeply patinated. It was also absolutely elegant in its proportions and shape, without question one of the most exquisite tools I have seen anywhere. Intending to verify its type, I asked her its name. She said *Ci wara.*

Ci wara means several things. It is the name of a farming association that used to be a secret initiation society. Zahan and Imperato discuss it at length as the name of an agricultural deity.[23] It is also a praise name for good farmers. As such it means "farming animal" or "farming beast," using a Mande praise formula that likens accomplishment to wildness, ferocity, and awesomeness, and often incorporates implications of great age and high levels of *nyama.* Musicians and dancers are frequently praised with similar formulas, and it is considered honorable indeed. Thus the woman applied to her hoe a form of high praise customarily used for extremely accomplished people, and in the process indicated that she found it beautiful.

Thus the concern for articulation we first encountered with apprentices at their bellows extends from the processes of making things to the products made. Good form permeates the blacksmiths' experience, and they pass it along in their tools and weapons to everyone else. Articulation, in several forms and several realms, is a central feature of the Mande smiths' identity, and we will explore it in another of its dimensions in the next chapter.

THREE

SMITHS AND THE SHAPE OF CIVILIZED SPACE

Many blacksmiths are deeply involved in the articulation of Mande social and spiritual space. Their position in the social system primes them for such enterprise, while the technical nature of their craftwork predisposes them toward acquiring appropriate kinds of knowledge. Smiths are not the only people who shape cultural space. They share the task with bards, cult leaders, politicians, and elders. Nor is every blacksmith interested in such work. Some are quite content to confine themselves to iron and wood. Others do not have the disposition or intellect to venture beyond those materials. Nevertheless, virtually every Mande town has at least one smith with the acumen to play a major role in his community's social and spiritual life.

The blacksmiths' craftwork offers us a model to interpret these other activities. It makes them intermediaries between nature and culture. Smiths provide the tools and utensils people need to change important aspects of their physical environment. Agriculture is a good example. Seeds become sustenance through the use of a long chain of blacksmith products. These products help articulate nature, making it more useful to people.

Smiths shape social and spiritual life from this same vantage point, as intermediaries. They intervene and negotiate. They disseminate information and generate beneficial events. We can characterize them as coming between individuals, between individuals and situations, and between individuals and the forces at work in the Mande universe. Hopkins and Sidibé provide an appropriate example with reference to lineage structures. Smiths and the other *nyamakalaw* have the same kind of lineage systems as the rest of the Mande population. Normally, however, these systems are isolated from one another, and this isolation lends a certain political neutrality to smiths, enabling them to intercede in certain types of political situations.[1] This neutrality is largely theoretical. On the one hand, many blacksmiths aspire to political prominence and there are many ways they can achieve it. On the other hand, political allegiance with smiths is quite desirable and there are always means of arranging it. Still, their alleged neutrality is one of several criteria that qualify smiths to mediate.

Sorcery and herbal healing are the focal points of the blacksmiths' credentials as mediators. These two occupations interface in a system of knowledge and articulation that shapes reality through the activation of nature's resources and the energy called *nyama*. Organic substances are gathered, transformed, and assembled in configurations not found in nature. Spirit entities are called upon to offer up their special powers and capacities. Ritual is enacted to help make the assembly process correct and efficacious. At base, sorcery and healing are joined in a finely tuned body of procedures that rearrange elements in the practitioner's immediate vicinity so that vaster spaces may be reshaped.

Given what we have seen of smiths so far, it should not surprise us that large numbers of them become healers and sorcerers and that the entire profession is held to have a natural affinity toward manipulating nature's forces. The idea of secret expertise, "trade secrets," *gundow*, provides a rationale. The Mande say that every significant activity and profession has its secret expertise. Some professions, such as farming, make their expertise quite readily available. Others, such as hunting or smithing, apply more vigor to protecting their secrets, because the knowledge and skills involved provide power, prestige, and an aura of mystery. Still, nearly anyone can buy hunters' expertise by joining a hunters' association and partaking of the instruction and initiations it offers. The blacksmiths' trade secrets are by no means so readily available. Hardly anyone outside their clans can acquire them; endogamy is too deeply ingrained. People believe that the energy released in the activation of these secrets by outsiders would overwhelm and damage them. Furthermore, both blacksmiths and other citizens claim that the smiths' secret expertise is vast. No other profession has more trade secrets. Thus basic similarity inclines smiths toward healing and sorcery. Like smithing, healing and sorcery involve the use of *nyama* and arcane knowledge. Many smiths acquire a modest expertise in healing or sorcery and develop a small clientele to augment their incomes. Many others become so renowned in these practices that their clienteles extend over several hundred miles and they give up smithing altogether. Some smith clans even specialize to some degree in certain of these practices. While members of the Dunbiya clan most likely practice just wood and metal work, members of the Camara clan are likely to be herbal doctors, and members of the Kante clan are apt to be diviners, herbal doctors, or both.[2]

THE PRINCIPLES OF MEDICINE AND SORCERY

The Mande believe that illness, crop failure, unsuccessful commerce, and other calamities can be caused by the malevolent acts of people and spirits, or unguarded proximity to unbridled occult energy. Health and well-being can bè caused by the same agents acting benevolently, or the same energy properly manipulated.[3] The principles involved join a special kind of knowledge to particular types of articulation, in the hands of several types of experts.

The knowledge is called "the science of the trees" or "knowledge of the trees," *jiridòn*. It is grounded in the axiom that the world is full of useful entities; one simply needs to discover them. Close observation and experimentation with the savanna environment over many centuries have allowed Mande practitioners to compile an enormous traditional pharmacopoeia. It uses elements from the animal and vegetable worlds, and often inorganic matter as well. No single individual knows it all, or even most of it, and of course it is not written down. Rather, people acquire as extensive a knowledge as their practice requires, or as much information as they feel might some day prove useful. Sedu Traore liked to say that wisdom dictates the amassing of as much information about the natural environment as possible. One might never use it all, but if one's progeny find even a little of it helpful, then the effort was worthwhile. Sedu gave me a good idea of how much of this knowledge is to be had. He maintained what he called a modest practice as an herbalist, soothsayer, and sorcerer. I never learned the full extent of his clientele, but people sought his expertise in towns fifty miles and more from his home. I was with him once when an herbalist greeted us as we arrived in town to visit Sedu's brother, the gun maker. Evidently this fellow had learned of our trip and waited at the town entrance several hours for the chance to consult with Sedu on a particularly difficult problem. Sedu told me numerous times he considered himself to be only adequately versed in this Mande biology. Once, however, I asked him to name all the plants he knew and how they could be used. He laughed and asked if I had three days to spare.[4]

Although the precepts of its use differ, this knowledge is in fact rather like our biology. It calls for learning ecological zones and knowing what thrives in them, the growth stages of each inhabitant, and the uses to which each might be put. The leaves, bark, and roots of trees, for example, all have different properties, as do the bones, claws, skins, and organs of animals. How best to acquire these various elements and how to treat them once they are obtained comprise the principal interests of this "science of the trees."

Vast and valuable as it may be, this knowledge by itself is considered just the first half of a two-part system. To use it involves another important Mande idea: that information and materials can be arranged in practical configurations that allow people to accomplish things. These configurations are called *daliluw*. They are concise, goal-oriented clusters of information and instruction, recipes for the successful completion of an endless array of activities. Simultaneously they are the power behind human acts, the right to perform them, and their cause. Sedu says a *dalilu* is "the thing that can make something work." It is a form of articulation that draws knowledge into the realm of useful endeavor.[5]

There are *daliluw* for everything. Some are employed to diagnose and cure illness. Others help secure success in a business venture or a marriage. Others can be used to assassinate people. Still others provide the conceptual templates for the manufacture of amulets, guns, or any of the things that blacksmiths produce.

Normally, one acquires a *dalilu* by buying it. A special type of gift called a *kumaboli* is tendered, which balances the power that will derive from the *dalilu*'s use. In exchange the buyer receives what people call the *dalilu*'s tradition, *lada*. In the case of a medicine, for example, background information, ingredients, procedures for manipulating them, and proper applications of the finished product are all part of the tradition. A snake might be burned for its charred skin. Baobab roots might be pulverized and boiled and then combined with the fluids and powders distilled from other plants, insects, or animals according to an exacting formula that might include chanting, offerings to spirits, and other forms of ritual behavior. *Daliluw* that are not paid for are said not to be effective. One can receive all the necessary information, but without the gift of exchange somehow or other the recipe will not work.

A large percentage of *daliluw* can only be activated with the aid of "secret speech," *kilisi*.[6] This involves whispering or chanting a formula over ingredients as they are assembled, while rhythmically implanting in them a quantity of the speaker's spit. Speech is full of *nyama*. So are the chanted formulas and the saliva. The application of chanted utterances and saliva to the knots in a string or cord as they are being made can produce a potent amulet. In certain instances a single substance, like the karite oil used for cooking, is so empowered by the addition of "secret speech" that it becomes of itself a *dalilu*.

Ownership of many *daliluw* is restricted to certain types of individuals or certain families. Quite a large number are the heritage of smiths, and this is one reason why smiths are so often described as awe-inspiring and why they can be so influential in the affairs of their communities. There is also an interesting kind of knowledge, closely related to *daliluw*, with which people are said to be born. Sedu said it simply exists in people's heads at birth. It too is composed of knowledge activated by articulation, and it too is often confined to types of individuals or particular families.

Sedu Traore used to say that "good Bamana," that is, mature, sensible, and responsible citizens, made it their business to own as many *daliluw* as they could. Such acquisition is expensive and time consuming, however. It may also require long-distance travel, to contact a person in a faraway region known to possess a particularly desirable example. It may even be dangerous, because a person with a reputation for having large numbers begins to be viewed as a sorcerer and therefore becomes fair game for other sorcerers. For all these reasons, many people have little desire to acquire many of these units of useful information, preferring instead to pay for the services of those who do possess many. In a sense, Sedu was expounding upon the virtue and valor of his own profession, since large numbers of smiths make it their business to amass enormous collections, the fruits of which they gladly put at the disposal of their clients, for a fee.

These recipes for acts divide into a variety of types. There are, for example, a host of occult poisons called *kòròtiw*, which can be further divided into subtypes. Some are sent to their victims on the wings of insects. Others ride on sticks. Others are flung into the air or are sent long distances mounted on wind currents. Still others are slipped into a victim's food or drink. All of them are asserted to be potent, deadly devices that instill considerable disquiet among the Mande. Blacksmiths are reputed to have particularly vast collections of these unsavory items. In fact, they are said to have invented them. Another *dalilu* category includes the antidotes for these occult poisons, which are called *folifuraw*. Naturally, smiths have huge collections of these as well.

Some *daliluw* are designed to provide entertainment. One type in particular generates a spectacular response from audiences in both secular and sacred contexts. It makes performers appear to spit fire. I observed this fire spitting during a public performance by an amateur drum orchestra in Bamako. Several families in the western quarter of Ouolofobougou hired a band to perform one evening for the neighborhood. Amateur drum and balaphone groups are numerous among the Mande. Many young men enjoy the challenge of becoming good enough to earn reputations and extra money by performing at festivities such as weddings and parties. Some establish large followings in several towns, buy uniforms to enhance their image, and develop vary dramatic routines.

The band I saw was a competent local group, but as it happened a friend of theirs was visiting from the city of Ségou, and, since he was a terrific lead drummer, they invited him to play. He used a large heavy drum called a *jembe*, which stands about thirty inches high and is held between the performer's legs, with the aid of a strap that goes around his neck. This drummer was a virtuoso. His solos were complex, crisp, and very fast. He was also an acrobat, turning one-armed back handsprings every now and then to punctuate his playing. He also owned a *dalilu* for "fire spitting."

Suddenly, after a solo and a back handspring, he smiled, and his teeth glowed a bright reddish orange. This took the audience's breath away. He closed his mouth, performed another lengthy solo and smiled again, and again his mouth was aglow. The audience became completely still, and, as the drummer continued to play, he pursed his lips and exhaled with vigor. A fantastic spray of orange-red sparks poured from his mouth, traveling in a great arc some eight feet before hitting the ground or simply losing their luminosity. From the drummer's lips to the midpoint of the arch the sparks spread in a wide cone some two to three feet in diameter. The sheer volume of sparks emitted with each breath was staggering, and the master drummer continued to produce them for some five minutes. With each new blast the crowd shouted in awe and pleasant amusement. Fire, after all, can be dangerous. Yet, in contrast to the sparks that fly in a blacksmith's forge, these sparks that landed on my hand and on the faces of my companions produced neither a burn nor any other uncomfortable sensation. Considering the impact on the crowd, it was clear this master drummer had been most wise to buy a fire-spitting *dalilu*.

The type he bought is called "fire powder," *soro tasuma*. Its fabrication involves combining material from a number of trees whose names and habitats constitute the secret knowledge of the recipe. Once assembled, the powder can be inserted into the nose or mouth, where it absorbs moisture. In that damp state, air becomes a catalyst causing it to glow phosphorescently, thereby creating luminosity with no apparent source of light. Exhaling sends minute particles of this light hurtling from the orifice in great billowing patterns.

Although it is most dramatic, its owners are not numerous. Sedu Traore, who made a point of knowing who owned what *dalilu*, knew of two men living near Bougouni and a third to the north near Bamako who possessed it. This is largely because it has become expensive over recent generations. Sedu said that the most recent transaction he knew of cost the buyer a goat, a red rooster, and 3,000 Malian francs (roughly U.S. $7).

Under very different circumstances, a French colonial administrator at Kayes observed in 1943 what may have been a related means for generating luminosity. One night a seventeen-year-old girl began to glow, as if her body had been transformed into twenty to twenty-five luminous centers. The officer could learn nothing from the girl, but other informants suggested the glow might be an herbalist's cure for a problem that warranted psychological as well as physical ministrations.[7]

Another Mande *dalilu* for fire is more dangerous because it employs actual combustion. The roots of a particular tree supply the principal ingredient. A sufficient quantity is dug up and the bark removed. An organic crust that covers the bark is cut away with a knife. The bark is then placed in a mortar with the white, succulent portions of a certain type of savanna grass, and the two are pounded together. A small quantity of gunpowder may be added to the mixture. The final product resembles dried moss; and when lit, it smolders very slowly. When oxygen is forced through it, however, great volumes of minute sparks fly off, creating a dramatic orange cascade of "fire."

Part of this *dalilu* involves preparing a protective container that can also act as a nozzle to launch the sparks. A very small antelope horn, no more than two inches long, serves the purpose. The tip is removed first so that air can be blown through the horn. Then the horn's outside surface is wrapped with something sticky (today, bicycle tape is used), so that the person spitting fire can clamp it firmly between his teeth. Finally, the flammable substance is packed tightly into the horn. Now the user need only touch a match to the contents and place the device in his mouth, so that the narrow end protrudes just slightly from between his front teeth.[8]

A variant of this recipe employs the leaves and stems of another kind of plant, pounded to a pulp in a mortar that has been used to beat karite oil nuts. Small traces of the oil are absorbed by the pulverized vegetation, which can also then be put into a small horn and ignited.[9]

The horrific, horizontal masks that blacksmiths make and dance in the kòmò initiation association are said sometimes to spit fire as part of their dramatic performances. The art history literature has never discussed Mande "fire spitting," but it has pondered the phenomena just to the south among the Senufo, where masks very similar to kòmò masks are used in similar contexts.[10] The Senufo masks have come to be known as "fire spitters" because their wearers, like the drummer in Bamako, could generate the effect of fire. Scholars have never determined conclusively, however, how the Senufo version is accomplished. In the 1930s the Belgian anthropologist Albert Maesen reported that Senufo dancers blew sparks and little flames out the mouths of their masks. The technique involved igniting small pieces of resin-coated grass by blowing on a piece of smoldering wood apparently retained in the mask's mouth.[11] But lengthy debate has focused on the fact that no Senufo masks of the types said to "spit fire" show any sign of charring from smoldering materials placed in the mouth. The art historian René Bravmann offers a solution with reference to a Mande ethnic group called the Ligbi, who live east of the Senufo in the area of Bondoukou. Here too are masks that relate to those used in the kòmò association, and Bravmann notes that they spit fire with the aid of live embers set in clay cups that are glued inside the masks' mouths.[12]

If we return to the Senufo, however, an early report by the colonial administrator Maurice Prouteaux brings us back to the enigma. In 1914 he observed a masked dancer who from time to time would let two fistfuls of sparks and what he described as tiny glowing coals fall down the surface of his highly flammable costume. Furthermore, the dancer was capable of making the "fire" penetrate the straw roofs of "sorcerer's houses" without setting them ablaze.[13] Perhaps the dancer used a recipe like the Mande drummer's dalilu, a possibility made quite plausible by the many cultural and historical relationships that the Senufo have with the Mande.

A HIERARCHY OF PRACTITIONERS

The men who dance powerful Mande cult masks, such as kòmò, are always considered sorcerers. Often, if they also are administrators within the group, they are considered priests as well. Other masquerade dancers, however, and other types of performers may possess many daliluw but be considered sorcerers in only a limited way. Sidi Ballo is a good example. He is a well-known itinerant performer of the "bird dance," *kònò dòn*. Dancing inside a large cloth cone that is supported by a bamboo frame, he manipulates a carved wooden bird's head mounted at the end of a three-foot staff (Ill. 33). The masquerade is heavy and cumbersome, but Sidi manages nevertheless to perform some marvelous feats with it. He leaps over benches, bounds horizontally into walls, climbs bleachers, and even contrives to turn the costume upside down while he continues to dance. At one point in his performance he lays the whole masquerade on its side and opens up the bottom, challenging his audience to find him inside. They claim they cannot see him, and during the performance I witnessed I was able to see well inside the costume, but I could not find him in there, either.

Sidi claims he owns a *dalilu* that makes him invisible, to the point that he could walk down a street in broad daylight and no one could detect him. In fact, Sidi owns several of these devices. Some are intended to enhance his performances. Others are intended to protect him from dangers inherent in his work, such as tripping over benches and skewering himself on the bamboo frame of his costume. Still others are intended to protect him from anyone in his audiences jealous enough of his accomplishments to activate sorcery against him. This makes Sidi in one sense a sorcerer himself, and his fans often encourage people to see him in that light. Indeed, several told me that he was capable of miraculously leaping in and out of trees. But Sidi confines this sorcery to the arena of performance, whereas *kòmò* mask dancers use both their sorcery and the arena of performance to manipulate events in larger social, political, and spiritual contexts. How are we to differentiate these actors in the realms of medicine and sorcery?

The Mande use a variety of words to characterize them. We can begin with "wise persons," *domaw*, who in fact are not actors at all. These individuals have reputations for knowing much about the world, for being well versed in the "science of the trees," for example. They rarely exercise their knowledge on the plane of occult action, however, and so, while they are respected tremendously, they are not held in the awe or fear reserved for people who activate their knowledge.

Basitigiw are "masters of secret things," people with a large or small number of *daliluw* at their disposal. Sidi Ballo could be considered such a person. So could someone who owns a few herbal cures or amulet recipes and sells them to clients, most often to augment incomes in other professions. People more deeply involved in medicine and sorcery can be called "masters of the leaves," or "masters of medicine," *furatigiw*. These people are likely to have more extensive collections of recipes and remedies and may also be more skilled at making diagnoses. They may practice divination as well as medicine, and they may claim to affect both the occult world, through the manipulation of the world's energy, and the physical world, through the manipulation of herbal preparations. Such people can emphasize doctoring, or sorcery, or both in their practices, and the famous ones need do nothing else for their incomes.

When the Mande contemplate malicious sorcery they distinguish two basic types of sorcerers, although the distinguishing characteristics are often blended in individuals, and one name, *subagaw,* is often used loosely to refer to them both. Strictly speaking, the first type are called "sorcerers who eat people," *mògòdun subagaw* or *mògò domu subagaw.*[14] Such persons are said to be born with voracious appetites for human flesh, though many of them apparently do not know it until a chance set of circumstances or an act of divination reveals their true nature. Some are believed so hopelessly dominated by their appetites that they will eat their own children and then deny it, claiming that some other source caused the deaths. A *kòmò* cult song illustrates this, with the formula:

> Hard-hearted sorcerer-woman finished eating all her children,
> Saying chicken-pox is on my children.

Or, a few lines down:

> Small-pox is on my children.

Or, still further down:

> Diarrhea illness is on my children.[15]

These sorcerers do not devour people physically. Rather, they are said to dine supernaturally on the vital organs of their victims, most frequently at night while the unsuspecting souls are asleep. Some of these sorcerers are not even aware of what they are doing, but nevertheless the Mande claim that their victims grow sick and ultimately die, sometimes after lengthy bouts of progressive dissipation for which there seem to be no natural causes.

Sometimes these malevolent sorcerers attack their victims with special occult powders that induce illness. Other times they use supernatural spears rendered invisible through a *dalilu.* Often the sorcerers transform themselves into animals or even a mist that can penetrate thatch roofs or pass under locked doors. However they act, the reason for their actions is always the same. They prefer the taste of human flesh to any other form of meat.

Sorcerers of the second type do not devour people. Nor are they necessarily born into their avocations. Often they are capable of transforming themselves into other animals or entities, but their greatest sources of power are their mastery of the "science of the trees" and the extent of their repertoire of *daliluw.* Often they lay traps for people, "sorcerer's nets," *sujew,* composed of invisible force fields activated by *kilisi* secret speech. Crossroads are favorite repositories for such devices and are favored congregating places where these sorcerers can band together to plot the demise of their victims. Thus this warning in a blacksmith's song:

> Large crossroads, sorcerers meet each other there.
> A crossroads is never empty.[16]

Thus too the fact that most Mande approach crossroads with caution.

As in any other society, there are always people quite prepared to harness sorcery against their fellow citizens. Still, as we have noted, the same resources can be used by people doing benevolent works. And often enough there are those individuals who work malevolently in some situations and benevolently in others. The Mande call them all sorcerers.

Particulary powerful and frequently aggressive sorcerers may be called *somaw*. They are viewed as possessing all of the capabilities of sorcerers, and many more. In a sense they are like the magicians that populate our medieval tales. Often these individuals become the antagonists of malevolent sorcerers, quite frequently overwhelming them with their own supersorcery. Sometimes they are commissioned by individuals or communities to take up such a fight. Sometimes they simply decide to consider the work of another sorcerer as a challenge.

Somaw often aspire to greatness; they wish to become heroes, *nganaw,* so that their names and deeds will be remembered by the bards and become a part of Mande history. As a result their characters are full of a kind of unconstrained ferocity called *karo* that makes them unbelievably tough. This makes them effective at fighting malevolent sorcery, but it by no means prevents them from behaving malevolently themselves. Sometimes, through subtle combinations of treachery and sorcery, they secretly create serious problems, with the goal of subsequently being asked to solve them and thereby become heroes. That is why Mande say that "the hero is welcome only on troubled days."[17]

Many blacksmiths become *somaw*, and in former times they often asked a trusted woman friend to make a single braid for them on the tops of their heads, with the rest of their hair shaved off. The braid became a symbol of stature and power and served as an open challenge to anyone with the taste for a sorcerer's duel.[18] Mande sorcerers are always considered fair game for each other, and often they attack one another just to prove their ability. The approach can be with *kòròtiw* poisons or any means at their disposal. The approach can also be shockingly insidious, with lengthy plans developed that include layer after layer of strategy. There is never a moment or a place where sorcerers can feel safe enough to relax. That is why some try to remain anonymous. With their braids, however, *somaw* blacksmiths made themselves conspicuous.

The effect of those braids, aggrandized no doubt for the benefit of today's blacksmiths, is referred to in a smiths' song that honors several great practitioners. It includes these lines:

The blacksmith Satigi's braid has become something lethal.
If a *soma* were to see it,
If a good-for-nothing *soma* were to see it,
His ideas would become numerous.[19]

Satigi was an extremely famous *soma* blacksmith who passed away recently.
The lines imply that, faced with Satigi's braid, a less powerful sorcerer would
find himself thinking too much. He would become unsure of himself, inde-
cisive and afraid. The song goes on to suggest the purgative effect the braid
could have on the type of sorcerers who eat people:

The person-eating sorcerer who sees it,
Will spew his victim's blood and confess.

By confess is meant a thorough, painful revelation. Every serious antisocial
act such persons have committed would be confessed. The blood of their
victims, mystically retained in their bodies, would be disgorged along with
the names of everyone they devoured. The names of other malevolent sorcerers would also be disclosed, so that a chain reaction of retribution might
be set in motion. Finally, these people-eaters might themselves become victims, driven mad or killed by the powers contained in the *soma*'s braid.[20]
    A hierarchy of power is implied in these terms, from the wise persons
called *domaw* who never act to the most potent sorcerers called *somaw* who
act often and with ferocity. We must not consider the hierarchy rigid, however, because the Mande themselves apply these terms with considerable
variation. *Somaw* are called *subagaw* by some people, and both can be
called "masters of secret things." Nevertheless, it is worth noting that blacksmiths are often found among the sorcerers that garner the greatest praise
while creating the greatest fear. With this in mind we should now examine
some of the things that blacksmiths do as spiritual articulators and social
mediators.

RAINMAKING

Blacksmiths say they can bring rain, and in these savanna lands where agriculture is so important, rainmaking is a precious ability. Labouret and Dieterlen say the Mande attribute this ability to control over what they call the
"*nyama* of the sky." Allegedly that control can be so exact that rain can be
brought down, or suspended in the air at will.[21] The smith Seydou Camara
explained to me that he could literally direct the flow of rain across an area.
He claimed that once he was actually commissioned by a town to bring rain,
while simultaneously being commissioned by one family in town to keep the
rain away from their field because they were not finished with their planting.[22] The Mande believe that rainmaking is one of the skills smiths are born
with, although not all of them are good at it. Sedu Traore informed me that

often several smiths in a community undertake the procedures together. Although the precise mechanisms they use are held in the strictest secrecy, the act is accomplished through a combination of the special power smiths are born with and the secret knowledge they can acquire during their apprenticeships. Thus fortified, Sedu concluded, their level of success is high.[23]

Marabouts, the holy men of Islam, are believed by many to possess similar powers, and a kind of rivalry exists between them and the smiths. Especially in towns where the Muslim population is strong, a marabout may be called upon or, just as frequently, may volunteer his rainmaking services, for a fee which smiths claim is never refunded, even when he fails. In southern Mali, at least, marabouts are said to fail quite frequently, and smiths prefer to wait until that has happened before consenting to try themselves. They are asked diplomatically just to do a little of their work to make it rain. They respond by saying they have waited so that the authorship of the successful act would be clear. To me Sedu said that "even if you have some power, if you want to be useful to people, if you don't tell them, they will not know."[24]

DIVINATION

Great value is placed on divination as a process that can help solve problems, improve one's life, and, in general, assist individuals in living up to the full capacities that constitute their destinies. Several people in every town have special knowledge and special powers enabling them to ascertain events likely to occur in the future and to determine the cause of present situations. These talents are not unique to the Mande, for they share them with other practitioners throughout black Africa, from the *babalawo* Yoruba priests of Ifa to the Kuba, Luba, and Azande divination specialists in Zaire, known for their use of beautifully sculpted rubbing oracles.[25] The Mande view of their own divination procedures and practitioners must be distinguished immediately from our views of Western fortune tellers. We often attribute to such persons the powers of observation and simple psychological perceptions, usually joking that their vague or ambiguous predictions serve them well, and thinking very infrequently about those who seem quite successful. In the Western Sudan there are also those who pretend to know, but, as success comes to them only occasionally, the Mande's desire for practical results assures that such charlatans will soon be clientless. True experts are believed to arrive at their conclusions by using procedures that tap the natural order and operation of the universe.

Such experts are known commonly as "persons who know," *dònni kelaw.* Other titles provide insight into the ways in which they are perceived. *Kunnyininai* means "reason seeker," *flelikela* means "someone who looks," *lajelikela* means "someone who examines." The techniques they use to look and examine vary widely. Some employ an old pair of sandals. Others use a small black bag filled with occult materials.[26] In one type the practitioner uses no physical devices at all, but rather depends upon his relationship to a wilderness spirit. The spirit "haunts" him on prescribed days each week, and under its influence the diviner simply looks at clients to learn everything about them, instantly. People with this kind of relationship to spirits are called "masters of spirits," *jinatigiw*. Most frequently they are Muslim marabouts or smiths.[27]

Many blacksmiths practice divination. A variety of techniques are at their disposal, but a smith is likely to specialize in one or two.

Among the myths that Monteil collected, one relates the exploits of a smith named Fa Sine Dyara, who assisted a Bamana leader named Sounsan through soothsaying. Dyara understood the "language of the birds" and he was able to advise Sounsan on the area in which he might most beneficially settle. Sounsan, favorably impressed, then established an agreement by which Dyara would continue to provide the king and his descendants with divined information in exchange for gifts of horses and the promise of royal protection.[28]

Another divination technique involves the use of snakes. Masters of this method are believed to have the power to call serpents to them from the bush. During the foreseeing procedure, the reptile's movements constitute symbolic gestures that are mystically interpreted to provide the answers to a client's questions. The Mande author Camara Laye provides an eyewitness account of this divination method. He notes that it was practiced to great advantage by his father, who was a famous Maninka smith in the Republic of Guinea. A key to his success involved a relationship he maintained with a small snake, which Camara would see from time to time leaving his father's compound. The snake helped the metalsmith know in advance what sorts of work his clients would be bringing him. Thus, he was always prepared.[29]

A very famous Mande smith also divined with snakes. By the time he died in the late 1970s, Satigi Sumanguru had become one of the most powerful smiths in Mali. His name, Satigi, means "master of snakes" and he is said to have been capable of calling them to him and communicating with them whenever he liked. It is also said that his entire family was protected by his power from poisonous snake bites. In addition to divining with snakes, Satigi also performed with them at festivals. He would first pour sand from his hands into three neat mounds on the ground. Then, without touching the mounds, he would cause a serpent to emerge from each.[30] Be they sleight of hand or supernatural acts, such performances had the effect of graphically advertising Satigi's special abilities.

Satigi was part of a larger tradition of snake manipulating, a tradition the English explorer Alexander Gordon Laing noted in his 1825 account of travels through the area that is now Sierra Leone and the Republic of Guinea. Near the Mande Kuranko, in what he called the Soolima Nation— apparently part of the Mande Djalonke (or Jallonke)[31]—Laing was treated to a performance by a man who manipulated snakes. The man played a calabash guitar and sang that he could "cure diseases" and "make wild beasts tame and snakes dance,"[32] all through the power of his music. Then, stating that he would prove it, the performer picked up the tempo of his music. A large snake then crawled out from under some stockading and crossed a courtyard rapidly, heading for the Englishman. Again the performer changed the tempo and sang:

> Snake, you must stop; you run too fast, stop at my command, and give the white man service.

The snake stopped and the singer continued:

> Snake, you must dance, for a white man has come to Falaba, dance snake, for this is indeed a happy day.

Laing then described the snake's response:

> The snake twisted itself about, raised its head, curled, leaped, and performed various feats, of which I should not have supposed a snake capable; at the conclusion, the musician walked out of the yard, followed by the reptile, leaving me in no small degree astonished.

Malian snake handling cults have been described by Imperato; similar cults in Liberia have been described by the missionary George Harley.[33] Members frequently use herbal concoctions while catching and handling snakes. Such solutions are very effective at stupefying the snakes and making them much easier to control. In serpent divination, however, the union between seers and snakes takes this manipulation one step further, into the realm of a supernatural bond.[34]

Throwing cowry shells, *kolonw*, is a popular form of divination that Seydou Camara used frequently. It involves the tossing or scattering of twelve, twenty, or forty shells, which have had their backs removed so that they are as likely to land on one side as they are on the other. Practitioners look for configurations in the tossed shells. Each possible figure is associated with a variety of meanings, and from among them the diviner selects those that fit the client's situation. When the shells are cast, many will be scattered into isolated positions, creating no meaningful arrangements. Seers look for groups of up to four shells, aligned through contact or overlap (Ill. 34). According to the methods Seydou employed, balanced configurations carry positive weight; imbalanced configurations carry negative weight. Two shells touching in a perpendicular alignment suggest the existence of an enemy, someone bearing ill-will or possessing evil intentions. A similar configuration, with one shell facing up and the other facing down, suggests the existence of a friend or benefactor who may be involved in the client's predicament. The possibility of good fortune in the near future could also be indicated.

Balanced cowry configurations are referred to as "cool," *suman*. Other configurations in this category can project the possibility of a prosperous marriage, a forthcoming child, or the arrival of a stranger full of good will.

Four cowries in a row indicate the client will soon encounter a "soulmaster," *jatigi*, a protector and benefactor, a person who will provide assistance and education of a most valuable nature. Two shells side by side and facing down represent a call for sacrifice, to ensure something beneficial or detour something unpleasant. All the figures have names, and meanings that are fluid enough to symbolize types of solutions practitioners can match to particular problems. In Seydou's view, the configurations do not occur haphazardly. Rather, they result from the fields of energy through which the client is moving. Divination involves a sensitive monitoring of those energies by individuals powerful and skilled enough to encourage the cowries to provide an index of the state of things in the immediate spiritual environment.[35]

Stone throwing, *belejiki*, is another divination technique that Seydou favored. He regularly used it to check the results he obtained from cowry shell divination. The stones are quite small. When thrown, the important ones are those that remain in the hand, or which can be picked up instantly in a graceful, fluid gesture that continues the hand's original throwing movement. The quantity held in the diviner's hand determines the figures to be made with them (Ill. 35). Three will be arranged in a triangular pattern symbolizing a man; four, in a similar arrangement but with the fourth placed above the apex of the triangle, symbolize a woman. Three rows of two stones suggest kindness, goodness, a benevolent situation.

Individual figures do not tell enough, however, and the diviner will leave the first on the ground and augment it with three or four additional throws. He places these new figures next to the first, working left to right to make a narrative of future events, a story that develops with each new throw. If the first sign were *Kumardise*, the black man, and the second simply two stones placed in vertical alignment, an ambiguous situation would have been established demanding resolution by an additional throw. If the third figure is *Yarase*, the black woman, then the second becomes *maro maro*, a child in its mother's womb, and the configuration of three figures signifies that the woman has conceived and that a child has been created between her and the man.[36]

In another type of divination, practitioners draw their own meaningful configurations instead of using material objects such as stones or cowries to construct them. The technique is called "putting it down in sand," *cenda*. Laing observed a variant procedure called *saduk* when he visited the Soolima Nation in 1822:

> A quantity of fine sand being spread on the ground, a number of hieroglyphic figures are marked on it at random; these are examined by the elders, who pretend to be enabled thereby to foretell future events.[37]

Cenda is the divination method Sedu Traore favors. He keeps a pile of sand in his forge (Ill. 36) just next to his bellows. When clients call he spreads the sand with his hand to create a flat smooth drawing surface. After ascertaining the client's problem, he closes his eyes and tilts his head back slightly. Designs are then drawn in the sand, as if they were the product of a kind of automatic writing. Sedu examines the signs carefully, to assess the client's situation and best-advised course of action.

In *cenda* especially, the important nuances of balance and harmony are graphically depicted (Ill. 37). Figures comprised of three marks arranged in a triangle, the apex of which faces down, represent a negative sign. They allude to the earth and the downward pulling effect of ancestors, suggesting death. A similar arrangement with apex facing up implies danger, because it points to the realm of gods and, as Charles Bird points out, the principles of hazard and chance.[38] Balance is implied when a figure is comprised of two marks side by side, or four marks arranged in the shape of a lozenge. Here a visual metaphor is made between the harmony established in the sand composition and the benevolence that will characterize the client's situation.

Sedu once told me that compared to *cenda*, techniques such as cowry throwing are just playing. Seydou Camara would hardly have agreed, of course, and in the end such statements partially derive from the fact that diviners tend to take most seriously the methods with which they have experienced the best success. According to the findings of Sarah Brett-Smith, who worked in the Bèlèdougou area north of Bamako, the interpretation of *cenda* signs is based on standardized mathematical formulas.[39] This element of systematization may have contributed to Sedu Traore's feelings about the method.

Many more divination methods are available. Chickens can be used to check the efficacy of sacrifices for which they have just been killed. Their necks are cut, and their blood is used as an offering. They are then tossed several yards away, and when they come to rest, a seer examines their positions. If both legs are down, the earth, ancestors, and malevolence are suggested. If both legs are up, the sky, gods, hazard, and chance are suggested, and an additional sacrifice will be made to help convert that chance into benevolence. If the chicken lies on its side, with its top leg in front of the bottom leg, the forces of earth and sky are in harmony[40] and the sacrifice is judged a success.

Certain types of divination fall within the domain of blacksmiths. That does not mean that no one else can practice them, but rather that everyone else must learn them from a smith. Procedures controlled by the smiths vary from area to area. In southern Mali, and especially in the Wasoulou, these procedures include looking into water, cowry throwing, sand drawing, and rubbing old sandals with a smooth stone.[41] Another method employs a woven wicker fan, which is used rather like a divining rod. *Kilisi* secret speech is uttered over it and it will then turn either to the left or right in the diviner's hand, providing a yes or no response to questions.[42] In yet another method, cowry shells are placed around the edge of a small black wooden disk. When a cowry freezes in place, a question has been answered in the affirmative, similar to the way in which rubbing oracles in central Africa are used.[43]

Many smiths make a device that directs energy into its owner, who then becomes clairvoyant. Called "black bag," *bòròfin*, it is composed of an animal's tail, the base of which is set in a cloth or leather bundle. Cowry shells and brass bells are attached to the outside, while *dalilu* recipes are hidden inside. In use the device seems to possess its owner, who dashes about and reveals things.[44]

Divination deals in probabilities rather than certainties. Thus many practitioners check their findings in one method with another. I have seen Seydou Camara begin divining with cowry shells, then switch to small stones, and finish by throwing halved kola nuts. If the nuts corroborated his other findings, he made them into a sacrifice to encourage accuracy further.

DOCTORING

The blacksmith Sedu Traore is an herbalist, *furatigi*, or "doctor," *dòkòtòrò*, a term transformed from the French. Like other herbal practitioners, he has a reputation for treating certain illnesses successfully. Since he is frequently called upon for them, he keeps a supply of the necessary materials on hand (Ill. 38). Among the medicines Sedu makes regularly are two, *dono turu* and *siyo*, prescribed for general stomach disorders and one, *nte*, for menstrual cramps. Another medicine, called *pompo mpogolo* or *jabi da fura*, was also prepared for a particular stomach problem. Called *ken kun*, "big belly," it is believed to be inflicted by sorcery and is serious enough to cause death if not countered. While fabricating its cure, Sedu utters *kilisi* secret speech to supply it with *nyama*.[45]

Sedu treats rheumatism with a solution he calls "medicine for broken bones," *furakoloci*. In cases of temporary impotence he prescribes a small branch from a particular tree, to be used in the manner of a chewing stick with the pulp extracted and the juices swallowed. As a general tonic restricted to blacksmiths' use, Sedu prepares a drink he refers to simply as "liquid medicine," *fura ji*. Finally, among the more complex preparations is another ambiguously titled mixture, "smith's powder," *numu soro,* made on the basis of knowledge that some blacksmiths are born with and which is not available to anyone else. It combines materials from six trees and a form of mushroom, all of which are burned together in precise proportions with the resulting powder extracted and stored in a small antelope horn, *binye*. As a prophylactic, the powder is carried to prevent the bite of poisonous snakes, and it serves, too, as a general healing agent for cuts and scrapes. A medicine in ointment form, which may be related, was recorded by Raffenel in 1847.[46]

Some healing procedures can only be carried out by blacksmiths. Sedu described one to me that is particularly fascinating. He was approached by a Fula family with a very sick child, whose symptoms were familiar. Although neither he nor anyone in town knew the ailment's name, it had been seen before and never known to be cured, not even when the young patients were sent to the hospital in Bamako. The Fulas insisted, however, that they had heard blacksmiths alone were able to cure the disease, by cleaning out the forge's charcoal pit, placing the child in it, and working the bellows to engulf the child in smith-enriched air. Sedu says he managed to cure the child in this manner, although he never learned the name of the ailment.

The research of Eugenia Herbert and Pascal James Imperato has brought to light a widespread and ancient medical practice that Mande smiths share with other African doctors. Smallpox variolation, carried out in traditional African contexts, was first noted by non-Africans in Boston when the Reverend Cotton Mather observed scars on slaves and inquired after their meaning. At that time, 1706, epidemics were frequent in both Europe and America, but variolation had not been tried. In this particular area of disease control, then, Africa led the Western world and, given the matter-of-fact manner in which the procedure was explained to Mather, we may assume that it was already well established in Africa by the 1700s. Variolation is known to have been practiced throughout the Western Sudan. To the south, it was also used in portions of the rain forest, such as southwest Nigeria, where Yoruba priests of the cult of Soponnon, god of smallpox, controlled the practice.[47]

Among the Bamana it was observed initially by the French explorer Louis-Gustave Binger in the 1880s. Six decades earlier Laing had made a naive observation which, nevertheless, suggests a possible familiarity among the southern Mande with variolation. Having himself vaccinated a number of children, he noted:

> . . . it is in itself an interesting fact, that a nation so far in the interior of Africa, should have so readily submitted, at the instigation of a white man, who was almost a stranger to them, to an operation against which so much prejudice existed for so many years in the most enlightened and civilized countries in Europe![48]

The use of a traditional Bamana variolation procedure to contain smallpox epidemics in 1913 and in 1963 was documented by Imperato, who also recorded its use among the Mande Bozo to the northeast. The procedure consists of applying the tip of a hot poker, the type used by smiths at their forges, to the deltoid area of the arm, and then rubbing the vesicular fluid from an active case of pox into the burned area.[49]

Mungo Park, who was himself a British doctor, made the earliest European observation on the surgical aspects of Mande medicine. In the late 1790s he found their techniques for dealing with dislocations and fractures quite successful, their splints and bandages "simple, and easily removed." Patients with broken bones were well cared for, being positioned upon a comfortable mat with the area of fracture washed frequently in cold water. He observed that abscesses were opened and cauterized effectively, in the same motion and with the same instrument.[50] He also remarked that medical dressings were variously composed of soft leaves, karite butter, or cow dung and indicated that the choice was up to the doctor's judgment. He documented the use of vapor baths to induce extreme perspiration and thereby effectively alleviate fever, and he noted that the ceremonies often associated with treatments were superstitious by his standards but of psychological benefit to the patients.[51]

Among the southern Mande, Laing found the use of numerous, potent herbal medicines to be effective. In contrast to the northern Mande, however, he noted that their surgical procedures were poorly carried out.[52] In the Gambia River basin, medical practices of the Mande state of Wuli impressed Gray, whose own expedition suffered great hardship from fever and dysentery, the result being the loss of apparently over half his men. He said that "in some cases I had recourse to the remedies made use of by the natives of Africa, and whenever those were resorted to in time, the disease soon gave way."[53]

AMULETS AND SECRET DEVICES

Amulets, sometimes known as talismans or charms, are made by smiths and are exceptionally important components of traditional life. Many resemble metal jewelry or knotted lengths of twine, but others are distinctive in appearance, constructed in the form of supernaturally charged materials protected inside a small leather packet. These packets can be rectangular or square and come in various thicknesses and sizes. Some are mounted on a cord and hung from the wrist, neck, waist, or over one shoulder and under the other arm. They may be hung singly, in clusters, or in evenly spaced groups. Other amulets are sewn to the outside of clothes or pinned inside them. Some are hidden in a pocket or purse. Some are even made in the form of stuffed leather tubes that become bracelets or belts.

There are hundreds of different kinds of amulets, each designed for a specific function. The Mande believe they can protect the young and old from certain diseases. They can enhance a merchant's chances for financial gain, or help deter serious loss or accident—one in the form of a thick leather belt is even said to guard against the hazards of frequent long-distance travel. They can inspire love, or trust, or friendship from others. They can amplify one's political acumen or make one impervious to the attacks of others. Hunters, especially those who spend much time in the bush, possess large numbers of amulets. They use them to help track and kill animals, to protect themselves from the dangers of *nyama* released upon an animal's death, and to preserve themselves from perils such as poisonous snakes and lions. Amulets are, in short, prominent physical manifestations of Mande beliefs about the world's deep structures and the practical access that human beings have to them.

The Mande commonly call amulets *sèbènw*. The same world means "writing," which suggests in part the nature of some amulets' contents, and, conversely, reinforces the fact that most Mande written scripts are secret and intended quite often for spiritual use. Someone who makes amulets is generally referred to simply as an "amulet maker," *sèbèn dlan la*.

As in the case of sorcery itself, the names applied to these products of sorcery can be used with considerable flexibility. In my own experience, a *basi*, strictly speaking, is very much like an amulet (*sèbèn*), except that it is likely to be larger and is often composed of exposed animal parts, or sizable pieces of animal hide rolled around secret contents (Ill. 39). A *boli* is contructed of similar materials, but it may generally be distinguished by a heavy coating of earth or mud, and pronounced traces of blood sacrifice (Ill. 40). All of these creations are power objects, and the distinctions between them tend very much to blend. Thus people often use the terms interchangeably.[54] They are spoken, however, only in private, restricted conversations, because even though the objects may be openly displayed, they are still secret and dangerous things, and it is simply not wise to talk about them publicly.

The term *saraka* refers to the manner in which many amulets are set into operation. It has been translated variously as alms giving, a sacrificial offering, and a kind of tax, which, according to Henry, must be given to the "fetishes" and spirit beings of Bamana belief.[55] It is the gift or offering necessary to make something work. In a sense it parallels the term *kumabo*, which is the payment necessary to implement a newly acquired *dalilu*.

Kilisi secret speech can be very important in amulet making, where a supernaturally potent formula of human sounds and the speaker's own energy-laden saliva join forces as they are lodged on some kind of material support, the power object. Sometimes the blood of sacrificed chickens, instead of human saliva, is deposited along with an uttered formula. Sometimes kola nuts are chewed and expectorated on the support object, again in the midst of properly formulated ritual phrases. Although these amplifying substances are generally preferred, words alone will often suffice, because they have been in intimate contact with—indeed, they can hardly be distinguished from—those complex forces that animate the speaker's material self.

Blacksmiths say that physical contact with them gives power, because they have been considered for so long to be very richly endowed with occult energies. When I began to work intensely with Sedu Traore, he felt that my constant proximity to a blacksmith and his forge might do me harm. I had not been born a smith and so could not possess the extra energies that are their heritage. To fortify me, to begin to make me more like a smith, Sedu started making presents of some of his tools. Through prolonged contact over the years, they had become reservoirs of Sedu's personal powers. In Sedu's view that power would now, under controlled and beneficial circumstances, become a part of me.[56]

At least two types of nonalphabetic, graphic writing are used to make amulets. One resembles the figures made during *cenda* sand divination. The other is much more curvilinear and aligned horizontally instead of vertically. It resembles the secret script forms used by blacksmiths in their *kòmò* initiation association.[57]

Some amulets bring organic matter together, sometimes with script or secret speech, sometimes with both, sometimes with neither. The procedures for making them quite closely resemble those used for herbal medicines. Herbs may be combined without much alteration, or they may be reduced to powders or pulp. In certain instances substances such as gunpowder might be called for, ultimately to be combined with script on folded paper and then packed away in leather. Some amulets are made in liquid form. They are not packaged but rather are intended to be drunk or applied to the body, where they operate on behalf of the wearer until washed or worn away. Love potions very often come in this form.

Finally, some amulets are metal, *nègè*, either wholly or in part. Metal is a particularly suitable material for an amulet because it contains high levels of *nyama*, which were released and then directed back into the metal by the smith during forging. One type, in the form of a belt comprised of a thick tube of leather, contains iron and is worn by smiths during the middle stages of their career development. It is said to help them develop to their full potential and become masters. Blacksmiths make thin copper or iron sheets called *walaw*, which stand five to seven inches high and are rounded at the top (Ill. 36). Smiths may use them themselves or sell them to Muslim marabouts, as slates for the writing that is subsequently washed off and swallowed by clients or rubbed on the body. Simple bracelets (worn by Sedu Traore in Ill. 5, 7) and more complex forms consisting of two twisted lengths of iron are also made as amulets. A number are made of brass, *denye*, and copper, *nsira*, in the form of thumb and finger rings, *bolokoni nègèw;* miniature models of slaves shackles, *jònnègèw;* and miniature volutes (Ill. 41). Some amulets are even composed of tiny replicas of blacksmiths' tongs, *balanw*, made of either copper or iron (Ill. 41) and designed either to be amulets in themselves, or to be incorporated into something larger.

A most interesting group of metal amulets is made in part by uncircumcised apprentices. Copper sandals, *nègè sabaraw*, and miniature hammers, *nègè maratow*, are forged by these young blacksmiths if a client is advised through divination that such objects, fabricated by the purest of hands, must be acquired as a kind of sacrifice, *saraka*, in order to achieve certain ends, such as becoming famous in one's work or becoming the head of one's town or region. Before they can be activated, however, they must be handed over to a mature smith, who will "give them their *daliluw*," as Sedu Traore said.

One example is called *nègè haya* (Ill. 41). It is solid iron and its central rectangular core is "the work of an uncircumcised smith," *numu bilakòrò baara*. Often it is constructed from precious stores of traditionally smelted iron, called *gwa nègè*, which is believed to make it more powerful. When the amulet's core is complete, an iron frame is made to hold it, and this is fashioned by an adult smith into a twisted bracelet. The device is supposed to protect its wearer from being pierced by any weapon composed wholly or partially of iron. It has fallen into disuse in recent decades, but formerly it numbered among the principal possessions of soldiers. Indeed, Sumanguru Kante is said to have owned one, along with another that protected against the attack of wooden weapons—the two together made him invincible, at least until his secrets were discovered. Mungo Park encountered similar amulets, but it was Laing who related a fascinating encounter with them while visiting the court of the Mande "Soolima" king. During the reenactment of the military accomplishments of a hero named Yarradee, the bards sang:

> "Follow me to the field" exclaimed the heroic Yarradee, "fear nothing; for let the spear be sharp or the ball swift, faith in the greegrees will preserve thee from danger." [58]

Then the hero himself pantomimed his deeds against 10,000 Fula soldiers. Finally,

> . . . and with sword in hand [he] opposed himself to twelve musketeers, who then made repeated attempts to fire at him, but in vain, the priming always burning in the pan, Yarradee at the same time laughing and shaking his gree grees in token of defiance; at length overcoming them all, and making them kneel at his feet, he commanded them to discharge their muskets in the air, which to my great surprise they did, and not a single musket missed fire. I of course knew that they had some sleight of hand method of stopping and opening the touch-hole at pleasure; but although I witnessed the same performance repeatedly; I could never detect them, so expert were they in the management of the deception.

The Mande smiths who made these amulets insisted that their clients test them before taking them home. Placing it around a mango or other type of fruit, the smith would tell his client to take any knife he wished and try to pierce the protected fruit. If it could not be done, the transaction was completed.

Some blacksmiths manufacture a supply of metal amulets to be sold at the markets, while others work solely on commission. Jacques Daget and M. Konipo described acquisition by commission among the Mande Bozo: In this instance the amulet maker was not a smith, but he sent his clients first to a blacksmith's shop to procure miniature tongs. If the situation dictated copper tongs, the smith charged more. If the situation dictated that the smith work nude, at night and in the client's presence, the smith charged a bit more. When finished, the tongs were taken to the amulet maker, who transformed them by packing their tips into a leather case that could also contain additional substances, such as pieces of roots, bark, or leaves. [59]

The old smith Magan Fane once described to me the amulets and power objects used in the sorcery war between Sunjata and Sumanguru Kante, the legendary king who tried to build a great empire out of the Mande Soso state upon the collapse of the Ghana Empire around the beginning of the second millenium after Christ. Kante's power, *fanga*, derived from his secrets, *gundow*, and from the fact that he was a blacksmith. When he marched as King of the Soso into Mande country he wore clothes fashioned from the skin of human beings to show he could kill even kings with impunity. One room of his palace was full of the artifacts of his power. They included the skulls of nine defeated leaders, an enormous balaphone with which he maintained mystical communication while away from his residence, an equally large serpent, and numerous weapons constructed in odd shapes and with three cutting edges. These things (and more) were his *ceya minaw*, "the things that make you a man," and they were the sources of his power. Sunjata realized that to defeat Sumanguru Kante he had to neutralize them.

Early in the war Sunjata made a prayer beseeching God's assistance in a fight which he did not have the earthly means to win. His prayer was answered with a formula for killing Kante, the Sorcerer King. Using this formula, Sunjata prepared a substance that Magan called *nasi*, "power of darkness, a thing used to harm someone." Sunjata placed it inside a small calabash, *bara*, and asked who was bold enough to pour it over Kante's power things. His bard Bala Faseke, *Jeliw Bembake*, "ancestor of the bards," took the calabash. Bala went to live in the court of Sumanguru, and through cunning and his professional ability as a musician became Kante's praise singer. On a day that Kante was in the forest, Bala, through deceit, gained entry to the king's chamber and poured the *nasi* over all the power devices. Then he made his escape. When Sumanguru returned he found the sources of his supernatural powers no longer of use to him. He exclaimed, said Magan, that he had been effectively neutralized by a person who was a *cenyon*, "someone like him," someone potent enough to be a worthy challenger.[60]

During the early years of contact Europeans noted the Mande use of amulets. In 1620, some 400 years after the Mali Empire was founded, Jobson encountered great numbers of "gregories" along the Gambia River:

> The gregories bee things of great esteem amongst them, for the most part they are made of leather or severall fashions, wonderous neatly, they are hollow, and within them is placed, and sowed up close, certain writings. . . .[61]

All along his route inland to the Bamana state of Ségou, Mungo Park noted the use of objects he called "saphies," which were comprised of materials such as the blood or body of chickens, written verses from the Koran (for Muslims), stones, and even a few sentences "muttered" while spitting. One of Park's hosts asked him for a lock of his hair for an amulet, while another requested that he write a "saphie" in his own European script. Still another asked him to make an amulet by writing on a special wooden board called *walha*, from which the words would be washed off and taken internally. Park found sheep horns to be a favorite container for the solid types of amulets.[62]

Some thirty years later Gray noted that the king of the Mande state of Wuli sat upon a lion skin covered with "grigris." Gray's colleague, the surgeon Dochard, went all the way to Bamako, and during his lengthy stay there had the opportunity to record an interesting fact regarding Koulikoro, a town some twenty miles to the northeast, where the Niger River cataracts end and large-scale boat traffic down the Niger can begin. He wrote:

The population of Kooli-Kooro, which is a considerable town, is entirely composed of murderers, thieves, and runaway slaves, who live there exempt from the punishment their crimes merit in consequence of their wearing about their persons, a stone (taken from a hill in the vicinity of the town), and which, from a superstitious belief amongst the Bambarras, would immediately kill anyone who should touch them. . . .[63]

As it happens, the legendary Sumanguru Kante is said to have vanished into one of the hills at Koulikoro after his final defeat by Sunjata. Today he is honored there by the Bamana, and it is said that he still has the power to grant any request a person would care to make.[64] Stones are often considered the abodes of ancestors, and the stones that Dochard recorded may well have been empowered by that very potent ancestor, Sumanguru Kante.

Today blacksmiths fabricate a wide range of amulets and power objects for a large number of clients. Among the more common ones is a type, kept hidden in a pocket, designed to protect against another person's hostility. The Mande believe that should its owner be drawn unwillingly into fisticuffs, his opponent would find himself thrown mysteriously to the ground as he threw his first punch. Another is meant to be secreted beneath the pillow of the person one wishes to marry. There, it is hoped, the device will radiate just the right energies so that the hopeful party becomes irresistible. Another popular amulet protects against snakebite, and another against misfortune while traveling.

An especially ominous type of amulet works to protect against theft. Different smiths make their own variations and one often encounters the amulets suspended above the entry to their forges (Ill. 39). They are large; one variant, *besi*, includes the skull of a wild pig, while another, *tonso*, consists of a bat's head with a stake protruding from its mouth. Any individual foolish enough to steal something from premises protected in this way will allegedly fall ill in a most unpleasant manner. Shortly after the act the thief will find it impossible to swallow, and begin to foam at the mouth. Total dehydration will follow, resulting in death if the thief does not return the objects. Only the amulet owner possesses an antidote, called *lakari*. It is rubbed on the victim's throat and taken internally with water, and in these ways it counters the effect of the talisman.[65]

The *masa sèbèn* (Ill. 41) is an amulet that used to be reserved for kings and smiths. Its benefits are multidimensional; it prevents snake or animal bites, death through warfare, and nearly every other kind of calamity. Sedu Traore has one himself (Ill. 5) and said it saved his life when a boat in which he was traveling was wrecked, killing everyone on board except him and the boat's operator. During World War II, when the French conscripted Malians to fight in Europe, a great many *masa sèbèn* were made. Today they can also be owned by wealthy as well as royal persons.

Finally, some amulets are reserved for smiths alone. One kind, called a *tongono* (or *tonkono*), is made of a small cylindrical stone bead suspended around the neck on a knotted string (Ill. 8) and activated through the use of *kilisi*. These amulets protect smiths from lions and snakes and various other sorts of danger, but are especially noted for their ability to detect poisoned food. Before the arrival of the French, poisoning was a common means of eliminating a rival or responding in general to serious forms of jealousy. The Mande believe that when blacksmiths travel and have to dine on the food of strangers, the *tongono* preserves them; if a smith lifts poisoned food to the level of the bead, a small section of it is supposed to break off, making a loud, popping sound. In this way the smith is informed of treachery, without ever having taken a bite.[66]

As is the case with many activities of smiths, individuals become well known for their abilities in making amulets. Fame then broadens their clientele. A friend of mine who is Muslim and owns a garage in Bamako endured an all-day drive over back-breaking road to buy a certain type of amulet in Kolokani from a smith renowned for making it. A Malian businessman living in Dakar, Senegal, took the train to Bamako and then a bush taxi south to purchase a *masa sèbèn* from Sedu Traore. The trip cost him three days in each direction and a large sum of money. It was an act that paid great tribute to the powerful acts of smiths.

SOCIAL INSTRUMENTALITY

The Mande are very deliberate in their social lives. They are taught to value attentiveness and circumspection, to strive for an ideal disposition in which listening and thinking take precedence over speaking and acting. Age is respected. Polite greeting patterns are always followed. Innuendo and indirect references often populate people's speech. In general, the values of cooperation and accommodation expressed in the concept of "mother childness" serve as templates for proper social behavior, while beliefs about *nyama* provide a convincing rationale for employing them.

Such a social system places great emphasis on mediators, intermediaries, and advisers, individuals who can buffer the spaces between persons in conflict or negotiations, individuals who can fill those spaces with culturally sanctioned authority. Within those spaces these individuals work as instruments of moderation and reason. They reshape the conditions that define relationships between people, thereby articulating new relationships.

Blacksmiths do these things admirably. Their theoretical neutrality, their *nyama*, and their knowledge would seem to be just the characteristics required. Other people can also serve in these capacities. Hopkins reports, for example, that when a father in Kita sent his son on a business trip, the son accounted for himself with the use of a classificatory elder brother as an intermediary.[67] In serious matters, however, the stature of smiths would be more helpful. Hopkins also noted that the Maninka in the Kita area use bards in these capacities more frequently than smiths.[68] Kita, however, is a large cosmopolitan area, and I found that south of Bamako in the smaller towns and rural areas, blacksmiths were used quite frequently.

Thus, blacksmiths serve as advisers and interpreters, financial and social intermediaries, judges, spokesmen, and witnesses. As intermediaries they may be called upon to monitor obligations that have been established between community members or put an end to confrontations. In a society where jealousy can produce great danger and where financial responsibilities must be met by all because few are wealthy enough to suffer an unjust loss comfortably, blacksmiths are empowered by society and powerful enough personally to come between disputing individuals. In fact, smiths command enough respect to intervene in the midst of an actual brawl. To terminate the conflict they establish a forum for the airing of complaints and then ascertain who is most at fault. Continuing disputes involving debt also fall within the jurisidiction of smiths, and in all cases their judgments will be considered authoritative and final. Their anvils may be called upon to serve as the surface on which oaths or obligations are sworn. The anvil represents the authority of the blacksmith and his direct ancestry, and its use involves connotations of power strong enough to bind individuals to their word for fear of spiritual repercussions.[69]

For their services they receive gifts from those deemed in the right, most frequently in the form of food or kola nuts, and more recently in the form of Malian currency. If the person held to be in error is recalcitrant or vengeful, he might seek retaliation against the smith through sorcery or poison. In such a situation the smith's own capacity in that realm will serve him well, as will the bead amulet he may wear around his neck to warn against poison.

Arrangements involving marriage may also place the blacksmith in the role of intermediary for formalized communication between the two families, and for the negotiations regarding gifts to be exchanged. As importantly, smiths assist in the proper annulment of a marriage or the end of an engagement. In the latter case, for example, a woman unhappy enough with her prospective mate to wish the arrangement terminated may ask a smith to escort her to the home of her parents. A very private meeting will then take place in which the woman voices her complaints, and the smith substantiates them. The smith will advise the family as to the wisest course of action. If the grounds are considered strong enough to warrant separation, the woman will simply remain in the home of her family. Specifically, the blacksmith's role here is that of adviser, witness, and, to some extent, judge. Later he may be called upon to verify and validate the proceedings to the family of the other party.[70]

Every Mande town has a committee of elders mandated to maintain social and economic harmony and in general govern their community. A variety of matters may be brought before them. I once visited a small Bèlèdougou town and met an expert mud-cloth maker. I commissioned a large shirt and pants suit but before she could agree to make it she had to consult with the elders, because I was a foreigner and she had to be sure the elders agreed that working for me was in the best interests of the community. Individuals who wish to bring matters before the elders often ask a smith to be their representative. The smith will stand before the council and present the individual's request, ending by giving his own advice regarding its merits. Imperato had frequent opportunity to document this blacksmith role during his successful program of smallpox and measles eradication. Throughout the Bamana regions of Mali, vaccinators first approached blacksmiths, who then appeared on their behalf before the elders.[71]

Historically, many Mande leaders retained blacksmiths at their sides as advisers and interpreters. At court, kings whispered their decisions to smiths, who then repeated them aloud for the assembly. In the early nineteenth century, Laing reported a similar relationship among the southern Mande, by referring to a king's "confidential Noomo" who was present when all important business was conducted.[72] Much important Mande business called for authentication by a smith. Charles Monteil recorded versions of Ségou's oral tradition which suggest that in the early 1700s the young Mamari Biton Kouloubali, who would later found the Ségou state, was in the process of reorganizing the youth association, tòn, into an instrument of his own personal power. Ultimately, he fashioned that instrument into a tremendous political machine. But in the beginning, as "head of the tòn," tòntigi, his exorbitant partying and the pillaging his group carried out to support their excesses caused his father to order Mamari in the presence of a smith to stop his disgraceful style of life.[73]

CIRCUMCISION

While it is convenient to distinguish between the spiritual and social articulations smiths make in society, the two spheres often blend. Amulet making, for example, could be viewed as seated principally in the spiritual realm, but its effects are most certainly felt in the social realm as well. Circumcision, however, is a kind of shaping that is deeply embedded in both realms, and its effects radiate across Mande society most dramatically.

None of the activities examined in this chapter thus far are the exclusive domain of smiths. Often no one else can do them better, or even as well. But unlike iron working, these activities can be learned by other citizens if they like, and a fair number do learn them.

Circumcision is an entirely different matter. As with iron working, no one else in traditional Mande society is qualified to do it, and it is virtually inconceivable that anyone but a smith would try. Some children nowadays are circumcised in hospitals by doctors practicing Western medicine. But they are mostly children of modern Muslims, or parents who have broken with tradition. Conversely, many parents who live otherwise Western life-styles still insist that their sons be circumcised by smiths.

The operation of circumcision is considered by smiths to be the most hazardous of all the acts they undertake. It demands impeccable precision, as-tute observation, and an extensive command of herbal medicines.[74] Physio-logically and spiritually the operation is considered very dangerous, while socially it is absolutely necessary if the child is to grow up and function as an adult. The surgery is linked to deep social and religious ceremony. Its ramifications are immense, and smiths consider it one of their most impor-tant responsibilities.[75] Like iron working, circumcising effects a transforma-tion of monumental proportions.

For the Mande, circumcision constitutes a physical and psychic journey into adulthood. An uncircumcised male would simply not be considered an adult. In conversations with smiths and young men, I was repeatedly told that uncircumcised boys could not get married or have sexual intercourse, nor could they enter the important *kòmò* initiation association or accept the responsibilities families and communities give adults. Furthermore, they would be incapable of acquiring knowledge crucial to their spiritual and intellectual development. Finally, while they remain uncircumcised, no matter how old they are, they are conceived of as boys and are not held re-sponsible for their acts; they can carry out the most annoying of pranks and behave very nearly as they please. They are considered more animal than human, in the sense that the social refinements that begin with circumcision have not yet begun to civilize them. After the blacksmith circumcises them, however, this period of grace comes to an abrupt end. Boys become men and are expected to act accordingly in all situations.

In their adolescent initiation association, *ntomo*, and at home among their elders, young boys are told they will be circumcised and they look forward to the event with awe and fear, because they know it will be painful. They brace themselves, however, with a spirit of pride and the knowledge that they are being challenged to endure the pain and become adults. Friends informed me that when the moment came the operation hurt, to be sure, but what they remembered most vividly was not the pain but rather a glorious realization that they had just crossed the threshold into a new and long-awaited life.

While their status as uncircumcised makes them in theory immature and irresponsible, in practice boys are judged ready for the operation when their parents and elders feel they have learned enough about the world and be-come mature enough to accept the surgery's cultural ramifications. In former times this moment came when the candidate was in his late teens. Today it occurs in the late preteens or early teens. In general, operations are sched-uled every three years, but in some communities they occur more fre-quently. Once a group of youths is ready, their parents meet to decide which blacksmith they will employ. Past experience becomes, for the most part, the deciding factor. Smiths who have performed the surgery, who have done a good job and are confident about their abilities will be prime candidates. If no such person lives in their town, the parents are free to consider smiths in adjacent communities, and, in fact, the only geographic boundaries are their own knowledge of smiths and the ease with which distant smiths can be brought to town.

When a smith has been retained, preparations are made for the event. The night before is celebrated with a community-wide dance, which lasts until the sun's first rays indicate that the time for surgery has arrived. The neophytes have waited together in one of the family compounds and they are now escorted to a tree just outside of town, where the blacksmith awaits them. In some areas he may be playing a four-holed bamboo flute, performing songs that praise circumcision and the approaching youths. With him may be another smith who assists and, generally, community elders and membes of two important initiation associations, the kòmò and nama. Young men from the last group to be circumcised may also be present to observe and assist.

As each boy becomes a man, the foreskin is wrapped and given to his parents, who save it as an amulet. After everyone has been transformed, the group retreats to a restricted area away from the community, where they spend about two months receiving the initial portions of an education that befits their new mature state. Periodically, they march into town in single file, wearing white pants and robe and a special white, peaked cap. The bravest, eldest, or first in his group to have been circumcised is their leader, and he heads the group, carrying a sistrum made of a wood handle and calabash disk clappers. While he uses it to produce a cascading rhythm, all the new men sing circumcision songs, as they visit the homes and meeting places of elders. They kneel at the feet of these town leaders and praise them, being praised themselves and receiving gifts in return. As boys they were called "the uncircumcised," bilakorow. Now they are called "children of the circumcision," bolokodenw, a title meant to suggest the importance of the event.

The surgery itself is more critical than we in the West might imagine. Our standard is a simple, minor operation that is performed a few days after birth. It becomes much more critical when the patient is a teenager. At that point heavy bleeding becomes a serious and potentially recurrent problem, as does the likelihood of dangerous infection. These two elements are of the greatest concern to the Mande smiths. Immediately after each operation, the blacksmith makes an important judgment, based on the way the patient bleeds, as to which herbal medicines he will apply to the wound. Some of his patients prove to be heavy bleeders and in such cases the smith will have recourse to a wide selection of medications with which to stabilize the situation and deal with any potential complications. Smiths insist that for this physical aspect of the operation the two most important criteria are the ability to cut precisely with the knife and an extensive knowledge of appropriate daliluw.

There is another kind of potential danger that smiths must be prepared to address. Supernatural complications are a strong concern of parents and smiths alike, and although we can isolate them from the physical considerations for the sake of discussion, the two are not always so readily distinguish-able. A smith encountering difficulties must be prepared to deal with the two types simultaneously, by recognizing the manifestations of each and responding to them both correctly. The symptoms associated with super-natural interference often take the form of dizziness or light-headedness. If they appear, the operating smith must instantly suspect sorcery and act accordingly.

Occult attacks on boys being circumcised are often inspired by jealousy. Sedu Traore explained to me two situations he has encountered most fre-quently. If two women share a husband and one has a son while the other does not have a child, the former is likely to become the "favored wife," *baramuso*, a situation that could create extreme feelings of ill-will on the part of the childless wife. If she were inclined toward aggression she might decide to visit sorcery on the boy.

Likewise, if two men who were brothers, cousins, or otherwise related by family ties felt compelled to compete with one another for social or economic standing, this would constitute the kind of jealousy inspired by the concept of "father childness." At some point one of the two might wish to destroy things the other owned or loved. A likely course of action would be to seek the death of the other's son through sorcery.

A most opportune time for such an attack would be when the boy was being circumcised, because at that moment he would be under extreme physical and spiritual stress, an ideal time to try to kill a person. To accom-plish this kind of murder an airborne poison of the *kòròti* variety might be sent. The circumcising smith would be responsible for detecting the pres-ence of such substances and countering their effects immediately. If the smith expected trouble, he might take the precaution of applying a preven-tive lotion, *kolifura*, directly over the wound. If the attack were unexpected, he could counter with various *daliluw*, many of which would involve the use of *kilisi* secret speech. The most distressing encounter of Sedu's career as a circumciser came while he was performing the surgery in another town. As he began, ten of the boys suddenly became giddy. His assistant was terrified by this and lost his composure. Sedu, however, recognized the cause and knew where to find the leaves he needed to make a proper medicine quickly. Thus he saved the lives of ten new men and retained his good name.

A final harzard surrounding circumcision involves the high levels of *nyama* released at the moment of incision, and it is this aspect of the operation which smiths find most troublesome. The escaping energy is said to be po-tent enough to blind a smith who has not mastered all the techniques of the surgery, and a really clumsy smith could actually be killed. To protect against this power, blacksmiths utilize secret speech constantly. They also have at their disposal lotions with which they can cover their entire bodies to serve as a shield against the energy.[76] Impeccable performance is still crucial, how-ever, and the aged smith Magan Fane related to me an incident that made the point quite clear. One year in a town, just one boy was ready to be circumcised. The chosen smith charged his inexperienced son with the operation. The latter, according to Magan, coated himself with lotion and needed to succeed only once, but was nevertheless rendered blind by his own inexperience.

Most smiths will not learn to circumcise, and in countless interviews, the reasons they gave me were always the same. Completing the operation successfully was the most difficult and potentially dangerous enterprise in their profession. Just learning the medicine and the sorcery required could take an entire year. The greatest concern of smiths who do perform the surgery is avoiding the acquisition of a "bad name," *tògò jugu*, by always doing good work. The greatest concern of smiths who choose not to perform the surgery is the potential for blindness resulting from an inadequate performance. Magan Fane had been taught all of the necessary techniques and procedures by his father, but he refused to use his ability and, furthermore, was not willing to pass it on to his sons. Sedu Traore alone among twelve brothers had been trained to circumcise. In one town occupied by some twenty practicing blacksmiths, only two men circumcised, and these same two smiths were often called upon by more than seven other neighboring communities to carry out the operation.

Blacksmiths use various kinds of knives for surgery. Dieterlen has identified a "great circumcision knife," *boloko kumba muru*. It is distinguished by elaborate engravings on the blade, which she says refer to various aspects of the Bamana creation myth.[77] However, in southern Mali the smiths I worked with told me that the knives they use to carve wood are perfectly adequate for circumcision.

The tradition of circumcision is extremely important to the Mande. Even in Bamako, where Western medicine has made its strongest inroads and where many modern Muslims send their children off to hospitals for the operation, most neigborhoods retain smiths to circumcise their young. Smiths comment constantly on the hazards of the operation, but they also indicate clearly that they think it is among the most significant things they do. An old and very prominent blacksmith in the region of Ségou discussed with me the changes that had occurred in his profession in this generation. He said he had given up the smelting of iron without too many feelings of regret, because of the convenience of buying metal that was ready to forge. He could understand why his clients no longer want iron lamps, knowing that the imported kerosene lanterns with their flames protected behind glass can be carried from house to house at night like a flashlight and illuminate a room more thoroughly. He made it clear, however, that he would not stop circumcising, implying that it could never be appropriate to discontinue the enterprise, or take it out of the hands of blacksmiths. Magan Fane, living some 200 miles to the southwest, echoed these sentiments by stating that everyone is born a person, but circumcision makes one a Bamana.

Zahan says circumcision must be performed by smiths because they are the artisans of humanity's social aspects, by virtue of their authorship of the tools that allow agriculture and, therefore, create civilization.[78] Sedu Traore put the significance of circumcision and the need for smiths to perform it in a slightly different way. He said the operation makes people better. Specifically, he said it makes the *ja*, one's consciousness, intelligence, and spiritual double, better.[79] In his view only smiths could do this, and therefore smiths are essential to the good lives of human beings.

THE RELATIVE ROLES OF BLACKSMITHS AND HUNTERS

It is too easy and a bit dangerous to stereotype population groups in other cultures. Exceptions always qualify such proclamations, and misleading impressions are often generated. But a cautious comparison of Mande smiths and hunters might help us put the information in this chapter into a useful perspective. These two population segments are both engaged in vocations and possess special intellectual and spiritual capacities whose ramifications are enormous. They have more power to act in the world than most other groups, and that power, *nyama*, enables them to carry out difficult and often very dangerous undertakings. Hunters travel through potentially harmful terrain to kill animals, thereby releasing energies that could easily overwhelm lesser persons. Smiths release similar amounts of power when they carry out circumcision, for example, and they must protect everyone present from the severe supernatural disturbances that could arise from the act. Both hunters and smiths are associated with concepts of heat, in the Mande sense of staggering accumulations of power and the imbalance of aggressive action. Thus a favorite line in hunters' epic poems says that when great hunters die, "The world has cooled off," *Diyèn rosumannen.*[80] Blacksmiths are referred to as masters of fire, a title which should be interpreted both literally and symbolically.

Both also have extensive knowledge which is used to fortify and direct power. Hunters' knowledge of the bush is unsurpassed and their herbal abilities, founded in *daliluw*, are also impressive. They depend upon knowledge and amass it in a fashion similar to the smiths.

Theoretically, however, and often enough practically, there are some noteworthy differences between hunters and smiths. The abilities of hunters are often directed toward earning a name and establishing themselves in Mande oral history. They are not opposed to seriously disrupting social harmony and cohesion to achieve their ends, and they are perceived frequently as threats to social stability, in spite of their ability to save it in periods of acute duress. The heat of hunters, then, is truly aggressive.[81]

The heat of smiths is more often directed toward different ends, for in all of their roles they attempt to create or maintain harmony and balance for their communities. People wholeheartedly depend upon them to do just that. They are believed capable of bringing rain to maintain the balance needed for farming productivity, and their tools encourage that balance by facilitating economy in farming and enlarging the scope in which it can be carried out. In divination they seek to maintain balance in their clients' future activities, or to reestablish it after a calamity by wisely seeking causes and appropriate courses of action. As doctors they maintain the harmony of healthy bodies when they offer the fruits of their *daliluw* knowledge to every member of their community. In circumcision smiths alter the physical state of young persons, forcing them into the realm of adulthood and ending their days of irresponsibility. At the same time they protect the newly circumcised from the dangers of that transitional state.

When smiths make amulets they direct their "heat" and knowledge to act as a kind of preventive medicine, protecting the array of balanced forces in a person's life or helping to reestablish them during difficult periods. As mediators and advisers they are available to monitor social intercourse, to contain the heat generated by disagreements and to cool it. At times, they must even absorb the aggression of an individual who remains disgruntled and wishes retaliation instead of harmony and so resorts to sorcery.

All of these tasks allow us to establish an important perspective of another kind. If we ask why blacksmiths are also sculptors, we find an obvious answer close at hand. Good smiths are outstanding articulators. They understand the demands of shaping wood and iron expertly. But good art everywhere has always been much more than form. It is a part of the force of religion, ideology, psychology, and organized society. It is both abstract and instrumental; it gives pause and it allows implementation. It is a functional cornerstone of civilization. The collection of tasks associated with the institution of smithing touches all these things. Who, then, but the smiths could be so well equipped to make sculpture?

PLATE 1. Blacksmith's forge near Markala with clients and friends visiting in early afternoon, 1973.

PLATE 2. Blacksmith's forge in a small town near Kasaro, 1973.

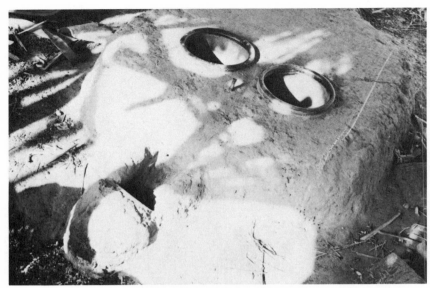

PLATE 3. Abandoned bellows in the form of two pots built into a massive clay platform, 1973. If the bellows had been in use, animal skins would cover the pots.

PLATE 4. Two young smith's apprentices working iron in a blacksmith's hamlet near Banamba, 1973.

PLATE 5. Sedu Traore carving knife handles behind his forge, 1973.

PLATE 6. Sedu carving a stool, 1973.

PLATE 7. Sedu using an adze to shape the bulb form at the end of a knife handle, 1973.

PLATE 8. Sedu using a carving knife as a plane to remove adze marks from a knife handle, 1973.

PLATE 9. Four adzes of various sizes and weights stored in the rafters of Sedu's forge, with his bow drill and an ax, called *sèmèn*, hanging on the wall, 1973.

PLATE 10. Sedu using a red-hot awl to make the hafting hole in a hoe handle, 1973.

PLATE 11. Patinated hand grip of a pestle, 1973. Above and below it are zigzag patterns.

PLATE 12. Some of Sedu's tools, seen from the position at his forge where he usually worked, 1973. His hammers are on the left and his awls are sticking out of the ground on both sides of the potsherd, which serves as a water basin. In the basin are his pincers, and on its edge is a stick used for splashing water on the coals. Two spatula-bladed knives for blackening wood are in front of the water basin. Part of his charcoal basin can be seen in the lower right corner.

PLATE 13. Sedu using one of his heavier hammers to form the haft of a knife blade, 1973.

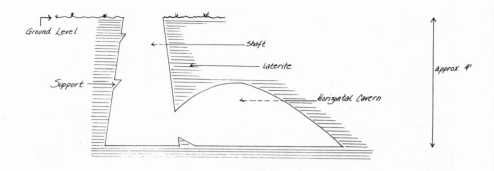

Drawing after M. Delafosse and Francis-Bœuf

PLATE 14. Cross-section of a type of iron mine found near Bougouni.

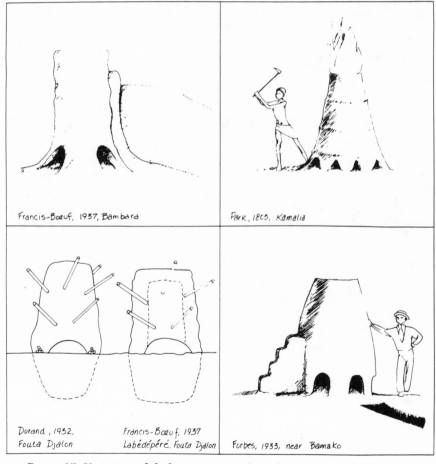

PLATE 15. Variations of shaft-type iron smelting furnaces recorded by several authors.

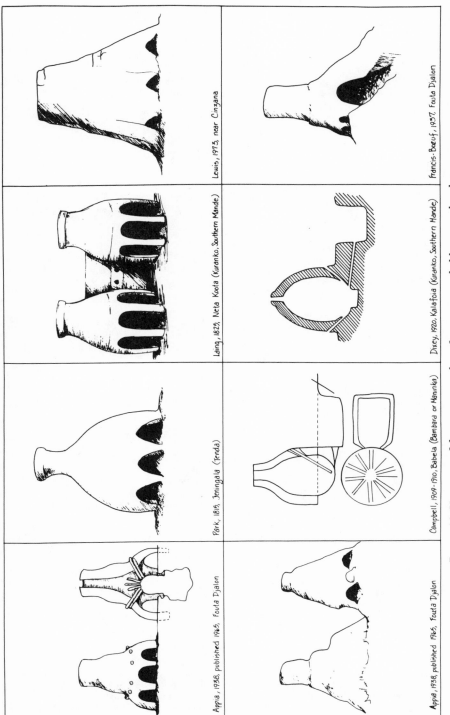

PLATE 16. Variations of dome-type smelting furnaces recorded by several authors.

Appia, 1958, published 1965, Fouta Djalon

Park, 1819, Jenningala (Irnda)

Campbell, 1909-1910, Babela (Bambara or Mannka)

Laing, 1822, Neta Koola (Kuranko, Southern Mande)

Dixey, 1920, Kalafoia (Kuranko, Southern Mande)

Lewis, 1975, near Cinzana

Francis-Boeuf, 1937, Fouta Djalon

Appia, 1958, published 1965, Fouta Djalon

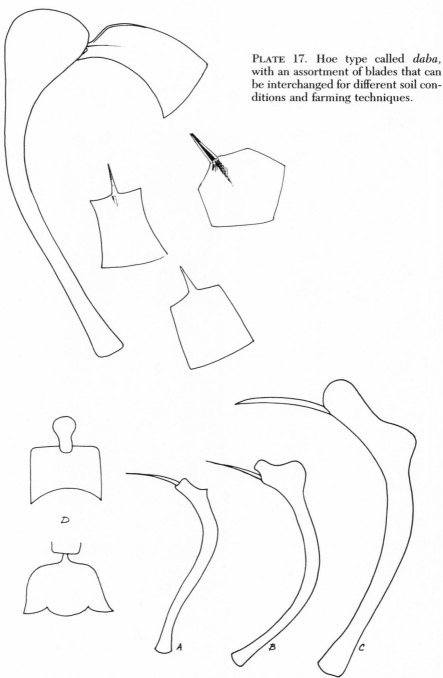

PLATE 17. Hoe type called *daba*, with an assortment of blades that can be interchanged for different soil conditions and farming techniques.

D

A

B

C

PLATE 18. (A) and (C) are a hoe type named *daba muso*, "woman hoe." The woman who owned (C) called it *Ci wara*, "farming animal," a praise name for good cultivators. (B) is a small version of *daba muso* called *masi masi*. (D) shows two *masi masi* blade variations.

PLATE 19. Small calabash called *bara den* used to
carry seeds for planting in the field.

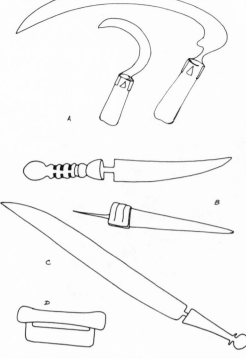

PLATE 20. Assortment of cutting tools. (A) Two sickles, each called *wòlòsò*, used to cut grass. (B) Variations of the all-purpose knife, *muru*, generally carried by any adult and often used to harvest millet. (C) Large knife for harvesting tobacco, named *muruba* or *sira baara muru*, literally "tobacco working knife." (D) Knife designed especially for harvesting millet, called *nyo muru*, "millet knife."

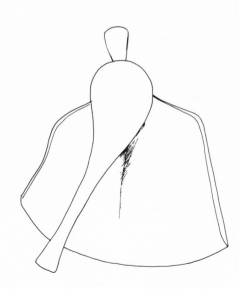

PLATE 21. Huge hoe-shaped implement, *njeruwe*, used to carry large quantities of earth. The blade is approximately two feet long and eighteen inches wide and is hafted into an enormous wood handle at an angle that causes it to be parallel to the ground when a load is being carried.

PLATE 22. Women grinding millet in mortars behind Sedu's forge, 1973. They often pounded in elaborate rhythms and combined them with hand clapping, which Sedu embellished with rhythms he made at the bellows.

PLATE 23. Bamana carved wooden door lock from southern Mali, 1973.

PLATE 24. Typical Bamana door, constructed of three large panels held together at top and bottom with smaller horizontal pieces, 1973. The door was being stored beside the house, with a well-used door lock still installed and ready for use, 1973.

PLATE 25. Water trough for cattle in southern Mali, 1973.

PLATE 26. Large indoor granaries in an abandoned and collapsing storage room in southern Mali, 1973.

PLATE 27. Bamana figural heddle pulley (h. 7½ in.). Private collection. Photograph by Jeffrey A. Wolin.

PLATE 28. Gun made by Cekòrò Traore, who specialized in their making and repairing, mostly for hunters, 1973.

PLATE 29. Cekòrò Traore assembling the parts of a percussion lock mechanism into a stock he had just completed, 1973.

PLATE 30. Detail of the gun depicted in Ill. 29. Note that the barrel is held in place inside the stock with wide hide straps.

PLATE 31. Bamana knife with janus head (h. 12¼ in.). Both faces are painted with pink pigment. Private collection. Photograph by Jeffrey A. Wolin.

PLATE 32. House door, southern Mali, 1973.

PLATE 33. *Kònò dòn*, "bird dance," masquerade making its first of many appearances at an evening performance in a town on the Mande Plateau, 1978. The dancer is the blacksmith Sidi Ballo, who carved the bird's head, assembled the costume, and performed as an itinerant dancer.

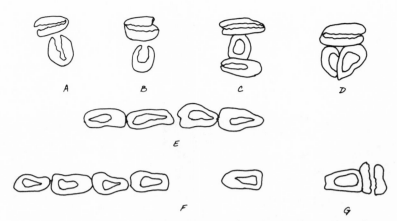

PLATE 34. Cowry shell divination. The letters depict canonized configurations that can be read as characters to be interpreted after the shells are thrown. The ideas they symbolize are considered to have an important bearing on the situation brought before the diviner. (A) suggests an enemy, (B) a friend, (C) someone wise and kind, (D) a gift, and (E) a journey. (F) suggests that the client will find a benefactor, while (G) suggests that the benefactor will be most helpful.

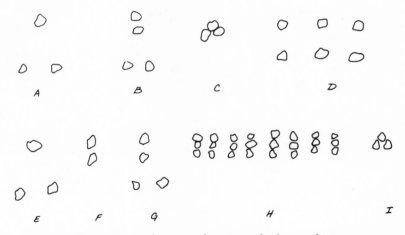

PLATE 35. Divination by stone throwing. The letters depict configurations determined by the number of stones left behind in the diviner's hand. The resulting signs are very abstract and depend upon extensive interpretation by the diviner. (A) indicates Kumardise the black man. (B) indicates Yarase the black woman. (C) indicates a prayer or sacrifice. (D) indicates goodness, kindness, or benevolence, often interpreted as receiving money. The bottom line suggests a typical sequence of figures. (E) indicates a black man is involved. (F) is ambiguous until (G) a black woman, is suggested. Then a scenario of marriage and pregnancy is indicated. (H) suggests that everything is good. (I) completes the sequence, which Seydou Camara interpreted as indicating a healthy pregnancy had occurred in a family, and that everything would be well if proper offerings were made.

PLATE 36. The pile of sand in Sedu Traore's forge, which he used for divination, 1973. The two copper plates, *walaw*, set in the sand are slates for writing amuletic messages that can be washed off and consumed or rubbed on the body. The bottle contains ink for writing similar messages that will be wrapped in leather amulet cases. The string is used to wrap folded paper amulets before they are encased in leather.

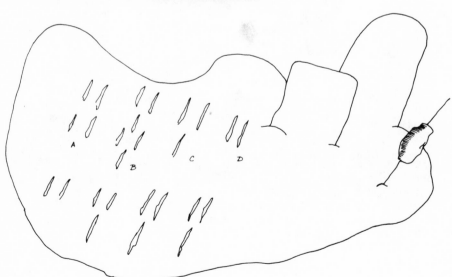

PLATE 37. Sand divination. (A), (B), and (D) suggest a good situation, a positive kind of balance. (C) suggests the pull of a force from the earth, the ancestors. It indicates a lack of balance, a bad situation, and the possibility of death.

PLATE 38. A selection of vegetable materials used in herbal medicines, stored inconspicuously in the rafters of Sedu Traore's forge, 1973.

PLATE 39. A large antitheft amuletic device composed of an animal skull and a hide sack full of secret ingredients, situated above the door to Sedu's forge, 1973.

PLATE 40. *Boli* shaped like a person, used in a *kònò* initiation association branch. Photograph by R. P. Dubernet, published in Henry 1910.

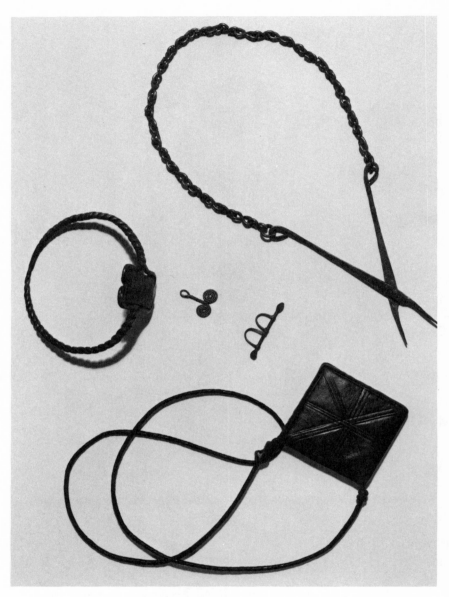

PLATE 41. Assortment of amulets, clockwise outside from the bottom: a leather-covered *masa sèbèn*, "amulet for kings" (l. 2⅜ in.); an iron *nègè haya* (d. 3½ in.); and a miniature iron smith's pincers (l. 4½ in. without chain). In the center are miniature copper shackles (l. 1⅝ in.) and a copper volute (h. 1 in.). Private collection. Photograph by Jeffrey A. Wolin.

FOUR

THE BLACKSMITHS' SCULPTURE

The Mande use many types of sculpture. Their doors are frequently graced with beautifully carved wood locks. Their stools are often enriched with subtle patterns of embellishment. Wooden dolls are carved for children. Wooden figures are carved for the souls of deceased twins. A great variety of mask and headdress types are made for use in the youth associations, *tònw*, and many more are made to be used in the spiritually oriented initiation associations, *jow*, as are some of the largest carved wooden figures known in Africa. Forged iron lamps were formerly used all over the Western Sudan, and iron staffs with figural tops are still placed near altars and used as important elements of ritual. In addition, idiosyncratic art works of both wood and iron are made for hunters and other individuals who use them as part of their occult practices.

All of these are made by blacksmiths. Sculpting seems to be an extension of their craft work, and for the most part they own the rights to such work as part of their heritage. In some instances other individuals can carve wood sculpture. Zahan notes that the *kule* group of wood workers can make masks and figures,[1] at least in certain Mande regions. Mary Jo Arnoldi reports a few instances where youth association masks in the Ségou and Markala areas are not made by smiths or *kule* carvers but by ordinary association members. This is exceptional, however, and the sculptures tend to be simplified versions after blacksmiths' models.[2] There are no exceptions in the making of iron sculpture. Like all other iron working, forging iron sculpture is the sole prerogative of the clans of smiths. Not all smiths make sculpture, and few smiths make every type available in their region. Often a blacksmith will specialize in making one type, or a few. Many of them establish extensive reputations making door locks, for example, or the carved wooden heads for bird masquerades. People generally know which towns have smiths who make especially fine examples of each type, and many people will not hesitate to spend a day or more traveling to get exactly what they want. Magan Fane was so old when I met him that he was practically blind. He had stopped working iron a long time ago and allowed his forge to fall into rack and ruin. Carving wood was extremely difficult for him, and he had given up making most things. He had a flair for carving the bird masquerade heads, however, and was loath to give that up. People still commissioned them from him, because his pieces were absolutely beautiful.

Sculpting is more difficult than making the tools and utensils that constitute the smiths' craftwork. More details are demanded, smaller and more complex surfaces must be articulated, and more intricate combinations of volumes must be established. It takes more finesse to carve or forge sculpture, but there are fewer opportunities to develop the skill, because it is not commissioned nearly as often as hoes, knives, and other implements. Thus sculpting is like sorcery in the sense that a limited number of blacksmiths practice it.

Although there is tremendous variation between and even within regions, we can characterize Mande sculptural style as sharply reduced to the point of being spartan. It groups austere bodies of shapes and volumes in ways that are unmistakable, once one has visited a few museums or examined the plates in a few African art history books.[3] The elements of form that establish compositions are allowed a life of their own, so that sculptures very often seem extremely abstract and find appreciative audiences among students of twentieth-century Western art. Yet these works contain a degree of vitality, of integrated energy, that makes them most exciting. Both the abstraction and the vitality make a very interesting kind of sense, in relationship to all the other things blacksmiths do. This chapter explores that relationship, and then examines in some detail four types of Mande sculpture not commonly encountered in the literature.

THE CHARACTER OF SCULPTURE
AND THE OTHER ROLES OF SMITHS

At a certain level Mande sculpture generates and then manages visual energy, largely through its repertoire of forms and the principles of their association. If we carry that thought a little further we find a correspondence between the sculpture of smiths and their other works. They all deal with energies, be they derived from social situations, the physical environment, or the realms of sorcery and spirits. And they all seek to control those energies, to focus and bind them helpfully, to resolve them and reintegrate them benevolently back into human experience.

The foundation that nourishes the institution of smithing, so that it may nourish society, is the simple axiom that knowledge can be power when properly articulated. Behind most of the smiths' works are units of highly focused, very practical information, the *daliluw*, which themselves are grounded in smaller units, the bits and pieces of organic matter and other materials that derive from the "science of the trees." For the blacksmiths, making sculpture is much like activating *daliluw*. First, in sculpting they reduce their subject to a collection of highly abstract elements, just as in the use of *daliluw* they collect raw elements from nature and refine them down to essences. Next, in sculpture these elements are linked in dramatic but carefully controlled configurations through the acumen of smiths, so that a vigorous new entity is created. This too is like the use of *daliluw*, where essences are distilled and rearranged through knowledge to create something new and useful. In both instances, knowing which elements to use is important. It is equally important to synthesize them very carefully. A poor mix in art produces a flaccid composition or an artificial union of parts that clash rather then meld. A poor mix in a *dalilu* produces an entity too benign to be of any use or too potent to be anything but dangerous. Thus, in both cases knowledge well used becomes power that can be controlled and put to work for people.

The anthropologist James T. Brink noted that good *nyama*, energy generated intelligently and propitiously as it can be during Sidi Ballo's bird masquerade performances or the rural theater performances Brink examined, has a very positive effect on people. It pulls them together. It unifies them.[4] This is true generally of Mande art. *Nyama* is generated by human acts, and acts of making art, be they rural theater, a bard's epic poetry, or a blacksmith's sculpting, are designed to serve society. The entire careers of many smiths and bards are punctuated by such acts. No wonder the appellation *nyamakala* is so thoroughly appropriate to them. They are points of access to terrific powers, and they rearrange and transmit these powers in all that they do. From divination to the fabrication of amulets and sculptures, men such as Sidi Ballo and Sedu Traore remake the world by taking it apart and reassembling it. In the process they harness the unrefined world and translate it into a Mande frame. In the process they civilize it. Sedu's comment that when a smith circumcises, he makes the *ja*, the expressive part of the human soul, better, can be applied in a wider context. During both circumcision and carving, cutting away brings into prominence a core that is socially malleable. The same is true of iron working, from the reductive process of smelting bloom from ore to the refining process of deriving useful forms from useless pieces of metal.

We can better understand this correspondence between art and the smiths' other roles by examining sculpture. Let us look first at a carved wooden headdress, designed to be mounted on a basketry cap lashed to the head of a dancer. Two crude breasts and a neck that thickens to form a head rise out of two opposing zigzags (Ill. 42). From the front, this head seems no more than an anchor for two huge ears and a prominent nose and forehead. Indeed, originally the holes in the ears supported bright knots of red thread or shiny metal ear rings, adding emphasis to these extraordinary structures. But from the side the piece swells to resemble the structure of a human head in profile, and the forehead has been engraved with a cross-hatch design that is hard to distinguish from a distance but nevertheless gives the head the sense of having human hair. In fact, the image joins animal and human characteristics convincingly but enigmatically, and the carving is so minimal, so economical, that for a Western viewer steeped in a different sense of representation the image systematically crumbles away to its parts, to be rebuilt by the mind again as the parts recall the whole.

The Mande do not have this trouble. First of all, the sculpture is made to move around a dance arena, and so its traditional viewers meld the parts more easily. Second, a principal element of Mande aesthetics involves a crisp clarity that can be quite minimal. This piece is successful by Mande standards. It is forceful and to the point. It is also innovative and creative; the zigzag neck, for example, occurs nowhere in nature, while the union of such ears to such a head is also highly imaginative.

The sculpture belongs to the category of works called "little animal head," *sogonikun*. Such works are performed by members of the youth and farming associations. Among other activities these groups organize and carry out agricultural labor for the community and perform with masks and orchestras during peak agricultural seasons. The little animal heads are made for entertainment, the bold and often saucy entertainment of confident and inquisitive young people growing up and finding their personal places in society. Knowing all of this, we have a better idea of why Mande viewers see this headdress as well carved, why they say, "Its style is good, it is well worked."[5]

A carved mask (Ill. 43), looking not really human and not really animal, is a focused collection of broad curves and large planes. The nose sits wedge-like in long flat cheeks, at the top of which rectangular eyes are cut, deep beneath a vast overhanging forehead. Under the nose the cheeks rush forward, forming a large rectangular cavity, the mouth. The top of the mask is huge. It is composed of two curving surfaces that meet at the mask's center, forming a straight vertical edge. Ears in the shape of thick-edged loops catch one's attention and focus it in a way that seems to prefigure the volume and shape of the dome-like top. They lie against the sides of the forehead and contribute to an exciting pattern of vertical and horizontal lines.

All of these elements seem dynamic, but they are very carefully controlled. The large forehead is countered by the protruding mouth, and both are secured visually in the mask's thick sides, so that a very judicious three-dimensional proportioning is achieved. This mask is one of several types used by the *kore* initiation association in performances that express ideals, often by their opposites and often by exaggerating and endlessly repeating the pertinent behaviors of animals.[6]

Even if we know nothing about the contexts of these works or the smiths who made them we can perceive in them high levels of visual energy, often created through geometric exaggeration and generally controlled through compositional subtleties that systematically reintegrate the energy back into the art. Most Mande sculpture does this, and, although there is a great deal of regional and personal variation in the works, some of the finest are also the most successful at generating energy from distilled geometry.

Good art everywhere is full of energy, but it is achieved by different means. Fang sculptors from the Republic of Gabon depend upon the union of stringent symmetry with a dynamic use of symbolism to create tremendous vitality.[7] European artists of the Baroque period depended heavily upon vivid, dramatic human gestures within a dynamic compositional field. Mande sculptors depend heavily upon the controlled collisions of prominent angles, curves, and planes. They reduce their imagery to an extremely abstract level and thereby provide a field upon which primary forms can play. Torsos are often reduced to irregular cylinders, limbs to irregular tubes. Both may be elongated beyond the point of resemblance to human models. Whole bodies are often reduced sharply, to give prominence to heads. Human faces very often feature huge protruding foreheads from which long, straight, monumental noses plunge. These two elements, foreheads and noses, become fulcrum points around which the other features are organized. Eyes may be set within the shadow of the forehead and work in consort with delicate mouths to create an almost pouty sense of innocence.

Certain animal masks are created along similar lines. Hyena masks used in the *kore* initiation association, for example, anchor a somewhat human nose high on a forehead, and then drop it in the shape of a large wedge down between the eyes and onto cheek planes that also seem somewhat human. Those planes sweep forward at the bottom, however, to form a most convincing muzzle and create a playful dialogue between human and animal form (Ill. 44). Huge occult masks used in the *kònò* initiation association often extend the muzzle and mouth of an animal beyond resemblance to anything in nature, thereby removing the reference from any specific animal and transforming it into an essence, an immense, gaping orifice (Ill. 45).

In many Mande sculptures human coiffures, antelope manes, and the ears and horns of animals receive the same kind of attention. They are often articulated in monumental scale and then incised with linear patterns. Puppet heads of animals and people may be extensively painted, often in sharp, geometric patterns that emphasize harsh juxtapositions of color. Other sculptures, such as wooden door locks, may be charred with a red-hot spatula in selected areas to complement patterns of pyroengraving and make the whole composition more lively (Color Plate I).

Generalizations about Mande sculpture style must not be overdrawn, because regional variations are extensive and many good sculptors put a premium on personal variations. The large wood figures used by the *gwan* cult and the *jo* association in southern Mali tend to be less geometric, although shapes are still reduced and sharply stated.[8] Many of the carved animal heads used by the Ségou and Markala area youth associations are composed of surfaces and volumes simplified to the point that they become themselves single primary forms instead of an assemblage of smaller ones.[9]

Quality is also relevant. The Mande have their fair share of mediocre sculptors, and very often these individuals are not capable of, or perhaps are not interested in, achieving the authoritative articulations good sculptors achieve with such elegance. Mediocre Mande sculptors generally produce lifeless representations with no interplay between the parts.

Once I showed Sedu Traore and members of his family a photograph depicting a carved wooden head from a bird masquerade. Perhaps the work was by an apprentice or a poor sculptor, because it lacked force and convincing form (Ill. 46). A lumpy, ill-defined bulb constituted the head, from which a long thin beak emerged. I did not think it was a terrible piece of sculpture, and the beak was even well carved in places. But on the whole the work could not be considered good.

Sedu agreed, diplomatically. He said that the work was all right but that we both knew of a carved bird's head that was better. He was referring to Sidi Ballo's bird masquerade (Ill. 47). Sidi's work is well known in the area, and his performances are much in demand. The carved head and masquerade costume are considered to be very well made, and Sidi himself confirms both these assertions. He describes the making of the costume and wooden head as having been a meticulous enterprise, and it shows. The bird's head, *kònòkun*, is about fifteen years old. The structure of the head is an elongated dome, with a thin ridge set prominently on top. The beak swells and curves near the tip, and near the head it too is graced with a thinly carved ridge. It is an energetic but nicely balanced carving, and when Sedu compared it to the one in the photograph I had shown him, he emphasized the difference in quality in a wonderfully subtle manner, by saying the two were not made by the same hand. One of Sedu's nephews said the beak of Sidi's was more extensively carved, and he made it clear that by that he meant it was better.[10]

This kind of response was typical of Sedu whenever we looked at Mande sculpture together. When the face of a sculpted figure, for example, was composed of clearly carved geometrically abstracted elements arranged in a stimulating format, he considered the piece to be good. When the hair style of a sculpture was large, sensitively shaped, and cleanly embellished with pyroengraved patterns, he considered the piece to be good. Pieces were poor when they lacked crispness and excitement or when they were not forcefully, authoritatively articulated. Generally, however, Sedu would not say so forthrightly.

In 1972 Sedu illustrated a rudiment of Mande art criticism for me by devising a technique to say in public how he really felt about another sculptor's work. For the Mande it is neither kind nor wise to criticize someone else's work in the presence of others. Instead, people issue platitudes. Sedu had me teach him enough English so that he could say a piece was fine in Bamana and then tell me instantly in English if he thought it was good or bad.

I once showed Sedu a finely forged sculpture of a female antelope with a baby on its back, another type of "little animal head" used in the youth and agriculture associations (Ill. 48). The way the two pairs of horns join the heads with rivets that become eyes, the way the necks and heads bend in thick rich curves, and the way the areas described by the bodies and legs form large and small rectangles that play off the curves to promote a gently moving kind of visual energy all make this piece elegantly beautiful.

Sedu's response to the piece was instantaneous and emphatic. He found the headdress absolutely beautiful, saying so in no uncertain terms. I kept asking why, and after marveling at the thought that I actually might not know, he directed my attention to the necks, horns, and heads.[11] He repeated his feeling several times that the sculptor was really a blacksmith, and in so saying praised the artist wholeheartedly, because in the Mande languages to link people to their professions with positive emphasis is to indicate that they have truly mastered it.[12]

I discussed sculpture quality with Sedu more than with anyone else. Nonsmiths focused on the same kinds of criteria, but their responses were briefer and less directed. Other smiths generally agreed with Sedu, while emphasizing their own points of view. Dramane Dunbiya, the senior smith in Sedu's town, always verbalized the importance of creativity and innovation, which he felt should characterize the details of a sculpture. An outstanding iron horse and rider figure, for example, might include delicate iron reins and a miniature rifle over the rider's shoulder. Magan Fane, an old smith from a nearby town, was more concerned with resemblance. He once criticized an iron equestrian figure by saying the horse was like a camel because it had an extremely long neck.[13]

Sedu used a number of words that focus on the concept of decoration to identify the attributes of good sculpture. *Jago* (or *jako*) means art or artfulness and style. It is generally used to indicate something decorated or embellished beyond practical necessity. Brink has described it as human vitality depicted through embellishment.[14] Smiths I worked with considered it the result of labor that made things attractive and desirable. Sedu sometimes described the effect of a sculpture or the painted decoration of a mud-brick wall by saying the embellished entity was pleasing to the eye, *nye la jako*. A Malian friend once described a colorful shirt with a vibrant repeated stamped pattern by saying, "The shirt has a lot of *jago*," *Chimisi jago ka ca*.

Masiri also means decoration, but Kalilou Tera notes that it refers most frequently to objects or materials that are added to a structure—such as the red threads and metal rings added to the ears of a sculpture—whereas *jago* refers to the decoration built into a structure.[15] Sidi Ballo made a similar distinction in describing his own bird masquerade. The cloth stretched over a bent wood frame he considered part of the basic form, although he quickly added, "That makes it beautiful," *O b'a cenye*. The fringe of white fibers near the bottom he considered *masiri*, and that too makes the masquerade beautiful.[16] Travélé and Bazin translate the term as "ornament."[17] The lexicon published by the Malian Ministry of Education translates the verb form as "to adorn, to decorate."[18]

Nyègèn means design, as in patterns of design engraved or painted on an object, again to make it look better. Sedu used it in the verb form to mean the act of decorating, even in the sense of the way a sculpted figure's hands are positioned to enhance the sculpture's appearance. The Ministry of Education's lexicon translates the verb form as "to draw, to paint."[19] Bazin defines *nyègè* as "to sculpt, to paint, to streak with color, to dye, to adorn with diverse colors."[20] Like the words applied to sorcery, however, these terms are often used flexibly, so that the boundaries between them begin to dissolve.

Another notion complements the Mande concept of decoration. It characterizes the core of an art structure before it is imbued with *jago*. The notion is *jayan*, which means clarity and precision, straightforwardness and discernibility. It connotes a quest for abstraction and reduction, in search of the real meanings of things.

This may complicate but it does not contradict what we have said thus far about decoration. For the sculptor, decoration is a final consideration; it brings a piece to fruition, to completion. First, a real-life form must be reduced conceptually to abstracted elements, which are assembled as the material is reduced and refined. The visual excitement is as much in this reorganization as it is in its embellishment, and this in large measure is what Sedu found so attractive about the iron antelope headdress. In addition, Mande decoration rarely consumes the structure to which it has been added. Patterns of pyroengraving on a figure's torso, a door lock, or a hair style do not obscure the sculpted form beneath. Rather, they enhance it, augment it. Red thread and earrings do not compromise the form of an antelope headdress. Rather, they civilize it by metaphorical extension, because those are the sorts of things human beings wear in their own ears. If decoration goes too far, it does so more likely than not as a symbol of something excessive in society.

In fact, there is a parallel to this when personal embellishment becomes excessive. A modest length of red thread knotted through a man or woman's ear lobe is fine. So is a beautiful hair style. So are attractive clothes. But when country people return home to a small town with a new big-city wardrobe, full of dyed linen and expensive embroidery, ostentatious display is considered to have displaced good taste. To correct it, other community members will confiscate the clothes and redistribute them.[21]

At the core of most Mande sculpture is a clear, comprehensible formal structure. The shape of iron lamps is immediately recognizable, and though they may be complex—with up to 100 cups—they will be carefully balanced. The structural components of iron figural sculpture are always clearly and simply designed, even when details of decoration are complex.[22] In

wood sculpture, too, a basic feature of masks, figures, and door locks is formal clarity, which emphasizes rapid viewer accessibility. *Kore* and *ntomo*
masks can be comprehended swiftly, no matter how ambiguous the imagery
may be. Antelope headdresses, though highly stylized, nevertheless capture
what is essential in antelopes: long horns and necks and a sense of strength
and elegance. Sculpted wooden figures, such as children's dolls, *jirimògòniw*,
and twin figures, *sinzinw*, are described by sculptor-smiths and nonsmiths as
good when they look like that which they intend to depict; that is, when they
capture the basic characteristics of human form (Ill. 49). The arms may be
too short and the hair style incredibly huge, but the core will be decidedly
human. Even in the monumental sculptures of the *gwan* cult and *jo* initiation association, the remarkable elegance captured by the sculptors does
not weaken the forcefulness produced through purity and simplicity of form
(Ill. 50).

This concern for clarity and real meaning goes beyond sculpture. Its value
is registered in terms that apply to Mande art and the Mande world generally. *Wòròn* means to husk or shuck. By extension it means to get to the core
and master something, such as music, song, speech, or any art enterprise.
Kolo means kernel or nut, and by extension the nucleus or essential structure of something. A bard may be praised with the phrase "He knows the
kernel of bardship," *A be jeliya kolo don.* Public speaking has long been an
important form of Mande artistic expression, and at its best it also partakes
of this quest for essences. Oral tradition says that Fakoli, the legendary ally
of Sunjata, was famous for his *kumakolo*, "the bone of speech, true speech,"
speech that is without ornament and goes concisely to the heart of the
matter. Fakoli knew how to convince people with words, with just the right
emphasis here, just the right understatement there. It is said that he won as
many supporters for the Mali Empire with his "true speech" as he did with
his sorcery and his military brilliance.[23]

A Mande apothegm addresses a condition—normally associated with
youth—that is in opposition to all this elegance and economy. One may say
of an exuberant, energetic young person, "He has wind up his nose," *Finyè
b'a nu na.* Frenetic, unfocused activity is thus referred to negatively, with
the implication that circumspection and an ability to find the center of things
must be developed if a person is to become a mature, effective society member. Thus the phrase *yèrè wolo*, which means to find one's true self, or the
true meaning, essence, essential dignity in anything, becomes important.[24]
A refrain in Seydou Camara's recorded version of *Kambili* acknowledges the
importance of this:

Thus to each slave, the sound of his awakening.[25]

The Mande believe that we are all slaves of God, and so the line applies to
everyone. To awake in this sense is to find one's true destiny, the path indeli-

bly set in the heart, but which may never be fully experienced if its possessor does not learn of it and act in consort with it. A Mande proverb makes the same kind of statement, but more directly:

> To know animals is good.
> To know trees is good.
> To know oneself is better than them all.[26]

The many forms of Mande divination are techniques that help human beings strip away the superfluous features of a situation, so that its basic structure may be understood and acted upon. Metaphorical descriptions attest to this. In a song that praises the accomplishments of a famous Wasoulou blacksmith-diviner named Red Musa and the wilderness spirit that was his benefactor, the bard Seydou Camara referred to social and spiritual difficulties as tangled things and to divination as the means of setting them straight. He sang:

> If things are tangled,
> The genie who cherished Red Musa will untangle them.[27]

Divination can also be described as scattering. In a song about himself Seydou sang:

> Scatter it, scatter it, yee![28]

In this way he likened divination to a chicken kicking up dust in the yard. The phrase implies that a problem is spread out or untangled so its source can be viewed clearly.

The Mande concept of clarity and precision extends into spiritual realms and to philosophies of action. Sedu Traore once spoke to me about the ways sculptor-smiths serve society. He was comparing the good work of smiths— as doctors, diviners, and amulet makers—to the bad work of charlatans, in this instance Muslim marabouts who seek personal gain by claiming to help people. He used two phrases like refrains in our conversation. He said: "Our path is really clear. The marabout's path is not clear."[29] Sedu said his elder brother liked to put it another way, by saying the way of Bamana smiths is singular, by which he meant true and pure. The way of charlatan marabouts, however, is not always the same.[30]

All of this should be kept in mind as we focus our attention on blacksmiths' sculpture. We will examine four types of Mande sculpture, so that we can relate our understanding of the smiths' creative activities to their art. The Mande do not use a word for "art" as we do. Of course, every kind of Mande sculpture has a name, and sometimes people use a word to refer to categories of objects. *Jirimògòniw*, "little wooden people," for example, can be used to identify small figural sculptures, such as the wooden twin figures and dolls.

Sogonikun, "little animal head," can be used to identify a variety of animal masks and headdresses, even though its precise application is to the masks and headdresses of a particular agricultural festival. I have even heard a blacksmith refer to his sculpture as *jiri,* "wood." But "art" as we conceive it—separate and distinct from other elements of culture—seems not to fit into a Mande conceptualization of sculpture.

Thus, the first two types of objects we will examine, spear blades and oil-burning lamps, might not be considered as art by every Western reader. This is especially true of spear blades. Yet, for the Mande their beauty, symbolism, and place in society takes them well beyond simple utility. They are especially interesting to us because of their association with a very important blacksmiths' enterprise, circumcision. Oil-burning lamps are also utilitarian, although many are graced with extensive decoration and some with abstract figures. They are a good example of a blacksmiths' product that was formerly in very wide use but has now become nearly obsolete. The third type, iron figures of women and equestrian men, fit most comfortably into Western categories of art, at least formally, and for the Mande their beauty is considered a significant part of their function. They exemplify an important aspect of Mande sculpture; they possess a particular identity, a collection of attributes that can be adapted to a wide variety of functional contexts. Finally, we will look at *kòmò* masks, horizontal helmet constructions of wood and organic matter than can only be owned and danced by smiths, and that illustrate very clearly many of the ways smiths act in and influence society.

Two qualities make these works particularly appropriate for us to examine. Three are made of iron, and so spring from the expertise that gives the smiths a major part of their professional identity. And three are designed to harness occult energy, and so become vehicles through which smiths bring their special knowledge and power to bear on society.

THE SMITHS' IRON ART

Mande iron sculpture has not been discussed in the literature nearly as often as wood sculpture or other art forms, such as cloth, architecture, or epic poetry. There are several reasons. Much of it is very secret, full of *daliluw* and so not really the kind of thing the Mande like to talk about or show foreigners. Much is also disappearing; that is certainly true of the three types we will discuss in this section. Finally, much is idiosyncratic, expressing a great deal of individual creativity in both the sizes and shapes of the objects.

There are, for example, small devices made of iron wrapped with cotton thread or fibers, designed to launch harmful *kòròtiw,* airborne poisons. The forged iron figure may be no larger than two inches in length, and shaped so ambiguously that only its owner can be sure whether it is a camel or a horse. This is fitting because only its owner knows exactly what it is supposed to do. Other sculpted devices are designed to absorb and defuse the harmful energies launched in the form of such poisons. Some take the form of small iron figures (Ill. 51) that combine clarity and elegance in the structure's core with a surface coating that is in no way decorative, but rather the dried materials of sacrifice that empower the sculpture, along with the iron itself. Other sculptures we rarely see are made by smiths for hunters as *basiw*, the secret and supernaturally potent devices that augment an individual's own energies and help enlarge his prowess (Ill. 52). Here too the surface may be absolutely blackened with the materials of sacrifice, and natural elements such as duiker antelope horns may be added both to symbolize and to embody high levels of *nyama*. Smiths also make iron sculptures to portray the wilderness spirits (*jinew*) who are their benefactors (Ill. 53).

As we discuss the three most common types of Mande iron art, we will move from the objects least likely to those most likely to be considered as art by Westerners.

TAMAW: SPEAR BLADES

Making them was not all; there were also *kilisiw*.
(Magan Fane, May 1973)

To the Mande, spears were much more than utilitarian objects. Very often they were embellished well beyond any practical necessity. They were vivid attributes of masculinity and male prowess, and so became symbols. They were used in the deeply significant ritual that accompanied circumcision, and so the ramifications of their symbolism were extended. In addition, as Magan Fane noted, they were full of the power that traditional occult science could give them and this made them special weapons.

Until guns became common in the Western Sudan, spears were used as the principal weapons of war. One sees them only rarely now, although they are still used quite often in circumcision ritual. Life, though, is calmer than it was in the days of state and empire building. Today other armaments take precedence. Hunters prefer their guns and rifles, and the special heavy axes they always carry. The rest of the citizens are happy to arm themselves with knives, or clubs called *berew* (or *tama berew*) that have a heavy, rounded business end and a metal tip so that they can be used as walking sticks. The Fula who live among the Mande sometimes still carry spears, and some elder Mande men use them as walking sticks. Sedu Traore said that in the last battles people remember around his town, in the days before the French, blacksmith-made guns were used almost exclusively, and that only the Fula still use spears as weapons.[31] So, the number of spears has dwindled over the years, and those that remain have been redistributed as families moved or sold them. I only saw a handful of examples during my stay in Mali, and they remained with families as keepsakes. But even from so limited a sampling it is clear that a variety of shapes were used (Ill. 54).

Many of these spear blades are very gracefully shaped. One is composed of a very narrow blade that swells elegantly near the base and is particularly beautiful. Severe rust has obliterated much of its surface, and it is alleged to date to before the time of Samory.[32] (In southern Mali, when an object is old, it is said to date to before the time of Samory; when it is really old, it is said to date to the time of Sunjata.) The rust obscures a delicate pattern of dot decoration that seems to have run around the edges of the blade and up the center. The old smith Magan Fane thought the dots belonged to a system of numerical symbolism that he, at least, no longer understands.

Most spear blades end in a thick-walled hollow socket, designed to fit over the sharpened end of the wooden shaft. Often a small hole pierced the socket, so that a nail could be used to lock the two together. I suspect these sockets were shaped by beating the hot iron around a very hard wood core. In fact, the cups of iron lamps are formed in this way. Very heavy wood from the *si (Bassia parkii)* tree is carved into a mold, over which red-hot iron is placed and beaten (Ill. 55). The wood holds its shape under the hammer blows, and, though it does ignite for an instant, the surface is charred but not seriously burned.

In some Bamana communities, ancient spears are presented to the circumcised youths, *solimadenw*, who carry them to call attention to their new status as men. Such a spear is considered an inheritance from the father. Originally it belonged to a male ancestor who brought it into the house where it then remained for generations. Acquiring the spear is seen as an aspect of becoming a man; it is a part of the *ceya minaw*, the "things that make one a man." In some towns miniature spear blades, one and one-half to two inches long, are now made and presented to the *solimadenw*. They are never shown, but rather kept secretly, sometimes on the walls of their owners' rooms. These miniatures assist their owners in becoming like their fathers or grandfathers, their bravest ancestors. They are signs whose symbolic content involves effectiveness in fighting.

The manufacture of spear blades involved more than forging iron. Certain *daliluw*, of the *kilisi* type that employ secret language and include the spit of smiths, were applied to give the spears special powers. In times of war they could be hurled long distances with accuracy that was guaranteed by the *daliluw* of their makers. The only protection available to an adversary facing such a weapon was the *nègè haya* amulet, another product of blacksmiths, designed to prevent puncture wounds.

Today, smiths say that the most important use for their spears involves combating the supernatural dangers that threaten the newly circumcised. In many towns boys waiting to become men are visited just before the operation by an elder bearing a spear. The latter plants it in the ground before the entrance to the compound where the boys gathered the night before. He then removes it, and they pass through, acquiring as they do so a power that will protect them from sorcery. In other communities, the procedure varies. After the operation an old smith will walk before the *solimadenw* as they leave the place of circumcision. He carries a spear which provides the same protection. Yet another variation puts the spear in the hands of the first to be circumcised, *nye mògò*, "the one at the head." While he holds it, nothing bad can happen to the others. All of these variants are held to be effective, and in the towns where they are used, smiths who perform the operation advise the youths' parents that there is no need for them to go to the expense of special protective sacrifices. The smiths, with their iron and their *daliluw*, have rendered the youths virtually invulnerable.

We must note two important facts about the use of these spears. First, the variations I have described are not regional. One town may put a spear in the hands of the first young man circumcised while its neighbor, perhaps no more than a mile away, will believe it better to have an elder carry the spear. Indeed, a third town in the same neighborhood may not use spears at all, preferring to depend on other aspects of a blacksmith's knowledge for the protection of their *solimadenw*. Such variation is seen by all as perfectly natural; everyone has personal preferences, and every smith has special procedures. On a map the distribution of these variations would appear as a complex mosaic intricately intertwined with one another.

Also important is the nature of these spears. Spears are made by smiths alone, and most of those used in circumcision were forged from traditionally smelted iron. Smelting and forging, as we have seen, involve great amounts of *nyama*. In addition, the spears are fortified with the application of powerful *daliluw*. The product is then put to work protecting young men during one of the most vulnerable moments of their lives. Blacksmiths are often seen as rugged individuals who fight fire with fire. It is no accident that the devices these smiths used to make, which were once considered formidable enough to be major weapons of war, remain major weapons in the war against malevolent sorcery.

FITINEW: IRON LAMPS

> In the old days, when a dance was desired, a huge *fitine* was stuck in the ground at the place and then everybody danced around it. (Magan Fane, July 1973)

> Intelligence is the *fitine* light. (Kalilou Tera, August 1977)

Iron lamps have also largely fallen out of use. Kerosene-burning lanterns are now available nearly everywhere, and most people find them advantageous because they can be carried when one goes outside at night. Up until the last generation, however, the traditional iron lamps were used in a wide range of contexts, and they were made in a variety of configurations, some of them quite lovely.

They were also widely distributed. One may still encounter them stored in homes throughout the Western Sudan. The western Bamana and those who live between the regions of Bamako and Ségou call the lamps *fitinew*. In the region around Ségou they are known as *futenew*. To the north and west, among the Soninke, Khasonke, and Maninka, they are known variously as *fetila, firine, firne, fitinew,* and *fitinaw*.[33] They were used as far west as the

Gambia Mandingo states. The Bozo and Sorko, Mande groups on the middle Niger River, used them, and Herta Haselberger photographed a magnificent example in Podo.[34]

The lamps were also used around the fringes of the Mande diaspora. East of Mopti and San, the Bobo peoples of Burkina Faso have used them. Closer to Mopti, along the Bandiagara plateau, documented Dogon lamps were simple, small, and single-cupped. Desplagnes illustrated a graceful example with a small iron hook projecting downward from the back of the shaft that supports the cup, which makes the whole lamp resemble the sacred Dogon iron insignia often found embedded in altars and in blacksmiths' forges.[35]

The Senufo of southern Mali and Ivory Coast make both simple and elaborate lamps. Anita Glaze was informed by Senufo elders that the more elaborate ones with many cups, which "gave much light," were used as part of the excision ceremonies of girls. These lamps are called *fetinew*, the name used by the Bamana immediately above them.[36] Further south, Maurice Delafosse found a simple, single-cup lamp among an assortment of wooden figures in a funeral chamber, in the south-central Ivory Coast town of Donko.[37] René Bravmann reports that among the Bobo, too, iron lamps play important roles during the funeral ceremonies of elders.[38]

Palm- or karite-oil lamps, composed of cup-shaped basins into which a cotton wick is dipped and which are most often mounted on iron shafts or rods, also occur well beyond the boundaries of Mande west Africa. At Bida, in the Nupe region of northwestern Nigeria, a number of very similar lamp types have been documented.[39] Iron lamps have been documented among the Yoruba in contexts which relate them to both Shango and Ifa, two important deities,[40] and von Luschan illustrates one found in the king's palace in Benin.[41]

The simplest Mande lamps consist of a single cup, *fitine daga den,* generally ranging from three to five inches in diameter. It serves as a basin for karite oil, *si tulu,* with a wick of twisted cotton thread, *fitine juru,* placed in the basin with its ends extending over the front of the lip. Most often the cup is forged to an iron rod, *fitine kala,* which is stuck in the ground to support the lamp. These rods range in length from less than a foot to several feet. Alternatively, a short spike will support a single-cup lamp; it is simply pounded into a mud-brick wall. Lamps made specifically for sale to Westerners usually have a stand attached at the base, because, as Magan Fane said, white people have cement floors.

This basic structure can be elaborated in a number of ways. First, the iron rod may be expanded into a broad shaft. This happened quite often in the regions of Ségou and Dioila, and it was most often associated with additional embellishment, the flat shafts being forged into a variety of geometric shapes ranging from diamonds to rectangles with indented sides (Ill. 56). Some are forged so that a thin ridge vertically bisects the rectangular units, while the shaft thins toward the outside edges, lending delicacy to what otherwise might be a somewhat ponderous composition (Ill. 57).

Just above the cups, the central shafts may also support a schematic forged iron figure (Ill. 58). On the one-cup lamps these figures are abstract enough to be barely discernible, and they are associated with a particular forging technique formerly used to attach the cups to their shafts. This was done by bending one and one-half to three inches of the upper shaft over the edge of the smith's anvil with hammer blows while the shaft was red-hot. When it had been bent nearly 180 degrees, a one to three inch tab, attached to the cup, was inserted between the two surfaces. Then, while all three elements were red-hot, the smith closed the gap and hammer-welded them into a single unit.

Generally, a fourth element would be tucked inside the space between the shaft elements. This was the tip of another piece of iron, most of which had been divided with hammer and chisel to form two long, thin extensions. When the gap was welded closed, this divided piece emerged horizontally from either side of the shaft, just behind or above the cup. On many lamps these pieces would then be bent to run upward, parallel to the shaft. They ended in small loops that held the chains and small iron utensils, *sira minaw*, used to adjust the wick within the cup and to spoon in additional oil.

After the top of the lamp was welded together, but before the side elements were bent upward, the shape of the top portion of the shaft would itself be altered. Hammer blows were directed at the center of that portion of the shaft that rose above the cup. The section was worked and reworked until gentle concave surfaces had been established. The hammering technique, using the oldest type of Mande hammer, is identical to that still in common practice for making the hafts of modern hoe blades.

This indented section of the upper lamp shaft recalls the stylized torso and head of a human figure, with the rods that flank it serving as arms. Generally, as the lamps grow more complex and the number of cups increases, these figures become more elaborate (Ill. 59).

Ample room for personal variation existed within this traditional scheme. During a trip to the Ségou region I saw, among the many lamps shown me, a variant of the single-cup with abstract human figure type that distinguished itself from all the others. The top of the shaft was forged into an oblong shape that projected slightly forward at its upper and outer edges, making it concave. It thus echoed in a perpendicular plane the shape of the oil-bearing cup, while adding interest to the head of the figure. It also resembled in conception the hair styles on many Bamana door lock figures. The maker of the lamp, a smith of the Fane family, said that he had made it many years ago.[42] He had been recommended to me by people in various river towns as someone who was very powerful, an outstanding amulet maker and, up until the past two decades, an expert iron smelter.

I saw another lamp in 1973 that was, in my experience, unusual.[43] Above a single cup a kind of scaffolding had been established, which supported two iron figures, one with hands turned up, the other with hands pointed down. Just below the cup the shaft had been twisted three times, according to a technique used by Bamana smiths.[44] This was balanced with two more twisted portions above the cup in the rod that connected the two figures. The cup was nearly lost in all of this. It lacked the prominence afforded the cups of most lamps simply because in most lamps, where so much iron work is present, that iron work consists of scaffolding for additional cups.

Indeed, many of these lamps were made more complex by the addition of cups and supporting scaffoldings (Ill. 61). Any number of configurations were possible. A single cup might simply be doubled, with its counterpart projecting into the opposite direction from behind. A horizontal shaft might be added to the vertical, with three cups mounted across it, or three cups in front and one centered behind, or three in front and three behind. This horizontal piece turned up sharply at both ends in some lamps, providing additional space for adding cups.

Creating lamp configurations seems to have been a regular preoccupation of lamp-making smiths. They were guided by the desire to build structures that were absolutely bilaterally symmetrical, and we would be hard pressed to find many lamps that violate this rule. At the same time, the rule became a foil against which marvelous complications were established in the third dimension. Along the vertical axis, a cup at any level in the front might or might not be matched with a cup in back, and some smiths created very complicated, sophisticated visual rhythms in the ways they played off front and back cups against each other. Such complexities in effect constitute a rich solution to the problem of incorporating into these kinds of artifacts both clarity and embellishment, the qualities which the Mande consider essential to a superior work of art. Clarity was set with bilateral symmetry, in as effective a way as one can imagine. Embellishment and compositional excitement were added with adventuresome placement of cups in the vertical registers, so that cups set in front and back generated a kind of positive-negative space. Bourama Soumaouro, a young, knowledgeable smith from the Wasoulou, explained all this to me. He said lamps with all their cups in front were all right. Lamps with a cup in back to match every cup in front were better. But the best lamps alternated front and back along the vertical axis.[45]

In a particular eastern city, where big lamps are still used, the prevailing aesthetic is a little different. Cups may occur on one side only, but they can occur in enormous numbers, so that compositions become quite complex without recourse to the interplay between front and back. A senior smith there named Ba Sinale Konate explained to me that more cups meant better lamps. He said the simplest lamps had a single cup. To improve upon them, lamps with three cups could be made, and so on up to 100 cups. He was clearly a man who lived by his own beliefs, because one lamp he had made had dozens of cups.[46]

Embellishment in the form of engraved designs, *nyègènw*, is also present on many lamps. These designs may be a simple configuration of short parallel lines running up the outside edges of the vertical shaft. They may be extremely complex, with many fine lines forming geometric designs including diamonds, "x"s and zoomorphic shapes such as lizards and crocodiles. One lamp I saw was topped with the forged iron head of a cow (Color Plate V). The smith Konate said that this was decoration, *masiri*, to make the lamp more attractive. When making a lamp one may, he said, add any decoration, *masiri*, or designs, *nyègènw*, one likes.

When lamps were still widely used by the Mande, they had a multitude of functions, in both individual households and entire communities. They were, first, the common means of illuminating rooms and courtyards at night. Imperato notes that new brides received them as part of their trousseaus. Women put lamps out along all the streets of town at night, and slaves kept them supplied with oil. They could also be placed at the entrances to communities. Sidi Ballo thought there used to be special lamps with seven cups for kings. Each cup represented one of the seven foundations of the leader's authority:

> Power is for him, the country belongs to him, the price of souls is paid to him, powder belongs to him, guns belong to him, people belong to him and cattle belongs to him.[47]

The biggest and most complex lamps lit nighttime performances of the youth associations, and the ceremonies of the initiation associations. Mama Konate, a smith who lived between Bamako and Bougouni, said the big lamps were used for wedding ceremonies, or when the young men felt like celebrating. He referred to such lamps as *yankadi*, "it is good here," and then clarified his meaning with the French phrase "la lampe de bonheur."[48]

In one major eastern city, wrestling matches are illuminated by six big lamps (Color Plates V, VI). Wrestling is a major popular sport in the Western Sudan. Wrestlers acquire, if they are good, a great deal of fame. Good ones have their own bards, who travel to matches with them to sing their praises. They also have their own sorcerers, who travel to matches and do everything they can to sap the strength, or at least the confidence, of opponents. The matches are thus spectacles, with musicians singing praises and technicians of the supernatural staging flamboyant rituals.

Ba Sinale Konate, a smith who had made one of the wrestling lamps, talked to me about them in 1978.[49] He said there were basically three kinds of lamps in the region. The simplest type, called *fitineda gansan*, was used around the house. A lamp with six cups, *konyo fitine*, was used for weddings. The most complex ones, and the only ones still in use, are called *bori baro fitinew;* they provide the light for wrestling matches. They can have forty, seventy, a hundred cups, or even more. Two sectors of his city are rivals in wrestling. Each has three lamps, and each wants its lamps to be the most beautiful. Previously, Konate's sector had used a single lamp of a hundred cups, but it had fallen into a serious state of disrepair. The smiths destroyed it and built three new lamps in its place, one of them with forty-four cups.

When not in use the lamps stay with the families of the smiths who made them.[50]

Symbolism in Mande lamps seems to have been quite variable. Because the lamps have largely fallen out of use, many people are simply not familiar with what they or their parts might have represented. In addition, the lamps as visual images are relatively neutral; that is, they are sufficiently abstract to accommodate a wide variety of associations. Many people nowadays say the lamps bore no particular meanings, while others believed they were symbolic but did not know what the symbolism might have been. An art merchant in Ségou, perhaps anxious to be helpful, said that the geometric shapes forged into lamp shafts represented the markings of certain snakes.[51] Sedu Traore disagreed, saying such patterns were simply decoration.[52] Kalilou Tera noted that feet and legs attached to the lower shafts of some lamps (Ill.60) may have reminded people of a moralizing axiom commonly used by the Mande. It is often said that if a human being is divided at the waist, the parts above serve reason, the parts below, serve passion. The head is the seat of intelligence. Hands support the head. They help it convert thought to action and they are controlled (at least within the metaphorical context of this axiom) by it. The sexual organs, by contrast, are the seat of potential mischief, and they are by no means always under the control of intelligence. The feet are also not always controlled by intelligence. Indeed, they may work in consort with sex organs and move unwitting souls toward mischief.[53]

The presence of feet on some lamps directs us toward another area of possible meaning. At least some of these lamps may have been intended to evoke human beings and the spiritual principles that animate them. We have seen that lamp tops may be shaped like humans, albeit very abstractly. The referents that do most of the work in establishing the connection are the thin rods that emerge from either side of the central shaft to become human arms held out and bent upward at the elbow. This motif—horizontal members turned upward at the ends—is often repeated in other parts of a lamp. Several cups on the larger lamps may have their own spatulas and spoons, for example, and these will generally be supported by the same horizontal rod bent up at the ends. In addition, the scaffolding that supports the cups may itself take the form of one or several horizontal elements that bend up at the ends. Given the precedence we have already established, it becomes rather easy to see in these lamps a multitude of references to the human form.

In the various Mande scripts a number of signs bear visual resemblance to this lamp motif, and the meanings of the signs cluster around the concept of a human being and, by extension, the spiritual principles or physical needs that animate all life. Zahan recorded a sign for "man, the male, the masculine principle" in one of the Bamana scripts (Ill. 61A).[54] Imperato indicates that one of the principal motifs in *bògòlanfini* mud cloth (Ill. 61B), which he calls the "Mali Pattern," is composed of the abstract representation of a human being.[55] Dieterlen and Cissé have catalogued a great many signs used in the *kòmò* initiation association, and several of these bring the lamp motif to mind. One (Ill. 61C), called "child of the tree," relates the wish for fecundity associated with newly circumcised young men.[56] Another (Ill. 61D), called "your two hands," recalls the hands of farmers and expresses the desire for agricultural abundance.[57] Another (Ill. 61E), called "master, or holder of truth," is used during important discussions or reunions.[58] Another (Ill. 61F), called "corpse of a very old woman," is employed when the deceased bodies of elderly women are buried.[59] Another (Ill. 61G), called "wind," represents the movement of the souls of all things.[60] Another (Ill. 61H) is called "offering" or "sacrifice."[61] Another (Ill. 61I) represents members of the Hausa ethnic group.[62] And another (Ill. 61J), called "flame or fire of the sky," is applied to altars by heads of families before fields are prepared for planting as a petition for adequate rain.[63]

Other factors support this possible interpretation of meaning in lamps. Imperato found that lamps connoted the human mouth and wicks referred to human tongues.[64] We should recall that both mouths and tongues are reservoirs of *nyama*. Cissé, in exploring the spiritual principles that give life to human bodies, describes three important Mande concepts, *nyama, ni,* and *nya.* We are already familiar with *nyama.* The *ni* is the principle of immaterial life, according to Cissé, and is connected in the minds of the Bamana with fire and air. It is also that aspect of human vitality contained within the breath and those bodily functions that we normally do not control at a conscious level. It is the heartbeat. It derives from ancestors. The *nya* is energy that radiates from the soul, source of life, to create an active field around a person. It exists in greatest intensity in the head, and when a person dies it reverts to *nyama.* Cissé notes that the Bamana, for example, liken the *ni* to a ball of fire in a hearth. The flames and radiant heat represent the *nya.* The heat that lingers after the hearth is put out is similar to *nyama.*[65]

Viviana Pâques presents a complementary notion. She says the *ni* is conceived of as breath, and is the heat that is the movement of human beings. It appears as a flame when the person bearing it dies, while in life it is the person's conscience, reason, and will.[66] Interestingly enough, Kalilou Tera indicates that intelligence can be likened to the light of an iron lamp,[67] and Imperato found that when a father or the head of a family died, a common funeral chant contained the line, "My lamp has gone out."[68]

These data are not conclusive. We cannot say that Mande iron lamps presented a constellation of symbols focusing on the physical and spiritual components of the person. It is reasonable to suggest, however, that many Mande individuals found it appropriate to contemplate ideas such as these when looking at or using the lamps.

NÈGÈMUSOW AND NÈGÈSOTIGIW:
IRON WOMEN AND IRON HORSE MASTERS

If people in a village knew an enemy was coming for war, they would hold an iron horse and rider staff with its back towards the direction of the enemy, with someone else holding a spear. In this way they would avoid war. (Magan Fane, August 1973)

They are to be admired. (A smith of the Kante family speaking about the staffs, September 1973)

In the judgment of smiths, making iron figural and equestrian topped staffs is the most difficult of all their sculpting enterprises. The medium of iron is hard enough to work into graceful shapes of two dimensions. In three, when one seeks believable forms after human beings, the task becomes quite arduous. Distributed across the Western Sudan and beyond, these sculptures are more than beautiful, for they, like spear blades, incorporate *daliluw* and can be used in a variety of critical situations. Sadly, they too have become much rarer than they were one or two generations ago. Also, like so many other types of Mande art, they have always been surrounded with a veil of secrecy. Thus, many details of their use remain obscure to us. We know, however, that they were, and to some degree still are, influential art works. Their significance and potency is well rooted in that rich interface between Mande beliefs about the world and the powers smiths possess to manipulate it.

Many artists of west and central Africa set sculptures atop staffs. Frequently, such sculptures proclaim the status or profession of their owners, elongation on the vertical axis being a favored means of arranging such insignia. In Zaire and Angola, the Kongo, Yaka, Pende, Luba, and Chokwe carry figural staffs as symbols of chiefly authority, and they often enhance that authority, or justify it, by portraying its source, a female ancestor.[69] In Nigeria, Igbo and northern Edo groups use iron staffs topped not with figures but with forged configurations of long tubular bells. Such iron works signal the titles of elder men, announcing and honoring their rank simultaneously.[70] Yoruba smiths place stylized birds, often forged from hoe blades, at the top of iron staffs that serve as emblems for herbalist-diviners. Another type, dedicated to the divination god Orere, consists of a single large bird over a staff with clapperless bells facing up.[71] The staffs share an important characteristic with the Yoruba lamps mentioned earlier, for they too reflect prototypes made substantially earlier by the metalsmiths of Benin.[72] The Fon in the modern Republic of Benin use a similar iron configuration, with a flat metal disk supporting various animal and human motifs. Such sculptures grace the shrines of important ancestors.[73]

At the eastern edge of the Mande diaspora, and strongly within its sphere of influence, Dogon smiths forge sacred iron sculpture in a variety of forms. Some are simply iron shafts that break open sensuously at the top to form cages that enclose beautiful pieces of amber or polished stone. Other shafts are chiseled open at the top to form branches that support small iron bells. Often, a reduced portion of the shaft continues upward in the form of a miniature or full-size spear blade.

Many Dogon staffs are topped with sharply abstracted forged iron figures. Most frequently, they emphasize the head and hands, while neglecting the rest of the anatomy. The arms sweep away from the shaft and upward in prominent displays that remind us of the scaffoldings in Mande iron lamps.

The hands are likely to be huge, often much larger than the heads. Articulated facial features are not the norm. Although a beard may be forged at the bottom of the head, details such as ears, noses, and mouths are usually absent; the head is a simple bullet shape. Sometimes these figures are mounted on broadly curved pieces of iron that look rather like sickle blades. They might be horses or serpents; they are too minimal to be comprehended outside their context.

Documentation for the Dogon staffs is incomplete, but mythical ancestors called *nommo* seem to be favored depictions. Staffs topped by spear heads are claimed by Marcel Griaule to depict the *nommo* created directly by God, who subsequently gave life to the others.[74] Other staff types apparently depict other *nommo* or the original Dogon smith himself. Occasionally, the smith is articulated at the top of a wavy iron shaft, which may signify his descent from the heavens.[75]

The uses of these staffs also remain minimally documented. Many seem to have been possessed by diviners and healers and by the leaders of Dogon sacred cults. Others were the insignia of the *hogon*, principal priests in Dogon communities.[76] Dogon town chiefs also own staffs to mark their status, but these are made of wood instead of iron, except for the bottom, which is tipped with a small conical iron sleeve.[77]

Iron staffs have been made and used across the length of the Mande diaspora, from its most easterly extensions, the Bozo and Sorko along the middle Niger River, to its most westerly, the Mandinka around the Gambia River. We can introduce the Mande versions with a beautiful Bozo example (Ill. 62). It is not figural, but rather ends in a forged hook that is capped with a small hemispherical boss. At three intervals along the shaft the iron has been spread with a chisel, so that a concise, cage-like structure interrupts the staff's axis. Similar openings occur in Bamana and Mandinka staffs, and even as far afield as the Igbo of Nigeria, where iron staffs with elaborately opened cages signify elder status and title taking.[78] Between these interruptions on the Bozo staff occur delicate patterns of linear engraving and sensitively articulated three-dimensional lozenge shapes. These bracket the cage structures and help to create a very stimulating but tasteful composition.

Bamana staffs are almost always figural. I suspect that in private they possess sacred names that reflect their power and their use in secret situations. In public they are called simply "iron women," *nègèmusow*, and "iron horse masters," *nègèsotigiw*. Imperato notes that they are called "iron rod," *bisa nègè*, and "iron staff," *kala nègè*, in the large Bamana area south of the Bani River and between the towns of Bougouni and Sikasso.[79]

These staffs occupy unique space within the Mande principles of form we have discussed. To be sure they are, like most Mande sculpture, minimal. But they establish that effect in a different fashion from that used to set the character of wood masks or the twin figures that correspond roughly in scale to the figural portions of staffs. We can instructively compare the two types of sculpture. The iron staffs (Ill. 63, 64) are not conceived quite as geometrically as are the wood figures (Ill. 49). More importantly, they are composed of smaller surfaces. Limbs and torsos are often thinner and more delicate. Where a wood figure's arms and legs are nearly rectangular in cross section, often with sharp angles at the four corners, most iron figures' limbs will be carefully rounded, an effect considerably more difficult to accomplish in iron than rectangular limbs would be. Details in fingers and facial features may also be exceptionally refined and more rounded, demanding the ultimate in the blacksmiths' technical skills (Ill. 64).

The energy and the drama so often achieved in wood sculpture are by no means absent in the iron staffs. They are captured in postures and proportions. Hands may be huge and held prominently before the body. Hair styles and hats are often emphasized. Necks are consistently enormous, while torsos and limbs are most often quite elongated. The resulting figures arrive quite effectively at that Mande balance between the bold and aggressive and the subtle and delicate. They do it, however, the hard way, because to achieve these kinds of forms in iron is most demanding. Smiths always emphasized the difficulty of making these sculptures. In fact, most blacksmiths told me they did not possess that kind of skill. This in part is what they meant when they told me that iron figural staffs were made to be admired.

The shaft portions of these staffs are sometimes pierced at intervals, the metal having been opened with a chisel, pulled with tongs, and pounded while hot to create the thinner strands of the cages (Ill. 65). More often, thick iron hooks emerge from the shaft in curves that sweep first down and then back up. The hooks end in hemispherical bosses, like the one on top of the Bozo staff, and rather like those that cap the cage constructions of some Dogon staffs. Generally, the hooks are formed by splitting and shaping the base of an iron rod, and so the shafts that support them are in fact composed of three or more separate pieces of iron. At that point, where the hooks curve away and each iron rod ends, a socket is formed to receive the tip of the piece below (Ill. 64, Color Plate VII). This kind of joining is difficult because if the shaft is to be strong and durable the iron at each joint must be in effect welded together with special techniques of heating and hammering. Thus, in the shafts, too, smiths have canonized configurations that are much more difficult to achieve in iron than any number of other forms would be.

Our evidence suggests that Bamana staffs were traditionally used in two kinds of overlapping situations, one political and one spiritual, both very potent. Kate Ezra and Viviana Pâques report that west of Bougouni in the town of Tennentou, four iron figural staffs were stuck in the earth above the tomb of the town's founding ancestor. Two were stolen in the 1880s, however, by Samory's army, while the other two disappeared in the 1960s.[80] Ezra was told too that similar staffs were put on display at the vestibule entrance to peoples' homes, when family members made offerings to their ancestors.[81]

Robert Goldwater has also noted the use of figural staffs along a corridor that began around Bougouni and extended toward San. They served as the family insignia of chiefs, but apparently they were more than symbols. Goldwater states that during ceremonies some were placed in the tops of trees while others were buried underground.[82] Such placements suggest usage that transcends authority symbolism, because, unlike the staffs used elsewhere in Africa to announce power, these were not necessarily even seen. In fact, they may have possessed power of a different sort, the kind that can be implanted in objects through the use of *daliluw*.

Imperato reports additional uses for figural iron staffs in this same general area, south of the Bani River. Here are found two initiation associations, called *jo* and *gwan*, unique among the Mande in that they seem not to be found elsewhere in the diaspora but rather incorporate many of the features found generally in the other Mande associations. Imperato indicates that during initiation ceremonies and the funerals of senior members, iron staffs played prominent roles. For funerals some were set in the ground under the branches of a sacred tree called *bana*, while others were placed in its branches. They were also either carried as wands or held high in the air during certain segments of funeral ceremonies, when members marched in procession from the association sanctuary to the town. For initiation ceremonies staffs were carried in similar processions and placed in the sacred groves where association sanctuaries were located, sometimes in the branches of trees that composed the groves' inner ring.[83]

In the area between Bougouni and Bamako these figural staffs were used in ways that clearly made them supernaturally powerful devices. Blacksmiths say the pieces were full of *nyama* and could be employed in various circumstances. Most frequently, representatives of the secret initiation associations, the *jow*, commissioned smiths to make the staffs. When complete, they would be placed around association altars in the sacred groves or shrine houses were only certified members could enter. The altars themselves were full of power supplied by the materials of *daliluw* and the substances of sacrifice, such as millet, kola, the blood of animals, or human saliva. The staffs were designed to extend that power. So, in addition to the energy produced in the act of working iron, blacksmiths infused these pieces with special *daliluw*. The elder smith Dramane Dunbiya said he used to make such sculptures. When the initiation associations commissioned them, he did not charge a fee, because he knew there would be numerous occasions when he would want to request the services of those associations.[84]

In this same geographic area, the staffs could also be individually owned. Dramane said he used to make them to sell to middlemen, who then sold them to other individuals. In fact, early in the present generation, the sculptures were sold by smiths at public market, amid the stalls of foodstuffs, craft items, and ingredients for herbal medicines. When private parties bought the sculptures, they used them in much the same way as the "children of the *jo*," *jodenw*. They put them near their power things—their "secret devices," *basiw*, and "the things that make you a man," *ceya minaw*—to honor them and expand their energies.[85]

In certain instances, circumstances demanded that the staffs be removed from their sacred places and put to use elsewhere. For example, before the turn of the century, when slave raiding was still a threat to every community, these iron sculptures provided a useful element of protection. When a town knew that an army was on its way to attack, town members would gather at the community's edge nearest the enemy's approach. One man held a spear. Another carried an iron staff. The latter held the staff up, exposing its backside to the approaching troops. By this action energy was believed to be released to counter military might, and the enemy would turn away, seeking another town to plunder.[86]

Fittingly, the imagery of iron staffs centers on power. In the equestrian pieces, the horse is the most obvious power image (Ill. 66, 67). Very few Bamana were wealthy enough to own one. In days of war, horses were tremendously important; the power of Sunjata's cavalry, often alluded to in most versions of his epic, leaves that fact in little doubt. So, too, explorers such as Gray and Park noted that the politically powerful in the Bamana kingdoms of Kaarta and Ségou were the ones who owned horses.[87] Charles Bird notes that the horse is also important in west African myth; it may have been the vehicle by which human beings first descended to earth.[88]

Smiths say spears and weapons such as large knives are important parts of the sculptures. Equestrian figures sometimes hold spears in upraised arms, and female figures sometimes carry them as well. I once showed the smith Sidi Ballo a photograph of an iron female figure from a private collection. The figure holds a spear in her right hand. Then, suspended from her right arm, her left hand, and parts of her hair, are four more knives, the number four connoting the principle of femininity in Bamana and other Mande systems of numerical symbolism. In spite of Sidi's famous bird masquerade and renowned dancing ability, he is a big-city person (from Bamako) and not accustomed to seeing the more secret things of traditional communities, especially when those things have nearly disappeared. He was not familiar with iron staffs, but he could respond to the imagery. He said this was a dangerous woman, even her hair style had become knives, and as an aggressor she would be unstoppable.[89]

Many of these figures, both male and female, wear hats that resemble quite closely the hats worn by hunters, hunters' bards, and sorcerers.[90] Here too the reference is to personal power, since in life the hats are laden with amulets and augment one's capacity to deal with the treacherous environments of bush and sorcery. The Mande are well aware of the fact that hunters became crack soldiers in periods of state and empire building, and so the paraphernalia of hunters become attributes of both hunters and soldiers. Hunters' hats on female figures are particularly noteworthy. Mande women are not normally hunters. Women of great prowess, however, who have acquired much personal power through, for example, force of character or ability as a sorcerer, can be affiliated with one of the hunters' association branches and so become eligible for the greatest respect. Ability beyond the ordinary is thus suggested by the sculptures.

Imperato acquired information that expands our understanding of these caps' awsomeness. He says they are called "crocodile mouth," *bamada*, were formerly worn by Bamana elders, and symbolize the power of the crocodile's mouth, apparently metaphorically, to neutralize the kinds of sorcery we have discussed as *kòròti* poisons. He adds that the small flaps at the back of the cap symbolize crocodile tails, while the large hands prominently displayed on some iron figures symbolize crocodile feet.[91] In addition to being powerful and more than a little fearsome, crocodiles are sometimes seen as agents of the supernatural. They can serve as oracles for soothsayers, for example, and are depicted in oral traditions as having helped human beings select the ideal site for the location of Bamako, "where the crocodiles spoke," which later became a most prosperous trade crossroads. Their association with iron figural staffs as vehicles of symbolism suggests the potency people perceive in these sculptures.

Finally, the material itself is part of the power imagery. These staffs could easily be carved in wood. Indeed, it would be simpler to make them in that material. Moreover, some smiths carve wood staffs; Issa Baba Traore illustrates a blacksmith in the northern Bèlèdougou region performing a sacred blacksmiths' dance with a short wood staff that ends in a zoomorphic form.[92]

Iron, however, as we have seen, possesses special connotations that fit the nature of these sculptures. First, when the staffs were still in widespread use, many were made of traditionally smelted bloom, the fruit of especially technical, arduous labor from the smiths' secret expertise. Second, iron is the military material par excellence. Four towns of weapon-making black-smiths are said to have circled the Ségou state's capital. Fields of smelting furnaces are said to have marked the gathering places of Sunjata's and Sumanguru's armies before their final battles. The hunter's chief tools are iron and the warrior's chief weapons are of the same material. The metal thus effectively augments the aggression and power implied in the symbolism.

As part of their function these staffs must possess occult power, and iron helps here, too. Smelting and forging release tremendous levels of *nyama*, which good smiths are said to direct as effectively as they direct their hammers. Each articulating blow implants the energy in the metal. Because these sculptures were so hard to make, the extra time and attention to detail devoted to them allowed for the accumulation of extra energy. Thus, the very fact that smiths chose difficult forms meant that in making them they also simultaneously enriched them with power. Once completed and put to use, the sculptures continued to gain energy, because in the process of paying their respects, owners made regular sacrifices to them. Millet, water, and beer were poured over the works during ceremonies, for example,[93] and this is one reason why so many of them become heavily rusted.

This last bit of information brings out one more aspect of the staffs' function. As one large group of blacksmiths told me, the staffs were to be ad-mired. They were placed around altars to add power and to honor them. During festivals they were brought out and held in dances to the accompaniment of drum orchestras and much hand clapping, and this was when they received sacrificial offerings. The works were highly valued by those who used them, as befit sculpture which a smith regarded as the supreme test of his forging skill.

Iron staffs elicited lively debate among senior smiths. The criteria of quality varied considerably but included proper postures, feasible proportions, and innovation. A horse's neck drawn out too long became confused with a camel and so was considered sloppy (Ill. 68). Human torsos could be elongated, as could limbs, but overall the proportions should suggest a person. The head of a horse would be weighed against its hooves, not according to any canon of realism but rather to see if the idea of a horse was conveyed efficiently. The image's accessibility was thus highly valued. And it was in the context of these iron staffs that Dramane Dunbiya said some smiths were excellent. In his view, little things such as reins in the hands of a mounted figure helped establish the difference between good and excellent sculptor-smiths.[94]

It is important to realize how flexible indigenous interpretations can be for the functions and symbolisms ascribed to artworks. These iron staffs provide us with an excellent example. Imperato asserts that in the Bamana area south of the Bani River, some Mande believe these staffs symbolize male and female ancestors. Others believe them to symbolize characters named Gwandusu and Gwantigi who appear in legends set in the mythic period after the world's creation. Still others believe they symbolize characters that played principal roles in the Mande creation myths as recorded by French anthropologists. Female figures represent Muso Koroni, the world's first female, master of creation, disorder, and sorcery. Male figures represent Ndomajiri, the world's first blacksmith, master of stability and medicines. Imperato suggests that this multitude of opinions is keyed to the varying degrees of esoteric knowledge individuals possess, but he also cogently notes that sculptures are interpreted differently by different people and that meanings change over time.[95]

In the far west of the Mande diaspora, along and around the Gambia River, Peter M. Weil has found that the Mandinka possess a rich tradition of powerful iron staffs, called *chono*, which they claim extends all the way back to the time of the Mali Empire.[96] The forms of these staffs vary extensively, but their meanings focus invariably on political authority and legitimacy of leadership. Made in hierarchical groups of three, they are manifestations of the flow of power in the expansion-oriented Mandinka kingdoms. They could be topped with other metals, such as brass or silver, but the most powerful pieces are a set of three made entirely of iron, and these, in fact, are said to be from the time of the parent political entity, the Mali Empire. Like Bozo and Bamana examples, Mandinka staffs are spread along the shaft to form cages. These are used to hold burning incense, which helps empower and purify the staffs. Hooks sweep up and away from the central axis, as they often do in Bamana examples. They often support figures that echo the figures set atop the main axis, but they also support medicines. Some of the organic concoctions are intended to protect the political office holder who is a staff custodian. In the past, others protected the kingdom and its capital.

Like the Bamana pieces, these staffs are considered extremely difficult to make, and blacksmiths charged a great deal for them—the fee commonly mentioned is five slaves. In fact, the expense is not surprising. After all, in addition to demanding the blacksmith's greatest technical skills, the sculptures symbolize an entire social and political system. They are elegant and effective markers of power, and the power that they themselves contain is believed to be sufficient to influence the course of future events.

South of the Gambia River is the area of Casamance and another ancient Mande kingdom called Kabu. Weil suggests that here, too, iron staffs had long been used.[97] Further south, the Maninka extend across the vast Mande Plateau, to end at last northwest of Fouta Djallon. There, a number of ethnic groups occupy the land to the coast. Among them are the Beafada (or Biafada) and the Badyaranke (called Pajadinca by the Maninka), who speak very similar West Atlantic languages and may in centuries past have comprised a single ethnic group that was split up by the invading Mande peoples. Fula groups also live there. Within this area these four ethnic groups possess an ancient tradition of iron staffs with cast bronze tops, a tradition that continued to thrive at least into the 1950s in objects of great temporal and spiritual power. The staffs are called *sono* (plural *sonoje* in Fula), and among them are some exceptionally complex, exquisite examples of African metal art. Traditions of origin suggest that the staffs came to these coastal regions from the inland Mali Empire and have served since then as emblems of political authority and religious objects within the non-Muslim cults. Their original context may have been the series of states founded by Maninka colonists between the Gambia and Corubal rivers, which are described in sixteenth-century Portuguese texts.[98] Oral history in the area holds that these state builders were "drinking Mandingas," that is, non-Muslim Maninkas and, possibly, other Mande groups who moved south to avoid conversion to Islam as the Mali Empire increasingly embraced that religion. To our confusion, much of the Portuguese literature refers to these groups as Soninka (Soninque), just as their informants did, and indeed some informants indicated that it was from the name Soninke that the term *sono* derived. In any event, these southern Mande states maintained at least a nominal allegiance to the emperors of Mali, and their leaders used the brass-topped iron staffs as leadership insignia.[99]

In the 1950s, these staffs came to the attention of the Portuguese Teixeira de Mota working in Guinea. He traced their distribution across all of the former colony and indicated that his informants in the upper Guinea coast were convinced that they existed in the surrounding nations as well. At one point in the late seventeenth century, the Portuguese themselves seem to have had a hand in increasing the scope of *sono* distribution. A thriving kola trade existed between the "Soninque" state of Braco in Farim and an area called Ro-Ponka in what is now Sierra Leone. Portuguese vessels served as the middle link in this trade, and historical evidence suggests that on one voyage they carried a number of bronze and iron pieces as gifts to the kings of Ro-Ponka. The latter preserved them into the twentieth century, using them precisely as they were used in Guinea.[100]

Like the Bamana staffs, those used in Guinea Bissau played both political and spiritual roles. They served as crucial religious objects within the non-Islamic cults. Normally stuck into the sides of a sacred tree, they functioned as objects of power and were used, for example, as divination pieces that were consulted before any major or potentially dangerous undertaking, such as war. Informants suggested that no distinction was necessary between these dual uses, for political power was grounded in the strength and force generated by religion, just as was the case with Mali's Sunjata.

Structurally, these staffs resemble their Bamana counterparts, though the figures are not iron and the staffs are frequently more complex. The brass figures at the top are often equestrians and often carry spears. Many of them wear headdresses that were identified by da Mota's informants as belonging to Mande of noble descent.[101] Hooks are present, generally in pairs, and there are generally more of them than occur on Bamana examples. In addition, here they are capped with small brass castings of human heads and half or even whole figures, while the figures at the top usually are part of a group, which might include more than one horse and rider, an accompanying retinue, and one or two dogs.

Clearly, all these staffs, from those used by the Bozo to those used in Guinea, partake of a very old tradition that may well prove to have originated in the old Mali Empire. While the forms of these pieces have varied substantially, their patterns of use seem remarkably durable. At their core must lie a concept particularly important to Mande culture. It would seem that the iron staff—beautifully articulated, impregnated with power, and employed in domains of religion and state where the acumen of blacksmiths might serve as an ideal metaphor—holds deep significance for the Mande.

KÒMÒKUNW: THE POWER MASKS OF THE MANDE SMITHS

The *kòmò* mask is made to look like an animal. But it is not an animal; it is a secret. (Sedu Traore, September 1973)

If you can't get a native,
Give me a stranger.
(Excerpt from a song sung by a *kòmò* masked dancer seeking a malevolent sorcerer)

Kòmò masks, called "*kòmò* heads," *kòmòkunw*, are potent images, carved of wood and covered with many different animal and vegetable materials that help them function as instruments of divination and destroyers of criminals and sorcerers. They are worn by high-ranking officials of the *kòmò* association, often the leaders, *kòmòtigiw*, and always men who have spent many years developing the power needed to dance within such creations and harness the energies believed to be embedded in them. These men earn their position but bear it as a responsibility, for they place important natural and supernatural resources at the service of their community. Each *kòmò* mask wearer is a focal point for these invaluable resources, and so he is a respected, sometimes feared, member of his community. He is important in another way, too, because almost invariably he will be a member of the profession of smiths.

The *kòmò* association is owned by smiths. While every Mande male can join, only blacksmiths can be leaders in it, and only smiths can make the masks and dance them. The cult gives smiths great political clout, because it is extremely influential spiritually, and political leaders cannot be successful without spiritual alliances. Nor can political leaders function without access to occult practices, and the *kòmò* association often amasses more potential for action in the political realm than any other institution or individual. Smiths cannot be town chiefs. But town chiefs cannot head *kòmò*, and may not have as loyal a following as a renowned *kòmò* leader. No wonder smiths are such good moderators, and so important to chiefs and elders when critical decisions must be made.

Like the smiths who make them, the masks used in *kòmò* project a strong air of inaccessibility. The coatings and other elements added to their surfaces, their ambiguous visual references, and the frightening aspect produced by the parts and the whole make them intimidating works of art.

Particulars of their use are not readily available to outsiders. Secret knowledge can be the most dangerous, and also the most important. These masks symbolize and assemble power. They portray wisdom while partaking of it. They reach to the very core of what the Mande hold to be the most significant, potent, and sacred aspects of their lives. Perforce, then, they are hidden away behind barriers of extreme secrecy and have not often been discussed in the literature. Even to say their names before the uninitiated is extremely unwise. Kept hidden in the home of the *kòmòtigi* or in the shrine, they are never brought out into the open except for sanctioned ceremonies. Even when the sculptures are in storage, members will not carry them past open doors, for fear that they might be seen by the unauthorized.[102] *Kòmò* is one of several Mande secret initiation associations called *jow*. It is a male association, but many Mande say it has a women's counterpart called *nya gwan*. *Kòmò* is one of the most widespread of the men's associations, known from the western Maninka lands to the Burkina Faso border. It may be as old as the Mali Empire; a variety of oral traditions associate it with the legendary Fakoli, blacksmith, general, and principal strategist to Sunjata.

Most young men join *kòmò* right after circumcision. In it they begin to participate in the deep affairs of their communities, because *kòmò*'s primary mission is to protect society from acts of natural and supernatural violence and to enhance the individual well-being and quality of life of every society member who petitions it. The leadership of each local *kòmò* branch is charged with the responsibility of accomplishing these tasks, and almost without exception the leaders will use a variety of resources, from psychological skills in handling people to a good grapevine that keeps them abreast of a community's social and political affairs. Also at their disposal are a potent array of *daliluw* to help with everything from divining the cause of a family's crop failure to correcting problems of impotency or infertility. The Mande feel that the blacksmith-leaders of *kòmò*, at least the very good ones, can bring rain, neutralize malevolent sorcerers, even subdue capricious wilderness spirits.

The most dramatic things done by *kòmò* leaders are accomplished with the aid of sculpture: *boliw* power devices, flutes, and masks, all infused with the potent *daliluw* that are the prerogative of blacksmiths. In fact, these sculptures are the most spectacular and the most powerful of a collection of power objects, *siriw*—often including whisks packed with medicines (Ill. 74, 75), large amulets that incorporate animal parts, even the mummified hands of creatures such as monkeys—owned and manipulated by *kòmò* blacksmiths in the fulfillment of their duties. All these devices harbor immense amounts of *nyama* which can be directed by their owners to help carry out important acts. It is in large measure because of them that *kòmò* is perceived by the Mande as being, even today, an exceptionally powerful institution.

The efficacy of *kòmò* and of all Mande power sculpture is based on principles we have already examined. *Kòmò* masks harness energy and control it on society's behalf. They do so through the blacksmiths who made them and the blacksmiths who wear them. An individual *kòmò* mask is, in reality, a wooden scaffolding onto and into which are packed a potent array of highly effective *daliluw*. They are very complicated amulets that are, simultaneously, an organized body of highly suggestive symbols. Similar collections of *daliluw* are also implanted in two other kinds of *kòmò* sculpture, the often ambiguous earthen constructions called *boliw* and the horns articulated in wood and iron called *kòmò buruw*. Let us consider them briefly before turning to the masks.

Boliw (Ill. 69) have attracted the attention of Western writers quite frequently since Father Henry first described them as abominations. As sculpture they are unique in Bamana art. Their shapes are solid and clearly defined; many seem to represent creatures such as hippopotamuses. Just as often, however, what they represent is not readily identifiable, and, more to the point, their full symbolic significance is not visually accessible, nor is it information to which the noninitiated are privy. Their surfaces are fully rounded, giving the impression that they are stuffed with unknown ingredients. Indeed, that impression is accurate because they are assemblages of many materials collected from the natural environment and held together with hard, thick coatings of earth, which shrink and crack as the sculptures age, enhancing the sense that they are tightly packed inside.

The clay coatings of *boliw* are impregnated with sacrificial materials, such as the blood of chickens or goats, chewed and expectorated kola nuts, alcoholic beverages, and sometimes millet. Inside are materials such as animal bones, vegetable matter, honey, metal, and, rarely, in former times according to Monteil and Henry, portions of human bodies.[103] Dieterlen has reported that the sum of these parts symbolizes the universe.[104] On another level the grouping of objects functions like a large amulet, becoming a reservoir of occult power for the association to harness. Sacrifices provide constant renewal, constant augmentation, because when administered according to proper procedures, they are sources of *nyama*.

The horns (Ill. 70, 71) are considered by *kòmò* members to be detachable segments or extensions of the *boliw*. Called *kòmò buruw*, they are often kept in groups of three that are stored with the *boli* in wicker baskets or separately in cylindrical containers of feline hide housed in the rafters of the *kòmòtigi's* room. They are thin cones with a diamond-shaped mouthpiece near the upper end and, often, with a head, ears, or animal horns articulated at the top. The three horns are in three sizes; the smallest is generally less than six inches in length, the largest averages between twelve and fifteen inches. Some evidence suggests that it is one of these horns, possibly the largest, that is played by the masked dancer during performances of the association.

As objects of power, the horns can also be used to carry out the tasks of *kòmò* such as divination and the elimination of sorcerers. In some areas, individual members of the *jo* own their own small versions, which they keep concealed under their shirts, lashed to a strap and suspended under the arm. Magan Fane indicated that these small horns facilitated a special kind of communication between members and the large horns stored with the *boli*. Messages could be transmitted occultly from small to large horns through *nyama* activation. The answer, generally the solution to a problem, would be returned to the member via his small horn.[105]

One instance in my own experience illustrates the force associated with these horns. A *kòmòtigi* in Bamako was approached with the news that a branch member was seriously ill. The smith placed his skin case with horns on the ground and carried out kola nut divination next to it. In this way he identified the source of the illness as a jealous individual who had sought the aid of two Muslim marabouts to visit disaster on the victim. Then the smith opened the container and, without removing the horns, chewed and spat the kola into it. He explained that this action would have serious consequences, and although I never learned the outcome, the smith assured me it would ultimately cause the death of the three guilty parties.[106]

In the northern Bamana areas, these horns are forged of very thin iron (Ill. 71). They generally terminate in two twisted iron elements that resemble animal horns. To the south they are usually carved wood, and their makers say the reason is that the mouthpieces are more comfortable in this material. Both wood and iron versions are held to be very valuable. Door locks comparable in size but possessed of many more carved details are valued at only one-eighth or one-tenth of the worth of a *kòmò* horn.[107]

The masks are the most dramatically powerful of the three sculpture types (Ill. 72, 73, 76). We can judge the dimensions and depth of this power by examining the way they are made. The blacksmith retreats to the bush to work, returning there day after day until the mask is complete. The actual carving demands less than an afternoon. Yet the mask is under construction for at least four weeks and often as many as six. First, a certain type of wood must be located—it is at that spot where the work will take place. Herbal components must be sought, reduced into various forms, and mixed in appropriate ratios. Hunting seems to be involved in the acquisition of horns, tusks, and quills, which are given prominent positions on the completed work. A well may have to be dug by the smith,[108] the fresh unblemished water being necessary for many medicines that will become a part of the mask. At the outset of the work, a chicken is sacrificed to ensure a successful finished product, and from that moment on, the process of construction is highly formalized and extremely demanding. It might be characterized as a complex enactment of *daliluw*, involving the utmost secrecy and the tremendous personal powers of the smith.[109]

A community knows where the smith has gone to work, and its inhabitants carefully avoid the spot. It is a place of active danger; *nyama* is unleashed in potent doses. The smith, while directing it, can also resist it. Nonsmiths do not have that power and would be killed by exposure to so dangerous a force. Should someone happen into the area, the resulting situation is referred to as *kunkow*, having one's "head in one's hands." Sedu Traore described the result of such bad luck: "If you see it [the work] and God helps you and you don't die, you will still be finished for the rest of your life."[110]

As is the case in all other enterprises, while making *kòmò* masks, smiths personalize their *daliluw*. A smith will have developed a corpus of these "recipes" peculiar to himself. Some he will share with other smiths in the area, but he may well have modified them. Others will be possessed by no one else for hundreds of miles. In addition, the mask will be designed with the capacity for specific activities, including, but not limited to, divination and sorcery detection. Sedu suggested the range of this adjustability with a terse statement: "It should do all the things the owner wants."[111]

These most impressive works are recognized by all as extremely valuable, and, in a society where value is paid for, the cost of a *kòmòkun* is high. In 1973 the smith's time, the materials, and the power generated by both were worth the equivalent of between fifty and eighty dollars. In one instance, a smith about to undertake such work indicated that he would receive 20,000 Malian francs ($40.00), one goat, one chicken, and ten kola nuts.[112] Such a sum is seen by blacksmiths as a modest one. Yet it amounts to three or four times the fee they would expect for six weeks' work producing farming tools or other craft-oriented implements.

Where newer masks are in use, the mask maker will be the mask wearer, because he alone knows the exact contents of the work.[113] The precise nature of the *daliluw* present, how many, which ones, and what sorts of personal variations, cannot be detected by anyone else. Thus, any other smith would experience great difficulty in controlling the mask, in reacting to or even observing rapidly enough its particular valences of *nyama*. Again, the likely outcome of such an ill-fated encounter would be death. For this reason, when a leader dies and no one has been trained to take his place, the mask will be carefully hidden until a new leader proves strong enough to wear it.

Age can be a large component of a *kòmò* mask's importance. When a new branch of *kòmò* is founded, a new mask may be made. Many branches have existed for generations, and some of their masks are believed to be several centuries old. In the Wasoulou, for example, when a *kòmò* mask wearer feels he is about to die, or is no longer able to perform his duties adequately, he hopes to pass his mask and his position on to one of his sons. Ideally, he will have been able to educate the successor over the course of several years, and a smooth transition of authority will then transpire. If no one is deemed ready to occupy the position of *kòmòtigi*, however, the mask owner will hide his mask, with all the other sculptures and implements of power, in a secret place deep in the bush. By doing this he also disbands the *kòmò* branch. Its members can find another branch, or, perhaps, join another initiation association.

The mask will remain hidden, sometimes for generations, until another man receives a sign that he has been chosen to assume the role of *kòmòtigi*. This man may be related to the former leader, or he may be unrelated and not even from the same community. He is chosen because he is considered capable; he possesses the personal strength and knowledge to become a new mask wearer. The sign he receives takes the form of a dream; in it the mask's location is revealed. The agent that causes the dream is a spirit, *jinè*, associated with the hidden mask.

The son of a *kòmòtigi* once described his father's dream to me; it was frightening. Enormous serpents guarded the mask and seemed to suggest its power. The dreamer found himself in various situations loaded with personal danger, a reminder that to accept the call implied in the dream, the dreamer would submerge himself from that moment on in a world where powers, spirits, and malevolent persons could kill him in an instant.

When a man accepts the call contained in such a dream, he retrieves the mask and gathers a group of followers who are willing to found a new *kòmò* branch. Through word of mouth most people will know that an old mask has been returned to use, and, because the mask itself sought and found a wearer, it is likely to prove quite powerful. A new *kòmò* branch with an old *kòmò* mask begins with an advantage. A major part of its credentials for action has already been proven.

Masks that have endured generations in use or in combinations of use and hiding are different from new masks in a basic way. They have been tested by time because their *kòmò* branches have experienced continued success. The power of one of these old masks can be compared to that of a *kòmò* leader. Each new one must prove his abilities. He will gradually enlarge them by acquiring many more *daliluw* and a great deal of experience doing the things that tax a mask wearer's capabilities, most notably discovering malevolence and destroying it without being destroyed himself. In general, the growth of knowledge and experience in people fills them with the capacity for success. *Nyama* is augmented. Power brings more power. Age brings more than durability, it brings potency and importance. For the Mande, a person who dies young builds nothing. But to thrive in old age is to be of great consequence, because it indicates the presence of much wisdom and power, both of which can be helpful or harmful to anyone else in the society.

Old persons can be praised with the name *dankelen*, as can younger persons who have already become renowned in the realms of sorcery or art. *Dan* means "isolated." *Kelen* means "one." The phrase equates people to impressive animals—such as elephants or bush buffaloes—that have grown very old and live alone, their power and potential for aggression being so great that they have become too dangerous to be accompanied. Persons so praised are respected immensely because of their accumulation of *nyama* and because they are perceived as having capitalized on opportunities they encountered during their lives, "opportunities taken advantage of," *mako nyalen.*[114]

Old *kòmò* masks have acquired power and command respect in just this way. They have been used successfully countless times in the service of their owners. They have received countless sacrifices, *sarakaw* or *sònniw*, of chicken blood and other substances of power. All of this increases the *nyama* that makes them formidable devices, and they grow ripe with the capacity for action. The famous old *kòmò* masks are often compared to less powerful masks in songs sung during *kòmò* performances. One such song repeats the refrain:

> . . . you've seen many *kòmò*
> You haven't seen the wild beast.[115]

The spirits associated with *kòmò* masks are also important attributes of the masks' excellence as supernatural devices. When a man is called by a spirit to be a *kòmò* leader, he will enter into an intimate relationship with it, just as he will with the mask. When he dances in the mask, the spirit will be present. It can help him when he divines, and it can serve as an additional agent of power when he undertakes difficult tasks, such as the destruction of sorcerers. Among *kòmò* members the spirits of some masks become well known for their power and for the effective union formed between them, the mask wearers, and the masks.

Kòmò masks have special costumes owned and worn by the smith when he dances. A framework of light and pliable wood is lashed into a rounded cylindrical shape about the height of a man. Cloth is stretched over it, and feathers are then inserted into the cloth. Around Ségou, guinea fowl and chicken feathers are used, according to Monteil and Henry. To the south, between Bougouni and Bamako, a more elaborate array of feathers is used, including those of the chicken, hornbill, and vulture.[116] Zahan illustrates the costume in use, and one can see clearly the wood rings pressing against the cloth, creating three visual action points from which the feathers flare out in a blur of motion.[117] These costumes are covered with amulets, the importance of which is evidenced by one of the names for the costume, "the largest amulet," *sèbèn den kunbaba*. Thus, if the forces of the mask are not enough, they are supported by those present in the costume.

Although considerable variety exists in the configurations of specific masks, in general they can be divided into three horizontal units: dome, horns, and mouth.[118] The wearer's head fits into a central helmet unit often shaped like a dome. This serves to anchor extensions to the front and rear. Large antelope horns emerge from the rear of this dome, first running horizontally and then curving upward in an arc that unifies the overall structure while amplifying the suggestions of ominous energy.

Horns are the archetypical symbol of the power of the bush. They suggest potential aggression in the form of danger for the unwary who venture unprepared into those vast and rugged regions. They also remind one of the marvelous durability and strength possessed by creatures who thrive there. Power is symbolized in another way because horns are often used as containers for traditional medicines, so they suggest by extension the Mande system of traditional knowledge.

Because it is long and sharp, a *kòmò* mask horn bears the name *binye*, "arrow," a term that has obvious aggressive overtones but in this context carries special qualifications, because the horns also symbolize knowledge, the prickly, potentially deadly knowledge of the *daliluw*. Horns associated with these masks bring knowledge and power together most effectively. They are ideal symbols, which many smiths take full advantage of by incorporating up to six into one sculpture.

Quills are frequently attached in tight bundles at intervals over the top surface of *kòmò* masks (Ill. 72, 73). Here, as with the horns, symbolism is aggressive and involves the capacity for violence. These too are *binyew*, and Zahan develops the symbolism. The quills allude to darts, arrows, or bullets—those used in the guns and rifles of traditional Bamana hunters. They also refer to poisonous substances which are made through the *daliluw* and propelled over long distances by insects. On *kòmò* masks, the smiths acknowledge their own sorcery abilities, their capacity to fight sorcerers through *kòmò* with the very means the sorcerers themselves use. Additionally, Zahan indicates that porcupines symbolize wisdom, the sage, one who knows much and is a protector of knowledge.[119]

A perfect example of a person possessing sharp and deadly wisdom is the legendary blacksmith Fakoli. Oral traditions state that he was one of the wisest of men, a tremendous fighter, and Sunjata's best strategist. Although he was described as very generous, he was feared for the catastrophe he could visit on a foe. Fakoli is imagined as having had a huge head (a *kòmò* mask, perhaps) covered with more than 300 *binyew.*

Fakoli of the enormous head.
Fakoli of the enormous mouth.[120]

The size of his head suggests the breadth of his intelligence. The size of his mouth denotes his capacity for action. Allegedly, he enlarged these attributes by wearing a cloth covered with vulture feathers and amulets, the perfect *kòmò* costume. Our image of him is thus as the quintessential *kòmò* blacksmith. In legend he blends with the devices that lend him power.

In front of the dome, a long, thin, ominous mouth is carved, occasionally with teeth zigzagging from front to back, more often with a series of paired, small antelope horns or wild pig tusks attached to the top and facing forward. The connotations of the mouth are unmistakable, though complex. Zahan associates the mouth with that of the hyena, an animal often used as a symbol of intelligence.[121] Children grow up with the idea that hyenas are buffoons, creatures hopelessly steeped in stupidity. They learn proverbs and hear stories that use hyenas to symbolize human foibles. In *kòmò*, however, their idea is transformed because here a body of lore teaches that hyenas possess tremendous stores of knowledge about the bush and its secrets. In fact, hyenas are considered so extraordinarily intelligent that hunters who track them claim that the animals are able to become invisible.[122] It is also said that hyenas devour sorcerers, and, furthermore, blacksmiths are believed able to become hyenas as part of their sorcerers' powers. The enormous size of the mouth is also significant, especially because it extends well beyond the length we could visually associate with hyenas. When we remember that mouths are sources for *nyama* and that speech is considered to be a potent force, we realize that the mouths of these masks are enlarged to depict the overwhelming power of the association.

The dancing smith holds in his own mouth a whistle-like horn made of bamboo or a larger one made of iron or wood. With this instrument he produces an extremely loud bellowing, which Henry described as a noise that freezes one with terror.[123] Thus the visual implications of the mask's mouth are borne out audibly.

A number of masks incorporate vultures' feathers gathered into massive bundles on the upper surface of the mouth or on top of the dome (Ill. 74). They refer to notions of wisdom. Bird and Tera indicate that birds mediate between the sky and human beings. They can make accessible the knowledge of spirits and of the celestial forces. As symbols, they connote the profound knowledge of the heavens, "celestial knowledge," *san fe donni.*[124] Another kind of knowledge associated with birds is divination, and one Bamana technique of divination involves communicating with birds. The presence of feathers on *kòmò* sculpture thus also alludes to the masks' power to divine.

Finally, we must consider the mask surfaces which are not specifically symbolic but by common consent constitute an attribute of power. Most *kò-mòkunw* are coated with the same sacrificial materials, often impregnated in earth, that coat *boliw*. On some masks, this surface covers every feature except the horns, quills, and feathers, producing a wavy, uneven, and cracked patina that grows thicker with each new sacrifice. As the surface grows, so does the mask's power.

First, the masks are made according to the dictates of the blacksmith's choice of *daliluw*. Later, their surfaces grow according to the dictates of additional *daliluw*. These coatings are a kind of visual record of power harnessed through knowledge. They become energy symbolized and energy actualized. When one understands the connotations behind them, the masks take on a conceptual quality resembling our own mental images of dangerous radioactivity.

Given the association of so many materials from a variety of animal sources, how can we reasonably say which animal *kòmò* masks depict? Occasionally, some smiths say the masks look like horses' heads, but they mean "resemble," not "represent." The idea these masks promote most effectively is one of general animal nature—potent, dangerous, and evasive.

Kòmò masks, then, assemble discordant organic elements that would never be so intimately associated in nature. For a society familiar with the bush and its inhabitants, the masks become a body of visual non sequiturs grouped to create a kind of chimera. This creature orientation is reflected in the songs sung at *kòmò* dances, when the greatest masks are praised as being wild beasts. But there is more to their composition, as Sedu Traore noted when he told me they are made to look like animals but are in fact secret and powerful things. Their appearance suggests both vast stores of harbored energy and the processes used to produce it. They are visual testimony of the *daliluw* formulas and their effectiveness.

These two important components, generalized animality and stored energy, are united very skillfully in the finest masks, leaving no doubt about the power of blacksmiths as sorcerers and the skills of smiths as artists. One splendid piece can serve as our example (Ill. 76). In profile it is constructed beautifully, through a combination of formal harmony and compositional dynamism. Huge upturned antelope horns at the back cause the viewer's eyes to pause, and then sweep back into the other parts of the sculpture. At the same time they provide ballast that helps balance the large open mouth in the front. A small pair of horns and two bundles of quills are set on top of the mouth, attached with sacrificial matter and twine, and aligned so that they meet at right angles, creating an elevated jag and a sense of energy. The mask seems immense because of an enormous quantity of long black feathers set atop the central dome. Even in its museum context, without its costume or its dancer, the mask is an impressive piece of sculpture. When one faces it, however, and imagines it charging toward spectators at a *kòmò* dance, the mask becomes electrifying, with huge mouth, horns, quills, and feathers combining to create a tight, compact composition that radiates energy and animality. A good Bamana dancer could manipulate a mask like this to raise the neck hairs of even the most stoic observer.

When the *kòmòtigi* dances, all that the mask is and all that the mask wearer can do come into dramatic focus.[125] In the Wasoulou, an evening performance begins with a warning. A drum signal goes out to inform all the uninitiated that they should conclude their business and move indoors. Two more warnings will be given before the mask appears. Now the members begin to assemble. As they arrive, they make sure they have complied with certain stipulations set by their leader. If they have made love that evening, they must wash thoroughly before they attend their meeting. When they arrive, they must set their shoes aside, leaving them off until morning. It is wise to arrive well-rested, for it is said that if you fall asleep at a *kòmò* meeting you will sleep forever. Some dancers of the mask make special stipulations. They may, for example, forbid the wearing of anything red; the color symbolizes heat and power, and the dancers want nothing to lessen the effect of their own controlled energies.

After the third drum warning the masked-dancer appears, followed by his bard. The bard will spend the rest of the night following the dancer closely, no matter where he goes or what he does. Were the dancer somehow to fall into a well, for example, the bard would be obliged to jump in after him. The assembled membership will also dance, but they must take great care at all times never to cross in front of the mask. If they do, they are likely to die. If men from out of town are present, they will be tested by *kòmò* members by being asked to interpret a series of signs. They will be confronted and tested again by the masked dancer himself, to be certain they belong to a *kòmò* branch and thus have the right to be present.

Power is activated at these meetings, defensively, offensively, and for the procedures of divination. It may become dangerous for anyone present, through an accident or in the heat of events. To free himself from liability and possible retaliation, the *kòmò* dancer may sing a song at the very beginning of his performance that excuses him from blame. It is also a matter of politeness. Should anyone find offense in the songs he sings or the things he says later, he will have already apologized. An excerpt from one such song shows the artful manner in which a *kòmò* dancer presents himself and his capacities to his audience:

> Eee genie-woman . . . free my hand
> So I can play a little for the world. . . .
> Slander is not between someone and his feelings,
> Leave my hand so I may speak to the world.[126]

The genie is a spirit associated with the dancer's mask. He calls upon her, an outside agent of terrific power, to show that all that transpires may not be completely within his control. The phrase that distinguishes slander from feelings points out that a person's feelings are honest and immediate. They emerge from the heart and have not been polluted by unkind intentions. The kòmò dancer wants his audience to know that he is being honest. Finally, there is the desire to "play a little for the world," to "speak to the world." Such lines bespeak the artist's ability to articulate aesthetically the formulas dictated by kòmò ritual. Through the use of songs such as this the mask wearer succeeds in balancing his power with his art.

As the night unfolds, the masked dancer will address three kinds of business: vigilance and self-protection, the activation of energy, and the dramatization of that energy. First, he will be on guard constantly against the presence of challengers and disguised sorcerers and against the activation of power devices that might be used to do him harm. The performance is an ideal setting for a sorcerers' duel because the masked dancer has set himself apart and made himself quite vulnerable to attack. He will thus scrutinize all persons present, noting what they carry and searching for what they might conceal. In an instant a person can activate kòròtiw poisons against the dancer, leaving him senseless or dead. The instant of enactment must be recognized and countered quickly with his own power devices or with the forces of his mask.

Another kòmò song illustrates another aspect of the mask wearer's vigilance. It also reveals his capacity for clairvoyance and his ability at divination.

> Hard-hearted sorcerer-woman Hari missed her time of coming.
> Saying she has come to watch things.
> Matured sorcerer-woman Hari missed her time of coming.[127]

Hari, it is said, was a sorcerer killed by a famous kòmò in ancient times. Disguising herself as a small animal, Hari attended a kòmò meeting. The song reconstructs her mistake, and indicates by implication—the phrase "missed her time of coming"—that she was killed for her error. Her "time of coming" was any time except the one she chose. She should have visited the mask wearer at his home during the week, for that is the appropriate way to secure an audience for an individual who does not belong to the cult. Sorcerers, however, are often bent on seeing things and doing things they should not. Hari wanted to see the mask dance and to show that she was clever enough to do so with impunity. She was well known for her abilities and power, and she is honored in the song with the phrase "matured sorcerer-woman." The mask wearer detected her at once and took her act as a violation of kòmò tenets of privacy and as a challenge to his own abilities. So he composed this song as he danced and then killed her. The song is now sung when a kòmò mask wearer detects a woman sorcerer disguised among his membership. After he sings the song, he may stop and name the sorcerer, who is then well-advised to leave immediately. Before colonial times in the Wasoulou, a kòmòtigi would then kill the intruder with a spear he always carried while dancing.

The way this song is used today typifies one element of the second matter *kòmò* dancers address, that of activating energy for purposes of divination. When a *kòmòtigi* divines while dancing, he gives his mental faculties over to the energies possessed by himself, his mask, and its genie. He indulges in a kind of free-association process and becomes an oracle for all the *nyama* at his disposal. Responses to the questions put to him by clients during the week now simply come into his head. He then verbalizes them by choosing from an extensive repertoire a song that best expresses the solution he will set forth momentarily. He may also compose a new song. He sings through an instrument that dramatizes his voice while rendering it unclear and difficult to understand. The bard interprets the song by recognizing the tones and phrasings of the singer. Then the singer stops and speaks through the same instrument, specifying the solution he has just alluded to in the song, and again the bard interprets his words for the audience. In this technique of divination, soothsaying skill is imbued with drama and art, and the results have made many men famous.

Another song that a *kòmò* diviner may sing appears to extend comfort to people down on their luck and a warning to those who are fortunate:

> Fortunate slave do shut up,
> All mornings don't bleach the same way.
> A man may walk,
> Then finish by crawling in the world.
> All days don't bleach the same way.[128]

The fortunate slave is the individual who has sought the *kòmò*'s aid by complaining of personal misfortune. "Shut up" means be patient. This phrase, coupled with the reference to "fortunate slave," signals a change in luck for the *kòmò*'s client, thereby transforming the song's apparent meaning.

Just as songs herald divination and announce its results, so too songs announce the use of power against antisocial sorcerers. Dancers do this subtly, through metaphor and a marvelous ability to be inexplicitly explicit. One imagines their victims admiring the art that announces their demise. The specific means a mask wearer uses to destroy another sorcerer will not be revealed, although aspects of their effects may be referred to in the song. These means will be based on the use of *daliluw*, but a *kòmò* leader's corpus of those power sources constitutes a major portion of his *gundow*, the secrets that make him successful. If they become common knowledge, they will cease to be useful.

The techniques Mande sorcerers use to defeat one another focus primarily on the discovery of an adversary's source of power. They say: "I will dip my hand into your means,"[129] and, though the use of the word "dip" makes the phrase sound almost delicate, it signals the most debilitating and conclusive kind of personal violation. To discover the knowledge behind another person's power is to render that person totally vulnerable. It is a matter of learning the other person's *daliluw* and then acquiring the *daliluw* that can be used most effectively against him. This is an important task of the *kòmò* leaders who achieve renown as fighters of malicious sorcery.[130] We should realize that the destruction of accomplished sorcerers is rarely easy, and a *kòmò* cannot guarantee that he will be successful. One epic recounts the story of Sumoso Yiraba, "Sorcerer-Woman Yiraba."[131] In ancient times many *kòmò* dancers were called upon to destroy this person, and none of them succeeded. The last two, who were also the most famous, were Ngonkòrò, "The Old Baboon," and Gwaranko dibi, "The darkness of the town Gwaranko." Both sought to determine a course of action against Yiraba through divination. As they divined, both composed a series of songs that foretold the stages of their battle with her and predicted as well their ultimate failure. The songs became an epic now sung sometimes by *kòmò* dancers to amuse their audiences.

In the story, Yiraba first delivers a series of insults to the *kòmò* dancers and their bards. She then transforms herself into a fox, thinking no *kòmò* can catch such an animal. Her adversaries become hunting dogs, who can easily catch foxes. She then becomes a pigeon and attempts to escape by flying. But the *kòmò* leaders pursue her as hawks. So she changes into a snake and hides in thick swamp grass, and the *kòmò* mask wearers transform themselves into yellow foxes, who eat snakes. Finally Yiraba changes herself into wind, and the *kòmò* dancers give up. Ultimately, no one succeeds against Yiraba. Members of her town later trick her with false compliments and then club her to death. Her body is burned and the ashes cast into a river, but she is not defeated and her ashes become leeches that take revenge upon the population.

The final form of business a *kòmò* dancer addresses is the theatrical dramatization of his power. It is part of the proof that he is an effective leader. These men very often are outstanding dancers, and they must perform in that capacity, encumbered by a heavy mask and an enormous costume, for most of one night each week. Their movements can be swift and impressive, with costumes and masks lending an awesome and intimidating quality to the spectacle. Some mask wearers are said to augment their dancing abilities with acrobatics that captivate their audiences; indeed, Monteil described the dancers as being capable of fantastic acrobatic feats.[132] Other dancers mount their masks at the ends of long sticks and thrust them up through the tops of their costumes. Both Henry and Monteil reported this in the Ségou region,[133] and informants told me it is done around Bougouni as well. This trick produces the dual illusions of great height and unnerving elasticity. At the same time it demands greater skill from the dancer, who must control both his costume and a long, heavy pole. I have been told by some *kòmò* members that their leaders may even dance with the masks while on stilts, and others say that some *kòmò* mask dancers can "spit" fire while others "spout" water. I do not know the means by which the latter is accomplished, but Bamana observers report that the dancer stamps his foot on the ground and a fountain of water emerges from the spot. When hunters dance in groups, some among them become well-known for being able to do the same thing.

All three of the components of a *kòmò* mask performance are impressive even in isolation. Each demands special abilities of the mask wearers, and they all demand great presence of mind and tremendous stamina. Together they are especially grueling, and necessitate enormous stores of personal discipline and fortitude, along with much intelligence and the capacity for action. The qualifications for dancing a *kòmò* mask would seem beyond the capabilities of ordinary men. The Bamana agree, however, that *kòmò* leaders are by no means ordinary.

A quick review of all the art forms common to the Bamana leaves *kòmò* masks and the sculpture types related to them peculiarly isolated. The principles of clear composition we examined earlier are not appropriate to power sculpture, and, in fact, the differences are so glaring and pervasive that the masks of *kòmò* seem to embody a kind of antiaesthetic.

Kòmò masks are neither accessible nor rapidly discernible. They do not fit the pattern of reduction, economy, balance, and harmony we have found in most other types of Mande sculpture. They do not partake of the concept of *jayan*, "clarity and precision." To be sure, the carved wood portion that serves as foundation for the entire mask is executed with a crispness of shape and clarity of volume. That foundation, however, is altered by augmentation, and what is produced is the most radical of transformations. The stuff of power is applied with an eye toward variety. Thus, large and small horns may well appear together with the tusks of wild pigs, the small ones often lashed to the mask with rag or twine so that they wobble slightly when the mask is in motion. Even the skull of a bird may appear on the upper surface, along with massive groupings of feathers or tightly bundled quills. This composite imagery does not produce the impression of economy or harmony. One must look several times to find the bird's skull, for example, hidden amid horns and bundles of porcupine quills.

Both *kòmò* leaders and lay members refer to these added animal elements as decoration (*masiri*), and they classify the large mouths and carved teeth in the same way. Excessive decoration seems to be impossible in the context of *kòmò*, however. More horns and more quills, for example, make the images better, because they make the portrayal of raw, vicious animality more effective and make the masks more frightening. I had the opportunity to show four *kòmò* members illustrations of ten *kòmò* masks. Two of these men were leaders in the association, one was the son of a leader, and one was just a member. They were all impressed with the masks most heavily embellished with animal elements. One mask, especially praised, contains two large antelope horns, six small antelope horns, and eight large bundles of quills (Ill. 72). This same mask also contains the thickest and most pervasive coating of sacrificial materials.

The Mande recognize a counterpart or complement to *jayan*. *Dibi* is an

abstract concept denoting "darkness, obscurity, a very dangerous place."
Sorcerers, thieves, murderers, and spirits (*jinew*) can be found lurking there
in abundance. Massive amounts of *nyama* are also associated with *dibi*, and
the malicious beings that frequent this region are believed to augment their
personal power by feeding on that energy. *Kòmò* masks are believed to bear
a special relationship to *dibi*. They are "an affair of obscurity," *a ye dibi la ko
ye*. With their blacksmith-wearers, they are able to enter that murky, dangerous place to fight fire with fire, and there is certainly ample heat in the
things the sculptor-smiths make.

Thus, *kòmò* masks depict "obscurity fighting obscurity," *dibi kèlè dibi*,
and in appearance they are quite the opposite of *jayan*, clarity and precision.
They are designed to be unclear. In a sense they are similar to certain Yoruba
masks, which have been described by Robert Farris Thompson as being
used for satire, moral inquisition, and psychological warfare.[134] These masks
purposefully defy aesthetic criteria, and so do the wild beasts of *kòmò*.

The goals that define the form of *kòmò* masks, then, produce a kind of
sculpture that is antithetical to the general tenets of Bamana aesthetics. To
truly judge the quality of a mask, however, the Bamana evaluate more than
its form. One night in Bamako my colleague Kalilou Tera and I were talking
with a Bamana farmer named Yaya Traore, who had recently moved to the
capital from the region of Bougouni in the hopes of earning more money for
his family. Because he was a *kòmò* member, we asked him how to distinguish
a good *kòmò* mask from a bad one. In his response Yaya united the mask with
its dancer and, in effect, described the criteria for a good *kòmò* performance.
First, he substituted the adjective "sweet," *duman*, for "good," *nyuman*,
using the word as many Bamana do to applaud people who are brave, hard-
working, or beautiful. He then listed his criteria for a sweet mask and
dancer. To begin with, he said all masks are not carved in an equally nice
manner, and the way they are carved makes a difference. Second, he said the
daliluw are not the same in all *kòmò* masks and this too makes a difference.
Third, the abilities of the *kòmò*—both mask and dancer—to carry out divination accurately vary substantially from *kòmò* branch to branch, and good
divination is extremely important. Yaya said: "Some *kòmòw* say a lot of
things, others can't." Fourth, he said some *kòmòw* can "show many things,"
that is, have the abilities to cure illnesses, advise clients on what sacrifices
will produce the best results, and activate the powers that battle malevolent
sorcerers. Fifth, Yaya said that the adeptness with which they execute the
extraordinary feats, such as spitting fire, makes a difference in their quality.

Yaya summarized all of this by saying: "The *kòmò* whose *Bamanaya* lies
down outside, that is the sweet one," *Kòmò min ka Bamanaya mana da kènè
kan, O de ka di*. By *Bamanaya* he meant the things of Bamana culture,
everything that *kòmò* stands for. By "lies down outside" he meant reveals its
capabilities most clearly. Kalilou and I translated his sentence like this: "The
kòmò who knows the most, and shows it most clearly, that is the best one."[135]

Kòmò masks and *kòmò* blacksmiths thus break their society's criteria on behalf of that society. When smiths make these masks or dance them, they cull vast segments of their special credentials—the capacities and abilities to which this book has been largely dedicated—and focus them on a performance context where ordinary reality gives way to extraordinary imagery and actions. It is true, as Sedu Traore noted, that every aspect of a *kòmò* mask and its performance is intentionally horrifying. Yet, everything about Sedu and the way he leads his life suggests that he, and men like him, could create such an illusion while successfully dealing with the reality of deadly energy behind it. In a sense, there is no greater tribute to the Mande sculptor-smiths than the fact that they are *kòmò*.

FIVE

THE MANDE SMITHS AS
MEN OF MEANS

In Mande oral tradition the founder of the *ntomo* initiation association is often identified as a legendary blacksmith named Ndomajiri.[1] He was full of the kinds of knowledge and power to which so much of this book has been devoted, and he shared a great deal of it with humankind. Especially interesting, however, is the belief that he created the Mande association that begins the process of imparting knowledge to all young boys and initiates the very critical mechanisms by which these children—creatures whose natures are considered quite ambiguous at best and who are said to be at least as wild as they are human—are made into civilized social beings. The legend suggests what we have come to know in this book. Mande blacksmiths are perceived as creative well beyond the boundaries of art and craft, and they are associated with many of their society's most fundamental institutions.

THE PROBLEM OF EXPLANATIONS

Like art, society has form, and like its aesthetic counterpart, social form is complex and difficult for foreigners to decipher. Mande society is as convoluted as any other, with its mores and principles of social interaction intertwined with actual patterns of behavior not clearly explained by Mande ideology. Smiths are at the core of this social form, partaking of its principles and contributing to its ambiguity. Most importantly, from their vantage point at the center they make form themselves. They are chartered by their culture to build, construct, fabricate, create, in a wide variety of materials across an equally broad spectrum of human situations. Part of their mandate is, in fact, to build social form anew with each succeeding generation and to help maintain that form with all of the other things they do and make. Clearly, these blacksmiths are artists with a great deal staked onto the social contributions they make.

Yet their contributions as well as their social position are clouded with ambiguity, which makes the smiths hard to comprehend. The very first ethnographic reporters experienced this difficulty, as do the Mande themselves. Smiths reside conceptually at the core of their culture, but they are often described as outcasts living on the fringe. They are simultaneously high technologists and sorcerers. As a group they are busy indeed, even if we only look at their works as craftspersons making their society's tools and utensils. They do so much more, however, that one wonders how they could possibly be expected to make their society's sculpture. Yet sculpting is the enterprise for which we in the West have come to know them best, and they make it in two very different kinds of media. Thus, to all that is staked upon blacksmiths' activities we must add some of our own wonder at the prodigious scope of their enterprise, and more wonder still at the ambivalence with which the Mande greet it.

Such a concentration of vital activities seems puzzling, at least to a society such as ours, so oriented toward compartmentalized specialization. Our puzzlement is reduced somewhat when we recall that while all these enterprises are linked to the institution of blacksmithing, individual smiths most commonly specialize in one or several of them. It is the rare individual who practices them all. Our puzzlement diminishes further with the recollection that nonsmiths also have the right to practice some of the smiths' special activities, such as soothsaying, herbal medicine, and sorcery. Still, we are confounded by the fact that so many smiths are inclined toward these vocations while so few of their fellow citizens follow suit. There must be special aspects to these activities that find strong affinity in the characters of smiths. Some sort of symmetry must align the practices and their blacksmith-practitioners.

No explanation for this clustering of activities is provable, though several propositions come to mind. We could argue, for example, that such an abundance of roles in the hands of so small a segment of the population resulted from the need to maintain a very large agricultural work force while providing a corpus of social and spiritual services deemed critical by the culture. The expediency of such a theory is attractive, but societies are rarely so clearly or simply motivated. The factors that thrust so much into the hands of smiths are likely to be far more convoluted. We could also argue an historical explanation, based on the importance of iron. If the material changed African civilizations as much as we think, then it might follow that the technologists who manufactured it into valuable tools and weapons were afforded a supernatural stature. This in turn made them the natural choices for tasks involving supernatural processes or possessed of supernatural ramifications. Thus would the prophecies of smiths become desirable and the will of smiths compelling.

It is certainly true that the Mande afford a primacy to the technical tasks of working iron when they characterize their smiths. The term *numu* has nearly always been translated first as iron worker to foreigners, and only later as woodworker, sculptor, herbal doctor, or sorcerer. Smelting, when still practiced, was even more fundamental to the essence of the blacksmiths' professional identity. And, while iron forging is contemplated by the Mande as an extraordinary activity as well as a technical one, iron smelting was held to be exceedingly awesome and mysterious. We might argue, then, that through a kind of mental and emotional osmosis typical of human beings, the technical and the supernatural came to be associated in smiths, giving them license to expand the scope of their enterprise.

Just one query demonstrates the limitations of such a hypothesis. How can we say with certainty which first entered the ken of these smiths' earliest ancestors, smithing or sorcery? We might suggest that the first Mande smiths were sorcerers who used their own skills and the perceptions of their society to acuire a monopoly on a new technology. Such an hypothesis may be less likely than one that gives primacy to the complex body of knowledge and skills composing iron working. It nevertheless qualifies our confidence in other explanations.

A related explanation also utilizes the preeminence of metal working as catalyst for all the other activities, but it emphasizes the entrepreneurship of Mande blacksmiths. My work with these individuals revealed their strong capacity for enterprise, coupled with willful industry. I rarely met a lazy smith, and a great many were avidly inclined to seek ever broader clienteles or extend their corpus of skills. The historian George Brooks has become convinced that Mande smiths played major roles in the history of the Western Sudan and Upper Guinea Coast as commercially adept enterpreneurs forever seeking new sources of metal, new markets in which to sell it, and new means by which they could maintain their monopoly on it.[2] We might argue, therefore, that over the centuries Mande smiths as iron workers sought and found ways to market themselves as proficient soothsayers, doctors, intermediaries, and other kinds of specialists. The proposition has merit, but we cannot prove it.

Since what we call the supernatural pervades the realm of smiths, we might argue simply that sorcery is the link between all the blacksmiths' activities. The technology of metal working is associated with phenomena such as secrecy, ritual, and wilderness spirits, while its practitioners are believed to radiate extraordinary amounts of the energy called *nyama*. If we ask what then of herbal medicine, for example, we could seek an answer in the union Mande perceive between medicine and the occult, a union widely commented upon by other authors writing on other African peoples. If we inquire about smiths' roles as advisers and intermediaries, we could argue, for instance, that fear of the smiths' occult knowledge would make them formidable in such service. In this way we might place every blacksmith activity, even the making of sculpture, in the camp of the occult.

THE UNITY OF ENTERPRISE

Invoking the notion of sorcery to explain the works of smiths elicits an obligation we dare not overlook. We must take care to incorporate the ideas that define sorcery's character and validity among the Mande. If our recourse is to a simplistic notion of sorcery as a body of superstitions and unfounded suppositions, or as an evil institution that generates unbounded fear, then uniting all the blacksmiths' tasks within its rubric obfuscates both the smiths and their acts. If we consider sorcery simply as an institutionalized response to social conflict, psychological strain, physical ailment, or general misfortune, then we will miss the pattern of vigorously embraced beliefs that shape Mande sorcery and join it to the smiths. If, on the other hand, we make the link between sorcery and smiths our point of departure and then explore their commonality in Mande terms, we can perhaps achieve not necessarily an explanation but an understanding of both the smiths' stature and their tasks within the broad, rich framework of Mande ideology. To do so we should first remind ourselves of all the things smiths do, and then seek elements that might unite them.

We can begin with craft and art, the most material manifestations of blacksmiths' expertise. We have seen that smiths make nearly every wood and iron product used in Mande society. Many of their products, such as furniture and farming tools, are utilitarian. Many of them, such as *kòmò* masks and iron altar staffs, are also sacred and supercharged with potent occult forces. Even in instances, such as boat making or leather working, where smiths are not the manufacturers, they make the tools the manufacturers use.

In a realm that uses material elements to achieve nonmaterial ends, smiths are masters at other types of manufacture. As herbalists they make medicines to improve the physical state of their clients. As sorcerers they make other kinds of medicines to improve the spiritual states of their clients. As soothsayers they use a variety of natural materials to make prophecies and proffer explanations regarding the present and future state of things. As circumcisers they use the human body to make fundamental changes in the human condition that affect forever the social and spiritual domains in which men operate.

Finally, in a realm that ignores material and balances spiritual and social elements, blacksmiths are masters at making, verifying, and helping to enforce arrangements among people. Their counsel is sought in important family and community matters. Their wisdom is sought when people compose new social or political alliances or break society's rules, and it is sought again when parents consign their sons to the smiths who govern *kòmò* associations, where the youths' education and socialization proceeds in earnest. With *kòmò* as our example we see how many of the works of smiths can blend into a single arena, because here sculpture is used, amulets are made, and soothsaying transpires, all with the goal of transforming boys into men.

All of these acts have many things in common, and we can divide them into two categories. The first is one of prerequisites, what a person must possess to carry out the acts. The second involves the effects of these acts on Mande individuals and society.

The prerequisites consist of knowledge, skill, and power. Each of the smiths' enterprises depends upon special expertise. Some of it may derive from a person's birthright but most of it must be acquired through lengthy periods of training. The basis of this expertise is knowledge of a special character, the kind of knowledge we have examined in our explorations of *gundow*, trade secrets, *jiridon*, the science of the trees, and *daliluw*, constellations of materials and procedures that allow people to accomplish things.

A principal characteristic of this knowledge is secrecy, because on the one hand such knowledge can be dangerous and on the other its difficulty of acquisition makes it more valuable for people who have troubled to acquire it. Another, equally important characteristic is what this knowledge makes possible. Almost invariably, as we have seen, it is oriented toward manipulating *nyama*, that spiritual force considered instrumental in shaping everything in the Mande world, from material objects to social and political situations. In addition, the knowledge makes the accumulation, articulation, and release of this energy safer for the manipulator and anyone else involved.

Yet another characteristic of the knowledge is its diagnostic capacity. It includes the training to perceive significant configurations in the natural and social worlds, to recognize meaningful patterns in an almost endless array of phenomena, such as illness, crop failure, family conflicts, and community torts. It is, therefore, active as well as reactive.

The Mande believe that almost anyone can acquire this kind of useful knowledge, just as they believe almost anyone can accumulate within and about their person high levels of *nyama*. Most people amass neither, however, to any pronounced degree. Such activity is time consuming, expensive, and dangerous. Nevertheless, all people find themselves in need of the fruits such knowledge and power can offer, and so, as we have seen, they seek the services of those who have taken the trouble to immerse themselves deeply in this world that melds science and the occult. Also, many people feel most comfortable dealing with practitioners they consider to be mystically endowed with spiritual force, and whose natural predilections are to seek more of this knowledge and power. The possession of knowledge and power as part of one's birthright is not exactly a prerequisite, then, but prevailing Mande attitudes make it very nearly so.

In addition to knowledge, practitioners must possess the skill to carry out the acts. It can be physical, as in the case of carving hoe handles and forging hoe blades or assembling the ingredients of an amulet. It can also be social, as in the case of mediating between feuding parties or helping to negotiate a bit of commerce between two communities.

The second category of elements that unify the acts of smiths involves the effects of these acts on individuals and society. The manufacture of iron hoes allows farmers to be more productive and efficient. Iron adzes and knives allow boat builders to construct better boats more quickly. Wooden masks used in the youth associations allow association members to express, ponder, and restructure the patterns of belief their culture hopes to pass on to them. Amulets allow individuals to expand their productivity, rearrange their links with the spiritual world, enhance their health, and improve their love lives and family well-being. Circumcision allows young males to become socially and spiritually whole, so that they may marry, raise families, and participate in their community's affairs.

In a variety of ways, then, each of these acts or the products they engender serves to aggrandize, refine, and reform, or to finish, bring to fruition, and make whole. Put most synthetically, they all serve to facilitate, articulate, and transform across a broad spectrum of Mande concerns, from the aspirations of individuals to the smooth functioning of the whole society. They create from potentiality. They shape or reshape objects, people, and situations by manipulating physical forms and their underlying structures of energy. They are as important to the Mande as successful annual harvests.

Thus we see that the Mande perceive a fundamental unity in all these acts. We see too a rationale for the affinity the Mande perceive between smiths working metal and smiths at work in these other arenas. As we have seen, these smiths are almost automatically subjected to lengthy and complicated training periods. They are perceived as inheriting enormous volumes of *nyama*, as well as several kinds of secret knowledge. The technology used in their smithing is complicated and often augmented with spiritual elements, while their readiness to collect more *dalilu* knowledge has given them the reputation of being prodigious sorcerers. Their reputations afford them social and political clout, by submerging them in an atmosphere of competence in dangerous undertakings. Thus the essential capacities of smiths are very well matched to the essential characteristics of their roles beyond smithing, which makes them ideal practitioners.

Given the affinity between these tasks and the smiths, it is natural that the Mande conceive of both in the same light. Thus the greatest significance of smiths lies in the fact that they are facilitators, articulators, and transformers. Their work takes place in two realms, the physical and the supernatural. First, as we have seen, blacksmiths are perceived as voracious manipulators of physical form. For us, this is most evident in their art, but for the Mande it is equally clear in their tool construction, amulet fabrication, circumcision, and even doctoring. When people wish to make good marriages or good business deals, grow good crops, or create healthy babies, they feel the smiths can help. While apprenticeship is the key to this hard-earned ability, and while we must not forget, for example, that mediocre sculptors exist alongside brilliant ones, nevertheless the Mande perceive their smiths to be natural articulators. Knowing that it is not, they still consider it almost automatic that blacksmiths will make things, as if they were born with the skill and cannot help themselves.

Beyond making is fixing. People think there is hardly anything that smiths cannot repair: hoe blades and handles, locally made or imported rifles, furniture, sculpture, and people. When the rains do not come and a crop is dying in the ground, people feel blacksmiths can fix it. When malevolent sorcery is practiced or there is trouble with capricious wilderness spirits, people feel blacksmiths can fix it. When citizens come to loggerheads or blows, people feel blacksmiths can intercede and make things right. Thus blacksmiths exercise their creativity all along an axis that begins with the inception of things and continues with their proper maintenance.

Smiths are equally busy in what we would call the realm of the supernatural. Remember, smiths are considered laden to the point of overflowing with *nyama*. This is vastly important, because *nyama* is the force that lies beneath the surface of all physical, spiritual, and social things, defining and activating them. It becomes, therefore, a kind of template, a substructure that must be changed to change what we see and know of something's surface. Smiths, who possess so much of it, become ideal choices for this deeper form of articulation and transformation. This helps explain the appeal of the etymology that describes the term *nyamakala* as handle, or, by extension, point of access to occult power. Thus the creativity of smiths extends across two kinds of space: the physical space on the surface of things and the conceptual space at their cores. This makes the smiths potent articulators indeed.

THE RESOLUTION OF MOVEMENT

The importance of the blacksmiths' fortes, facilitating, transforming and articulating, becomes clearer when we view them as elements in the conceptual underpinnings of Mande ideology. They are, in fact, major elements, because few societies place greater emphasis on the act of becoming. Personal development is stressed with vigor, and, irrefutably, with much success, if we use the history of Mande statecraft and commerce as our index. Children are considered as wild creatures that must become human beings. Human beings are of little account unless they become outstanding at some profession or avocation. Hunters, sculptors, leaders, and sorcerers, for example, will not leave this world in a happy state if they do not become so renowned for their skills that their names enter oral history.

Evidence of this ambition is everywhere, but nowhere more prevalent than in the performing arts. Songs abound that emphasize becoming through positive or negative example, as in this excerpt:

> Little smith who can't sculpt wood,
> Try to give the best of yourself.
> True smiths don't cultivate a cemetery.
> Little smith that doesn't know iron work,
> Try to give the best of yourself.
> A blacksmith does not cultivate a cemetery.
> Little smith with no distinction,
> Try to improve yourself.
> True smiths don't cultivate a cemetery.[3]

Any occupation could be substituted with the same effect, and the song addresses both young and old. "Little" is used as an insulting diminutive that points out lack of accomplishment by way of urging the sluggard on. Other lines in other songs also offer up such encouragement, by likening the unaccomplished to all manner of inadequacies. A person who has become nothing can be referred to as hot air, the one who comes when not called, a weak elephant in a group of elephants, or an elephant who can be carried on one's shoulders. Such an unaccomplished person can be said to be too light to do anything but float on water, or too lame to do anything but stay behind like the flesh of a young woman's buttocks. And there are more. Such unlucky ones can be likened to the deflated breasts of an old woman, a goatskin bag with a hole in the bottom, or human blood in a sack of human skin, with no heart and no bones. There is even a way of goading such people by changing the shapes of words used to characterize them. To call someone an elephant, for example, is to praise their strength and accomplishments. But to corrupt the word *samake*, "male elephant," into *samaka* is to generate a linguistic slur that proclaims the person to be like the false word, an inadequate illusion of the real thing. Thus bad form is likened to bad form.

Other Mande songs lament the passing of uneventful lives. Some bemoan the sadness of dying too young to use one's opportunities. Others state that to die young is to build nothing, which is like never having existed at all. Mande say a fruit not ripe cannot be eaten, and real death is to have been born for nothing and to die for nothing.

In addition to the artful insults, the Mande have a word for people of no account. It is *nantan* or *nantankolon,* meaning lazy, idle, slothful, ineffectual, good-for-nothing, and born-for-nothing.[4] People who suffer this appellation are said to be very weak, afraid of everything, unable to do anything, and, therefore, never successful. My colleague Kalilou Tera offered the etymologies: "he who is like one who did not come," and "someone without destiny," who is anonymous, and full of bitterness, frustration, and grief. Kalilou was fond of translating the word into English as "antihero."[5]

Ideology very often exaggerates its characterizations, leaving people to apply them to their neighbors as they see fit. Of course, many people, maybe most, live uneventful lives. A great many also, however, find inspiration or a challenge in messages like these, and for them Mande ideology conjures up the concept of the hero, *ngana*. The word means champion, a famous or celebrated person, someone of renown.[6] People who earn this appellation possess well-developed characters and an indomitable will to achieve. Charles Bird and Martha Kendall have written with great insight about this concept, showing how it works on peoples' aspirations and emotions, how it heats them up and compels them to attempt grand acts.[7]

The greatest heroes have been the legendary leaders, such as Sunjata Keita and Sumanguru Kante, but every region of the Mande diaspora has its oral traditions about famous hunters, warriors, leaders, and sorcerers. Furthermore, everyone can look around them, in their own town or towns nearby, and see people in the process of making names for themselves at sculpting, healing, masquerade dancing, soothsaying, and every other special activity that the Mande hold dear. Such people are also singled out in the performance arts with songs of praise that call them beautiful and brave and liken them to shining stars. For them are sung such lines as "may you be excused from death, from the death of your siblings," or "there are not enough words to praise you," or "ah, savage and solitary beast, we cannot finish praising you," or "my arms are on my back for you," meaning the praiser stands helpless before the person being praised.[8] For them too is the culture-bound hope that death will not be quite so complete, because the recollection of their names and deeds will live on in oral tradition.

It is worth returning to the praise line "savage, solitary beast," *dankelen*, which we applied earlier to *kòmò* masks, because its exegesis points us back toward complicated sorcery. One summer night when I watched Sidi Ballo perform his bird masquerade brilliantly for hours (Ill. 33),[9] this phrase was heaped on him almost endlessly in the songs that accompanied his dancing. No wonder. His articulation of masquerade and dance space and his transformation of the evening into an arena for contemplating great deeds and personal growth generated what the audience considered a most accomplished performance. The Mande say that celebration is an opportunity for education, by which they often mean socialization. Sidi Ballo's performance facilitated that opportunity beautifully.

The praise he received is used to liken very accomplished people to very ferocious animals, by employing a Mande formula of similitude equating the occult energies contained in two beings. Kalilou Tera explained the phrase as meaning isolated one, an animal grown very old and wise with bush knowledge and therefore very full of *nyama*. Such creatures are considered quite dangerous. They are likely to attack whatever comes near and so are invariably left well alone. The intent of the praise parallels that of another, *dankòròba*, which identifies a person grown equally old, equally wise, and therefore equally full of potent energy.[10]

People who elicit such praise are praised further by being awarded their own special time, the dangerous time between two and three o'clock in the morning when the world is said to be given over to wilderness spirits and the practice of malevolent sorcery. Anyone abroad at such a witching hour must be well versed in the knowledge of sorcery and well endowed with *nyama*. They are considered, in this mood of generous approbation, persons whose abilities to articulate, facilitate, and transform afford them a stature of awesome impeccability that sets them apart from fellow citizens of lesser ability. Artists like Sidi Ballo are often singled out this way. So are blacksmiths.

The Mande emphasis on becoming constitutes an interest in movement, from what one is to what one ought or wants to be. The interest necessitates an ideological avenue to help focus the efforts of people who want to move. An avenue is provided with the concept of "means," *nya*, which reformulates our three abstractions—articulate, facilitate, and transform—into a Mande social and spiritual framework.[11] The term refers to the manner or way of accomplishing things and by extension to their ultimate successful accomplishment. One can praise persons by saying they know the way of cooking, or sculpting, or healing. In this sense the term implies knowledge and control, paralleling on a larger scale the Mande equation that knowledge in the form of *daliluw* is power in the form of *nyama*. It connotes a deep, thorough, and practical understanding that endows one with the ability to manipulate people, situations, or things. These means can be tremendously beneficial for individuals and society, but they can also be devastating. Professional musicians, for example, often worry that jealous competitors will discover the "means" of their success and try to undermine them with sorcery. When singers lose their voices or harp players' fingers go afoul, they will often blame the catastrophe on just such a train of events.

One can also use the term *means* in the context of learning something's defining essence. The implication is the same. Such knowledge produces the power to control or manipulate. Thus good blacksmiths have the "means" to master the manipulation of iron. Their mastery is grounded in knowledge that makes actions possible.

In the realm of people, *means* identifies the capacities of individuals, as determined by their birthrights and destinies, joined to their abilities, as determined by the quantities of secret *dalilu* knowledge and occult energy they have at their disposals. Thus the term measures and evaluates peoples' essences or resources. If one seeks to discover other persons' "means," it is a quest to understand what makes them what they are. Such understanding gives one tremendous power to enhance or destroy them, to transform them in the most fundamental ways. This is exactly what musicians, indeed what every Mande person of accomplishment guards against.

With so much emphasis on becoming, these special Mande means are as important as their ends. They are what makes everything happen. When Sedu Traore gave me amulets and blacksmiths' tools, he provided me with the means to cope with all the *nyama* he generated at work. The bead he put around my neck did precisely the same thing. The businessman who came from Dakar for one of Sedu's amulets, the farmers who petitioned smiths for rain, and all the other citizens who bought tools, medicines, or advice were acquiring the means to move within the ideological constructs of their Mande world. Thus on the plane of everyday existence individuals negotiate their ordinary lives through the social and spiritual channels their concept of means provides.

On the plane of great deeds, where people cast themselves to become heroes, these special Mande means are equally critical. In fact, they constitute a major theme in the epic poetry of Mande oral tradition.[12] When an empire is to be built, heroes in the making must find the means to build it. When antagonists have to be overcome the means that make them powerful must be discovered and neutralized. Invariably, these means reside in the arcane, occult world, where secret knowledge and special expertise articulates the hidden energies that transform the world.

In an elegant analysis Bird and Kendall demonstrate the fundamental vitality of this concept of means, as a central element in a Mande philosophy of action that emerges from a "social theory of inertia" grounded in the ideas of "father childness" and "mother childness" that we encountered earlier.[13] The broader social and spiritual framework into which all these notions are built cantilevers the will of individuals to aggrandize themselves modestly or largely with wealth, power, and renown, against the goal of the collective to absorb individuals and usurp the fruits of their gain. When the Mande ponder their aspirations and actions, when they consider their happiness and contentment, they are guided by the ideal of becoming, the complications of their social constrictions, and the facilitating potential contained in their special concept of means.

From their technological expertise to their familiarity with the occult, smiths are steeped in these special Mande means. No other segment of the population is so thoroughly blessed, and no other segment is so systematically at work sharing these riches, for a fee. Everything they do, be it circumcision, the forging of a hoe, the curing of an ailment, or the carving of a mask, offers avenues for movement in the Mande world. Their ability to shape things in both physical and conceptual realms makes them invaluable to people seeking modest movement in their ordinary lives and to people seeking spectacular leaps on a more heroic plane.

Thus smiths are bridges. They use the resources of their birthright and training to fill the spaces between what people are and what they want or ought to become. Oral tradition is full of smiths doing this, and so is nearly any Mande town one would care to visit. No wonder we can consider the smiths as inhabiting the ideological core of their society. And no wonder Harry Tegnaeus and other authors have gone so far as to call them civilizing heroes.[14]

THE CONTRADICTION OF POSITION

Still, there are the sticky issues of caste, the ambiguity of smiths, and the ambivalence many citizens harbor toward them. We must consider why a profession so central, so full, could be cast out simultaneously to the periphery of civilization and contemplated with distrust and disdain.

The issue of Mande caste cannot be separated from the larger issue of what castes are. Unfortunately, opinions abound; many have merit but none has emerged as the standard by which we all can evaluate social systems. The Portuguese first applied the term *caste* to Indian society in the mid-sixteenth century. Now, more than 400 years later, many scholars debate its applicability to societies elsewhere in the world, while many others continue to debate its actual meaning in India.[15]

Contemporary opinion is most conservatively represented by sociologist Louis Dumont and other scholars whose research deals with India. He sets forth the criteria established by another Indologist, Célestin Bouglé, in 1908:

. . . the caste system divides the whole society into a large number of hereditary groups, distinguished from one another and connected together by three
characteristics: *separation* in matters of marriage and contact, whether direct
or indirect (food); *division* of labour, each group having, in theory or by tradition, a profession from which their members can depart only within certain
limits; and finally *hierarchy*, which ranks the groups as relatively superior or
inferior to one another.[16]

Then Dumont adds a kind of ideological glue, a scheme of opposition between the purity reflected in the Brahman and the pollution reflected in the
Untouchable.[17] This is consistent with most of the best-known work on Indian castes. J. H. Hutton cites Shridhar Ketkar's view that purity and pollution constitute the modus operandi of the Indian caste system.[18] M. N. Srinivas says the concept of pollution is a basic component of the system,
combining with karma, or natal ritual status, and dharma, or conformation to
the law, to give the Indian system its unique character.[19] H. N. C. Stevenson,
in an article that examines the literature concerning Indian status evaluation, agrees, stating that the "Hindu Pollution Concept" governs the behavior of Indians and underpins their caste system.[20] Dumont interprets this
concept as the essence of hierarchy, the catalyst behind superior and inferior
and the rationale for separation. As an India specialist he makes no apologies
for effectively restricting the term's application to India and invites scholars of other areas to discover other terms rather than dilute "caste" by
overextension.[21]

Many scholars agree, though no other term, such as guild, class, or special
professional, seems adequate. So creative are human beings that we could
not expect other social systems to correspond exactly to India's. As a result,
many scholars try to bend the Indian criteria to fit the social systems they
study, while others try to bend the social system they study to fit the Indian
criteria. Too many use the term superficially, without really exploring the
systems they have observed.[22]

The anthropologist Gerald Berreman adopts a freer interpretation of the
term, beginning with the basic definition of castes as "ranked endogamous
divisions of society in which membership is hereditary and permanent."[23]
He then adds the following criteria, which he feels are implicit in the
definition:

. . . castes are recognized as groups . . . they are in some ways interdepen-
dent; barriers to free social intercourse exist between castes; there are cultural differences between castes; there are differential degrees of power and
privilege between castes. Associated with caste in many and perhaps all instances is a degree of occupational specialization. While all the members of a
caste are not often committed to one line of work, there is a particular occupation or range of occupations which is considered to be appropriate to
each caste.[24]

Berreman considers this an interpretation that can be applied cross-culturally and uses it in his work on northern Indian society, with the qualification that, to understand caste in India, indigenous concepts regarding ritual status, pollution, and purity must also be incorporated.[25]

It is a tribute to our mental lives that so much debate can encircle the term and its interpretation, but the result seems to be that we are left somewhat at loose ends when we try to apply it to African societies. Two anthropologists who have done so most successfully are James Vaughan and Bonnie Wright, who have studied peoples at opposite ends of the Western Sudan and whose findings can be useful to us in our examination of the Mande. For Vaughan, caste means a "hereditary endogamous group who are socially differentiated by prescribed behavior."[26] For Wright, caste means "endogamous specialized groups who inherit their professional capacities genealogically."[27] Both provide rich and useful analyses of the systems they observed and end up describing two very different kinds of caste system.

Vaughan considers hierarchy an easily jettisoned concept belonging more properly in the realm of India. He emphasizes the interdependence of groups in caste systems and asserts the value of focusing on both functional and ideological explanations. He examines Marghi blacksmiths in northeastern Nigeria and believes that their system is based on a division of technological expertise for the production of food.[28]

Wright asserts the applicability of Bouglé's original definition to west African savanna societies and notes astutely:

> The ideological basis of the system, or the network of philosophical tenets about the nature of human identity, together with the cultural emphases and expressions of human differences, can be expected to vary from society to society and within each with the passage of time.[29]

She believes that an emphasis on hierarchy as in the Indian system inhibits our understanding of west African societies and suggests that a more accurate analysis for those societies sees castes distinguished by culturally defined sources of capacity or power, so that inequalities in the system are more a matter of realms of power than of rank. Her research focuses on Wolof bards in Senegal, who exhibit stereotypical public behavior corresponding to the stereotypical opinions other groups maintain about them. These opinions—that bards are parasitic, lascivious, loud, uncontrolled, often liars, and often sorcerers—are clearly pejorative, but Wright interprets them as, first, a metaphor of public social distance, and, second, perfectly understandable, given human nature, as a vain attempt to diminish the tremendous social and spiritual power of bards by associating them with "unsavory qualities."[30]

The Mande are very different socially from the Marghi, but they share several important beliefs and institutions with the Wolof. Mande smiths, we recall, belong to a special category of artisans, the *nyamakala*, who are distinguished from the rest of society because they possess the birthrights to activities restricted first by endogamy and then by considerations of expertise and occult energy. Much of the smiths' professional identity resides in the technology of smelting and forging and the artistry of sculpting. The rest lies in their secret knowledge and the energy of action. The other *nyamakalaw*, bards and leather workers, also possess special techniques, for shaping words and leather respectively, while also being noted for their knowledge and power.

Thus people are first polarized according to their perceived inherited capacities for articulating, facilitating, and transforming and then divided according to the materials they favor. Essentially, this polarity creates two categories of citizenry who are at each other's disposal: the groups directly involved in sustenance, commerce, and statecraft, on the one hand, and the specialized art and craft groups, on the other. The precolonial institution of slavery complicated but did not obscure this relationship, because slaves composed a work force utilized by all the polarized groups.

If we combine Vaughan's and Wright's minimal definitions, the Mande smiths can be considered a caste within a caste system. Both definitions very nearly fit the Mande situation, and joining Vaughan's component of social differentiation through prescribed behavior to Wright's component of inherited professional capacities provides a useful thumbnail description of where the smiths fit into their society. Thus we can say the smiths are a specialized endogamous group socially differentiated by prescribed behavior and genealogically inherited professional capacities. The reference to behavior accommodates the restrictions and privileges linked to blacksmith status. The reference to professional capacities accommodates the scope of smith enterprise along with its foundation in *nyama*.

If we take one step beyond this definition we immediately encounter difficulty. We must grapple with notions of rank or hierarchy, then with ideas of purity and pollution.

Hierarchy implies a generally recognized system of ranking, complete with an ideological rationale. Both seem absent among the Mande. First, neither the aspersions many Mande cast on the smiths nor the ambivalence most Mande feel toward them constitute a ranking system. Second, the most likely ideological construct, the concept of *nyama*, does not work well as a rationale. Nowhere in the indigenous perceptions of this force—as an energy that governs, shapes, and acts or as an awesome, sometimes fearsome, even deadly occult power—do we find the grounds for ranking people. Also absent is any foundation for ascribing a system of purity and pollution to the Mande, unless we choose to confuse potency with impurity. Instead, we find in those perceptions a multitude of reasons for distinguishing people, according to the realms of power and capacity suggested by Wright in her work on the Wolof.

In my view, the interpretations of caste set forth by Berreman and Bouglé, with their references to rank and relative superiority and inferiority, do not fit the Mande situation. By extension, the schemes of purity and pollution so central to many Indologists' interpretation of caste have no corresponding feature in Mande ideology.

We are left, then, with the ambiguity of the smiths' position in society and the ambivalence that other citizens feel toward them. Several of the topics we have explored shed light on these phenomena. Our examination of joking relationships and responses to the presumptions of researchers provided helpful perspectives. So did the analyses of sorcery, *nyama*, and the techniques, technologies, and knowledge that smiths characteristically possess. We glean from these explorations an understanding of prodigious credentials—the same recognition that the Mande have themselves. Without blacksmiths Mande society would be in dire straits indeed.

From all of this emerges a kind of tension that centers on the capacities smiths possess and the resources they offer. For the general citizenry, so frequently busy enjoying the fruits of the smiths' labor, the blacksmiths' potency constitutes potential danger, while their dependency on smiths' products constitutes more control over them than they could possibly find comforting. The means that make smiths so important—indeed, make them civilizing heroes—also make them subject to the jealousies and resentments of everyone else. Thus, what Wright concluded about the aspersions cast on Wolof bards fits Mande smiths as well. The power smiths have to control others is in some measure mitigated, or at least rationalized, by rendering it unsavory. This means smiths can be valued and damned at once.

The tension embedded in the Mande's perception of blacksmiths, expressed by praise and disdain simultaneously, may seem incongruous to scholars who seek resolution in the systems they study. Clearly, the Mande speak in multiple voices about their smiths, and if this gives the impression of unresolved or inconsistent behavior, so it should. But that need not instill a fear of faulty methodology in us; individuals and societies often hold conflicting views and express them both.

The anthropologist Ernest Gellner notes that researchers too frequently fall into the trap of contextual charitability, attributing to the beliefs and actions of other cultures a coherence they do not actually find.[31] Another anthropologist, Ivan Karp, feels that social structures invariably generate difficulties for their creators; he cites authors ranging from literary theorist M. M. Bakhtin to anthropologists Gregory Bateson, Victor Turner, Don Handelman, and Bruce Kapferer to corroborate his position.[32]

Karp also provides us with a useful example, in an analysis of marriage ritual among the Iteso of Kenya. Participants, all women, express their feelings about the roles they play in society. They communicate with more than words. They use ephemera, the fleeting, transitory elements of performance such as laughter and gesture. Their messages are complex and contradictory.

They speak, as Karp says, in multiple voices, and "If the result is confusion, such is the essence of social life."[33]

As Iteso women express ambivalence through contradictions in their performed ritual, Mande citizens express ambivalence through contradictions in their stereotypical images of smiths. These images, we have seen, quite accurately represent the wonderful materials and hazardous energies smiths control, the impressive credentials smiths use to control them, the benefits all Mande reap because of that control, and the resentment they also feel because they are so dependent upon it. In an examination of another realm, anthropologist Martha Kendall discusses the ambivalence addressed to Mande bards. This ambivalence reflects the different capacities and roles of bards and of smiths. But its ultimate focus is quite similar: bards bestow great benefits on their society while exacting an enormous measure of control, and this is quite rightly interpreted as a mixed blessing.[34]

Oral tradition offers an image of blacksmiths' power unchecked. It takes the form of the legendary sorcerer-smith Sumanguru Kante, who, we recall, is said to have lost an empire to another legendary figure, Sunjata Keita. Sumanguru is remembered in the bards' epic poetry and by nearly everyone with great praise for what he was and what he accomplished. But his image is the essence of fearsome, death-dealing, unstoppable power. He wore the skins of the men he defeated, and after Sunjata finally defeated him, no one is sure he ever really died.

Sumanguru represents the darker side of the blacksmiths' gift. Smiths have the means to make life sweet. But they also have the means to consume it. Intelligent people can only find this disquieting.

When special population segments, such as Wolof bards or Mande smiths, are studied from the vantage point of the ideology and experiences that compose others' perceptions of them, it becomes quite difficult to make simple generalizations. Some scholars describe the status of African blacksmiths as marginal.[35] For Mande smiths I think the opposite may be closer to the truth. They are so embedded in the ideological heart of their society, so very much a part of the nuts and bolts of day-to-day living, and so very full of the energy that Mande consider central to their world and their lives, that other citizens must cull their impressions from a broad and confusing body of data, from which they simply cannot detach themselves. No wonder those impressions are forever changing, and no wonder researchers have so frequently felt confused.

THE RESPONSIBILITY OF ARTISTS

Finally, we should ask how all this affects smiths as sculptors, and what its ramifications are for art. As artists, smiths find themselves in the interesting position of being conscripted by their own inheritance. The Western cliché about being born an artist acquires a special meaning here, where sculptors are first born and then made. Their birthright provides the opportunity for an excellent training that can carry apprentices well beyond the mastery of form in the Western sense, into a grander scale of mastery altogether. Such training will be so broadly based as to offer the possibility of instruction in a host of related enterprises, all of which can generate revenue. In the West, sculptors teach to augment their incomes. Among the Mande, sculptors practice smithing or sorcery.

While this spectrum of opportunity includes economic security, it also includes clout. Sculptors partake of their profession's aura and can enlarge it exponentially through their own individual accomplishments. Thus they acquire the power and control we have discussed at length as means in the special Mande sense. In that sense they possess their own battery of voices, the institutionalized instruments such as soothsaying and amulet making they use to help shape society. We can say, then, that blacksmiths also speak in multiple voices, voices that guide in divination or threaten in the kòmò association. And this is communication to which the rest of society must listen.

Smiths' sculpture thus accrues its meaning in a most interesting milieu. Its production constitutes one of the blacksmiths' voices, part of that constellation of resources that make smiths men of means. Itself the product of sophisticated articulation and transformation, it becomes a major agent facilitating movement in Mande social and spiritual life. It is used by the young to help them articulate their thoughts and experiences and transform themselves into adults. It is used by farmers to facilitate the ever more refined articulation of their agricultural skills, to transform seed and soil into plenty. It is used by families of deceased twins to articulate their grief in ways that help transform it into ideological optimism. It is used by leaders of the secret associations to articulate beliefs, channel experiences, and transform the realities in which citizens live and the ways in which they behave. Like the smiths themselves, their art is instrumental.

Smiths' sculpture resembles its makers in another way as well. It thrives—indeed, it derives some measure of its influence—because it bears the same aura of ambiguity and generates the same kind of ambivalence. In oral tradition, we recall, the legendary blacksmith hero Fakoli is praised as the man with the enormous head and mouth. In effect, he becomes his kòmò mask and it becomes him. A similar kind of confluence is reflected in people's attitudes toward sculpture.

People conflate their exposure to the stereotypical imagery of blacksmiths with their experiences of actual, individual smiths and thereby create their own impressions, which change as their exposure and experiences change. The same thing happens with sculpture. I always enjoyed asking young Mande for their thoughts about photographs of masks and figures. Those with little personal experience invariably responded with caution or fear. They had been led to believe that these blacksmiths' fabrications were terribly powerful and could hurt or even kill people. Some would only peek at the pictures, eyes half closed and ready to bolt, just as some of us peek at the frightening scenes in monster movies.

Older, more experienced children were always more matter-of-fact. They had seen more masks performed, perhaps helped prepare dancers in their youth association, or even danced masks themselves. They liked to say what they knew about the pictured works. So did most adults. All, however, both young and old, expressed seriousness and respect when talking about the pieces, and they maintained identical attitudes toward the actual sculptures they experienced in their lives. Once, in a small town, a father told his son to show me the *ntomo* mask in his charge. The young fellow kept it carefully wrapped in cotton cloth and hidden among his possessions. When he unwrapped it for me, he made it plain through his statements and behavior that he considered the mask to be a special entity charged with a potency of its own. Most Mande feel as he felt. Sculpture is not kept hidden away just to protect it from thieves or the ravages of insects and weather. People perceive it to be important and powerful, just as they perceive smiths.

When blacksmiths spoke to me about sculpture, their interests ran toward the practical. They were interested in how well pieces were sculpted and what would make them serve their purpose successfully. Were the horns of an antelope headdress beautifully shaped? Did iron equestrian figures establish a proper degree of resemblance to a person or to a horse? Did *kòmò* masks possess enough organic attachments to make them awesome? Their concerns seemed strictly aesthetic and functional to me—and indeed, they were. But to the smiths they were also part of a larger regard, a regard for means in the special Mande sense.

Remember, Sedu Traore once told me that smiths, when they circumcise, make the souls of their young patients better. By *soul* he meant spirit, image, essential self. By *better* he meant that the smiths' surgery—their articulation of human flesh—gives boys new lives as men. It purifies and civilizes them and moves them into a new world.

The night I watched Sidi Ballo dance his bird masquerade I realized that betterment and growth are gained from the blacksmiths' sculpture as well as from their surgery. When Sidi retired for breaks, local youth association members came out and danced their own masks (Ill. 77 and Color Plate VIII). They danced with vigor and enthusiasm, precision and elegance, as a chorus sang about tradition, accomplishment, and the good life. The dancers' competence earned them a share of the same kind of praise that was heaped on Sidi. They were praised as beautiful, in the deep sense that acknowledges character as well as appearance. Their masks were finely carved and beautifully proportioned. The praise the boys received was addressed to them indirectly through their masks, so that the deep beauty of each amplified the other. Thus, just as Fakoli's power was conflated in praise with his *kòmò* mask, so the fineness of these young boys was conflated with the sculptures the smiths had made for them. Although wood and not flesh had been articulated, the carving of the masks, like the surgery of circumcision, made these boys better. It enlarged their souls and moved them closer to maturity and responsible adulthood.

The smiths, then, in their sculpture as in their other enterprises, concern themselves with means, and in so doing they illuminate for us a large portion of the Mande world.

PLATE 42. Southern Bamana carved wooden "little animal head" (h. 16 in.), designed to be mounted on a basketry cap strapped to a dancer's head. Private collection. Photograph by Jeffrey A. Wolin.

PLATE 43. Bamana carved wooden mask (h. 15⅜ in.) for the *kore* initiation association. Private collection. Photograph by Jeffrey A. Wolin.

PLATE 44. Bamana *kore* initiation association mask. Photograph published in Henry 1910.

PLATE 45. Large Bamana carved wooden mask, heavily patinated, used in the *kònò* initiation association. Photograph published in Henry 1910.

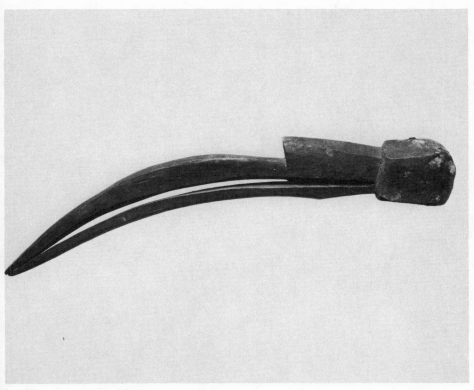

PLATE 46. Central Bamana carved wooden headdress for a bird masquerade. Study collection of the University of California, Los Angeles Museum of Cultural History.

PLATE 47. Sidi Ballo performing his bird masquerade, 1978.

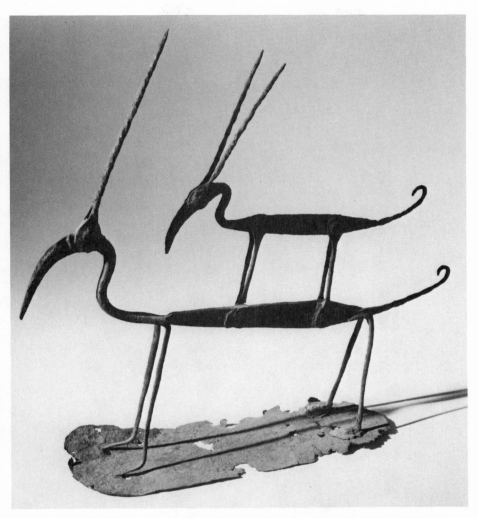

PLATE 48. Southern Bamana forged iron antelope headdress (l. 14⅛ in.). Private collection. Photograph by Jeffrey A. Wolin.

PLATE 49. Bamana carved wooden figure portraying a
deceased twin. Photograph published in Henry 1910.

PLATE 50. Southern Bamana carved wooden mother and
child figure (h. 45⅝ in.). The Metropolitan Museum of Art.
The Michael C. Rockefeller Memorial Collection. Bequest of
Nelson A. Rockefeller, 1979. 1979.206.121.

PLATE 51. Small Bamana forged iron figure coated with sacrificial material (h. 10⅞ in.), used to deter antisocial sorcery. Private collection. Photograph by Jeffrey A. Wolin.

PLATE 52. Northern Bamana forged iron figure with antelope horns and fur and a skirt of animal hide coated with sacrificial material (h. 20⅛ in.). Private collection. Photograph by Jeffrey A. Wolin.

PLATE 53. Eastern Bamana forged iron portrait of a wilderness spirit (h. 9 in.). Private collection. Photograph by Jeffrey A. Wolin.

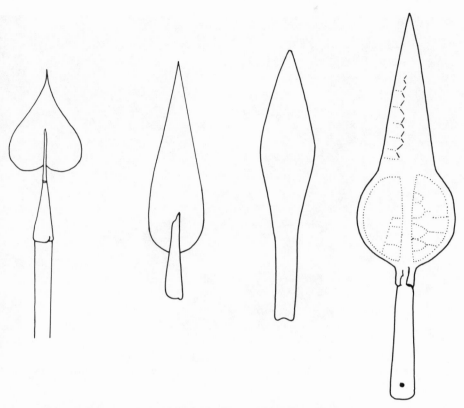

PLATE 54. Several types of Mande spear blades. Rust on the most elaborate
example had removed much of the dot-engraved pattern.

PLATE 55. Iron lamp cup-making mold, made from the same hard wood (*si*) smiths use to mount their anvils, and women use to make cooking oil or "shea butter."

PLATE 56. Simple one-cup Bamana iron lamp with elegantly forged shaft. Owned but no longer used by a blacksmith family in a small town near Ségou, 1973.

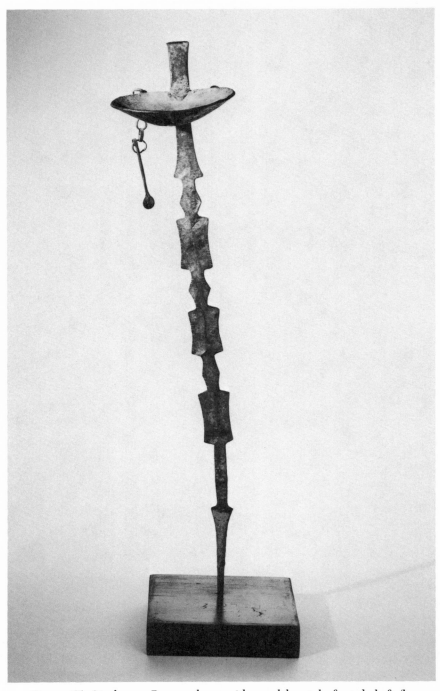

PLATE 57. Single-cup Bamana lamp with an elaborately forged shaft (h. 29⅜ in.). Private collection. Photograph by Jeffrey A. Wolin.

PLATE 58. Two simple Bamana lamps owned by a Malian art
dealer in Ségou, 1973.

PLATE 59. Beautifully forged Bozo iron lamp (h. 40⁹⁄₁₆ in.). Koninklijk Museum voor Midden-Afrika, Tervuren, Belgium. R.G. 65.17.70. Photograph courtesy of the museum.

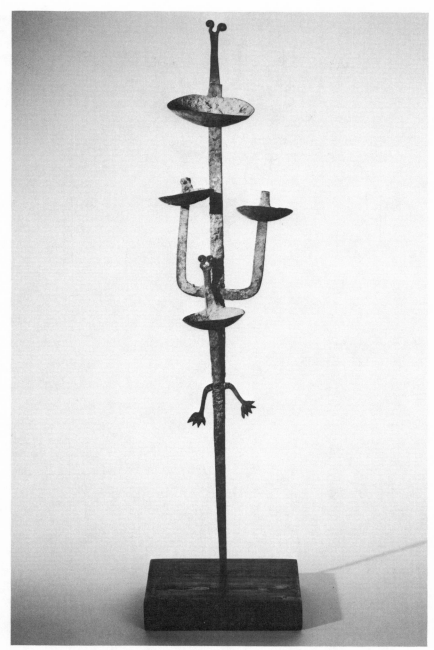

PLATE 60. Bamana forged iron lamp (h. 32⁵⁄₁₆ in.). Private collection. The lowest cup is riveted to a separate shaft that is riveted to the main shaft, holding the feet in place. Photograph by Jeffrey A. Wolin.

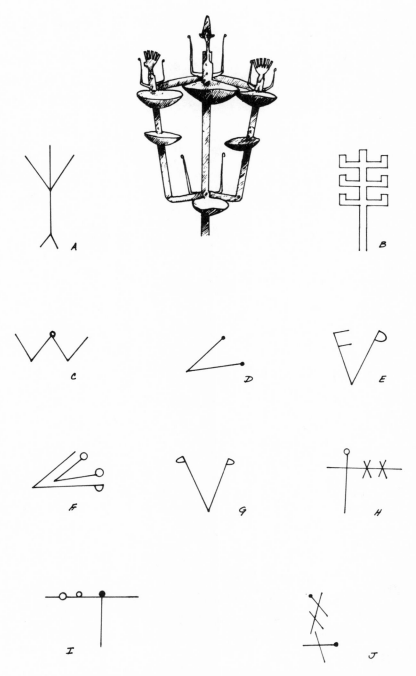

PLATE 61. Complex lamp, with symbols in Mande cloth and writing that resemble the configurations of Mande iron lamps.

PLATE 62. Bozo iron staff (h. 38⅝ in.). Koninklijk Museum voor Midden-Afrika, Tervuren, Belgium. R.G. 65.17.71. Photograph courtesy of the museum.

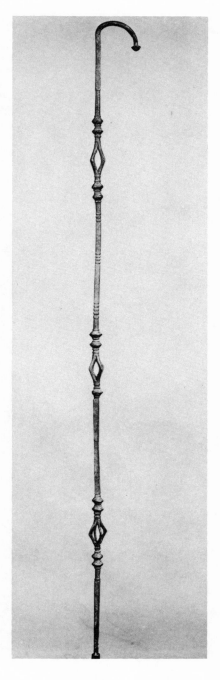

PLATE 63. Bamana forged iron figure (h. 9⅞ in.) originally part of an iron staff. Collection of Charles Bird and Martha Kendall. Photograph by Steve Sprague.

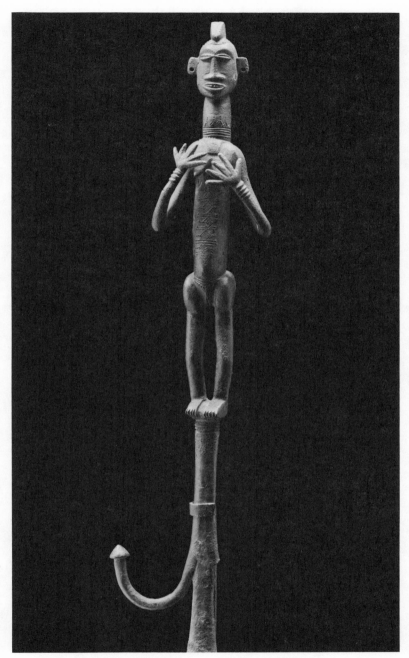

PLATE 64. Bamana forged iron figure and staff (h. 20¼ in.). Collection of Paul and Ruth Tishman. Photograph by Jerry L. Thompson, courtesy of the Metropolitan Museum of Art.

PLATE 65. Bamana forged iron figure and staff owned by a Malian art dealer in Bamako, 1973.

PLATE 66. Bamana forged iron equestrian figure and staff (h. 24 1/16 in.). The Metropolitan Museum of Art. The Michael C. Rockefeller Memorial Collection. Bequest of Nelson A. Rockefeller, 1979. 1979.206.153.

PLATE 67. Bamana forged iron equestrian figure on staff. Musée National des Arts Africaines et Oceaniens, Paris. Photograph courtesy of Service Photographique des Musées Nationaux.

PLATE 68. Old and corroded Bamana forged iron equestrian figure (h. 7⅛ in.) originally part of a staff. Private collection. Photograph by Jeffrey A. Wolin.

PLATE 69. Large Bamana carved mask used in the *kɔ̀nɔ̀* initiation association, with a *boli* in the background. The mask surface is heavily coated with sacrificial materials, and a *boli* construction supporting a bundle of bird quills is mounted on the mask's "forehead." Photograph published in Henry 1910.

PLATE 70. Southern Bamana carved wooden horn (h. 26⅝ in.) of the type used in the *kòmò* and *jo* initiation associations. It is wrapped with cotton twine that has become encrusted with sacrificial materials, in a fashion reminiscent of the bundles of twine often found in *boli* constructions, both new and very old. Private collection. Photograph by Jeffrey A. Wolin.

PLATE 71. Small northern Bamana forged iron horn (h. 7¾ in.) used by members of the *kòmò* initiation association. Private collection. Photograph by Jeffrey A. Wolin.

PLATE 72. Bamana *kòmò* initiation association mask (l. 27¹⁵/₁₆ in.), made of wood, antelope horns, bird quills, feathers, and a thick coat of sacrificial materials. Afrika Museum, Berg en Dal, Holland. 210-2. Photograph courtesy of the museum.

PLATE 73. Bamana *kòmò* initiation association mask (l. 27⅛ in.), made of wood, antelope horns, bird quills, cotton, and sacrificial materials. Teeth have been indicated in an ingenious fashion by the smith, who carved them beneath the lower jaw, with the result that the projections on the top are balanced underneath. The visual effect emphasizes the ambiguous, transformative powers of the masks, the association, and its blacksmith-leaders. Indiana University Art Museum, Bloomington. 72.111a. Photograph by Michael Cavanagh and Kevin Montague.

PLATE 74. Whisk made of animal hair, cotton twine, cowry shells, wood, and a heavy encrustation of sacrificial materials. This whisk and the one depicted in Ill. 75 were part of the paraphernalia associated with the *kòmò* mask depicted in Ill. 73. It could be called a "power object," *siri*, a "secret device," *basi*, or an "amulet," *sèbèn*, and resembles both the association mask and *boli* in its construction (an assemblage of organic materials that harness *nyama*) and function (the application of *nyama* to the accomplishment of tasks, such as combating malevolent sorcerers). Indiana University Art Museum, Bloomington, 72.111b. Photograph by Ken Strothman and Harvey Osterhoudt.

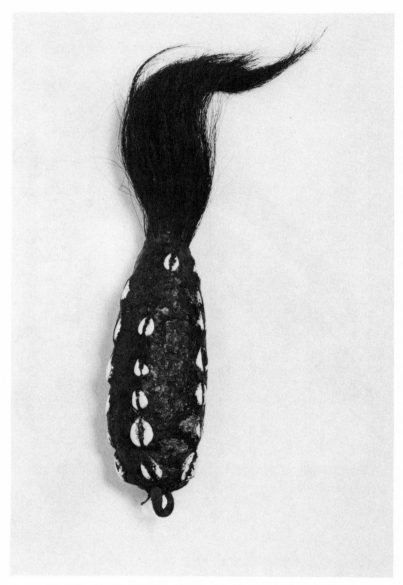

PLATE 75. Whisk made of animal hair, cotton twine, cowry shells, iron, and a thick encrustation of sacrificial material. Such whisks may be carried by a masked *kòmò* dancer as an important part of his choreography. Gesturing with it would symbolize, or actually signal, a supernatural counterattack by the dancer, the implication being that he had just detected the use of *kòròti* airborne poison against him. Indiana University Art Museum, Bloomington. 72.111c. Photograph by Ken Strothman and Harvey Osterhoudt.

PLATE 76. Bamana *kòmò* initiation association mask (l. 30¾ in.), made of wood, antelope horns, bird quills, feathers, and sacrificial materials. The cotton twine buried within the organic matter of *boli* and other *kòmò* masks is here used to help hold the feathers in place. Lowie Museum of Anthropology, University of California, Berkeley. 5-12980.

PLATE 77. Two members of a youth association branch dancing at a performance of the itinerant bird masquerader Sidi Ballo, in a small town on the Mande Plateau, 1973. The mask forms are borrowed from the *ntomo* initiation association, and, while dancing, both dancers and masks are called *ntomo*.

Notes

PREFACE

1. Makarius 1968:25. Cline 1937:114–139 and Barnes 1980:8–13 summarize much of the literature on the status of smiths in African cultures.

2. Murdock 1959:64–76, Greenberg 1966:8, Welmers 1971, and Fivaz and Scott 1977:21–22.

3. Charles Bird and John William Johnson, personal communications, 1986. Bird 1971:15 notes that *Mandeka* means "person of the Mande," *Mandekalu* means "people of the Mande," and *Mandekan* means "language of the Mande." *Mandeka*, Bird says, is the reconstructed form underlying the terms used frequently today to identify one of the principal Mande language speaking groups, the Maninka, Mandinga, Malinké, or Mandingo.

4. See, for example, Dieterlen 1955, 1957, and 1959; Pâques 1954:63–110; and Zahan 1963:116–120.

5. See Bird 1982:60–423.

6. See Ezra 1986:13–17 and Imperato 1983:16 for discussions of this variation in the southern Bamana region called Baninko.

7. See van der Merwe 1980 for a summary of iron working's history in sub-Saharan Africa.

I. BLACKSMITHS IN MANDE SOCIETY

1. For general discussions of Mande social organization see Hopkins 1971:100–117, Labouret 1934:105–108, Launay 1972, Monteil 1924:162–163, N'Diaye 1970a, Pâques 1954:62–68, Sidibé 1959, and Zahan 1963:128–133.

2. Bird 1972:292 suggests that bards, for example, may have originated in the era of the old Ghana Empire, sometime during the first millennium after Christ.

3. N'Diaye 1970b:102 notes that they are sometimes called *tòntigi*, as does Hopkins 1971:107.

4. Monteil 1924:190–193 and Pâques 1954:89. Sedu Traore also provided information on the life-style of slaves, in April 1973.

5. Mande family names, *jamuw*, often indicate professions and social niches, but not always. Names were frequently changed as a result of war or slavery. Such last names as Fane, Kante, and Dunbiya are nearly always smiths' names, as are Soumanguru and Soumaoro. Smiths may also be named Bagayoko, Ballo, Camara, Jara, Konate, Koulibali, Sissoko, and Traore, though several of these names are more closely associated with the clans of traditional leaders.

6. The smith was Mama Konate, in spring 1973.

7. Sedu Traore and Magan Fane were the smiths who provided me with the most detailed explanations of this practice, in summer and fall 1973.

8. Pâques 1954:63.

9. N'Diaye 1970a:79–83.

10. I interviewed a Somono canoe maker named Brema Fane several times in Ségou Koro in spring 1973. Additional data were acquired from Adama Timbo and Chiekna Sangare, research assistants, in spring 1973 and from John Lewis, an anthropologist who worked in the Markala area, in April 1975. See also Tymowski 1967.

11. See Cissé 1964, Sidibé 1930, and Travélé 1928 for studies of Mande hunters.

12. Charles Bird, personal communication, 1981.

13. Zahan 1963:127–129 and Labouret 1934:107 discuss these professional groups. John Lewis acquired corroborative data during his work in the 1970s (personal communication, 1975).

14. These women who repair calabashes seem to be an enterprising group worthy of scholarly research. During the year I worked in Senou a *kule* woman from another town came once a week to ply her trade. She always had much business, and indicated that she worked a different town nearly every day of the week.

15. Barbara Frank recently concluded extensive research on these leather workers, and her work promises to yield important new information on a profession that has been poorly understood.

16. Sedu Traore once lectured me on the importance of getting amulets covered quickly. Some amulet makers cover their own products, but most send their wares with their clients to the leather workers. Sedu also advised his clients to remain with the leather worker until the job was done. Otherwise, competitors or other persons of ill will might arrange a switch of materials.

17. See Bird 1976:89–100, Bird and Kendall 1980:13–27, Darbo 1972:1–14, Johnson 1978:92–130, and Kendall 1982:197–209.

18. N'Diaye 1970a:101–114, Sidibé 1959:14, and Diop 1971:50.

19. Aubert 1939:38.

20. Monteil 1915:340.

21. N'Diaye 1970a:14.

22. Bellamy 1886:81.

23. Monteil 1924:221.

24. Raffenel 1856:322, 418, 463.

25. Monteil 1924:143–148.

26. Durand 1932:47–48.

27. Hopkins 1971:106–107; N'Diaye 1970a:41–52, and Launay 1972 address the Mande specifically. Southall 1970:242, 257–258, and Vaughan 1970 address the notion of caste in Africa generally.

28. Hopkins 1971:106.

29. Raffenel 1856:272–273.

30. Labouret 1934:104. See also Doumbia 1936:358–362.

31. Labouret 1934:100, 101.

32. Wilson 1951:91–97.

33. Henry 1910:33–41 and Monteil 1924:141–156 provide useful information, if the reader allows for too much emphasis on the negative.

34. Bird and Kendall 1980:20.

35. Johnson 1978:109.

36. Bird 1976:97, Bird and Kendall 1980:14–15, 23–24, and Johnson 1978:94–95.

37. Henry 1910:27–28.

38. Monteil 1924:121.

39. Cissé 1964:192–193.

40. Labouret 1934:120.

41. Zahan 1963:133.

42. Bird 1974:introduction.

43. Monteil 1924:121 and Henry 1910:28.

44. Dieterlen 1951:63.

45. Labouret 1934:120.

46. Cissé 1964:193.

47. Cissé 1964:200.

48. Johnson 1978:95–97.
49. Zahan 1963:147.
50. Henry 1910:85–87.
51. Zahan 1960:168.
52. Johnson 1978:96.
53. Zahan 1963:127 translates *nyamakala* as "handle of *nyama*." Meillassoux 1973 provides a similar etymology, but finds it quite unclear and so prefers another, which derives from the Bamana term *nara*, meaning secret knowledge that can become dangerous. Camara 1976:75–76 examines the rich range of possible translations for *nyama* and *kala* and ultimately advises caution in their interpretation.
54. Zahan 1960:110–111, 127.
55. Roy Sieber, personal communication, 1981.
56. Monteil 1924:143.
57. Appia 1965:320–325.
58. *U maa don gwan tugu ye,*
    Kelen bi kelen kè soli kala.
    U maa don gwan tugu la,
    Kelen bi kelen kè kulu daba ye.
    U maa don gwan tugu la,
    Kelen bi kelen kè kolonnin ye.
    Suyatigi ye numudenw ye.
Song recorded by the author during a bird masquerade performance, June 1978. Transcribed and translated by Sekuba Camara and Kalilou Tera.
59. Thomas Heart, a Peace Corps volunteer who worked in the region, personal communication, spring 1973.

II. THE MANDE SMITHS AS CRAFTSMEN

1. The anthropologist John Lewis did encounter a town near Markala that refused to allow blacksmiths to live in it. It was a very conservative Muslim community, and the interdiction created numerous problems for the population. Hopkins 1971: 107 was told that an ideal Maninka community would have to include a lineage of smiths.
2. The *numu dugu* may be an outgrowth of the precolonial state-building days. People in Ségou told me that during the time of their great state several blacksmiths' towns surrounded the capital to arm the state's military forces.
3. Campbell 1909–1910:458.
4. Goucher 1981:183–189. See also Francis-Boeuf 1937 and Forbes 1933 and the illustration of a massive smelting operation in Binger 1892:I, 261.
5. Imperato 1972b:54.
6. Sometimes smiths pour water on their anvils, to cool them and the spirits of their fathers. In fact, smiths sacrifice kola nuts and chickens to their anvils just before the busy time during the farming season—or more often, if they like. They say this keeps the hammer from hitting them, the adze from cutting them, and the iron from burning them. They also say their water basins symbolize their mothers.
7. The section about smelting was written with reference to the following sources: Appia 1965, Archinard 1884, Saikou 1935, Campbell 1909–1910, Cline 1937, Forbes 1933, Francis-Boeuf 1937, Park 1799:283–285, and Raffenel 1856:56ff, 272–273.
8. Park 1799:283–285 and Desplagnes 1907:fig. 107.
9. I spoke with a group of Bèlèdougou smiths in January 1973 regarding ore gathering and smelting. The smith Bourama Soumaoro discussed Wasoulou smelting with me in March 1973, and Greg Polk, a Peace Corps volunteer, provided the information about western Mali in September 1973.

10. Francis-Boeuf 1937:411–414 and Forbes 1933:231, 233.

11. Schmidt and Avery 1978:1085–1089 and Avery and Schmidt 1979 have shed some interesting new light on African iron smelting processes, based on their research concerning Buhaya metallurgy in Tanzania.

12. Campbell 1909–1910:460–461.

13. Archinard 1884:250, 252 and Campbell 1909–1910:459–461.

14. Jobson 1968 [1623]:56, 152–153 and Moore 1738:41.

15. Gray and Dochard 1825:181–182.

16. *Diyen fòlòta ci lè ma. A la bana ye ci ye.* This passage is from a manuscript of the Kele Monson Jiabate version of the Sunjata epic, lines 97–98, in the possession of Charles Bird.

17. Legassick 1966 and Bouys 1943. The reader may wish to consult the *Journal of African History's* 1971 special issue, devoted entirely to firearms in West Africa.

18. Archinard 1884.

19. Imperato 1979.

20. The names I recorded in the southern Bamana area between Bamako and Bougouni are as follows: *kemito*, the shortest barrel but of high caliber; *gwasaa*, a longer barrel and also of high caliber; *lònga*, a medium length barrel and of high caliber; *buga*, a slightly longer barrel and of high caliber; *sonyori*, a long barrel of short caliber; and *losi*, the longest barrel but of low caliber. I would expect the names to vary in different areas.

21. Jamie Wickens, Peace Corps volunteer who lived in northern Ivory Coast, personal communication, spring 1973.

22. Imperato 1972b:52–56, 84.

23. Zahan 1980 and Imperato 1970.

III. SMITHS AND THE SHAPE OF CIVILIZED SPACE

1. Hopkins 1971:107 and 1972:99 and Sidibé 1959.

2. Charles Bird, personal communication, June 1977.

3. Henry 1910:29–61, Labouret 1934:130–132, Monteil 1924:142–155, and Tauxier 1927:87–114 provide an idea of the constellation of beliefs and practices that focus on the health and well-being of people.

4. Traore 1965:9–624 reinforces Sedu's statement with an extensive compilation of herbal and supernatural formulas.

5. See Bird and Kendall 1980:16–17 and McNaughton 1982a for more extensive explorations of *daliluw.*

6. McNaughton 1982a:491–492.

7. The informants, who were a Bamana, two Wolof, a Toucoulor, and a Mossi, suggested leprosy, *kounatio* or *baguitio*, or possibly eczema, *zaufala.* See Malzy 1943 and Monod 1943.

8. Interview with Sekuba Camara, June 1978. He noted that he possesses the *dalilu* but has never used it. The proper names of the plants are secret.

9. Interviews with Sekuba Camara and Kalilou Tera, July 1978. Again, the name of the plant is secret.

10. Glaze 1981a:137, 140, 256, 257.

11. Maesen 1940, as cited in Goldwater 1964:18.

12. Bravmann 1974:125.

13. Prouteaux 1918–1919; and McNaughton 1982a:496–498 (I thank Martha Kendall, editor of *Anthropological Linguistics*, for allowing me to use those materials here).

14. Sidibé 1929.

15. *Sumuso karogelen y'a denw ban dumunna,*
    Ko nyoninsa ye n' denw kan.
    or: *So bana ye n' denw kan.*
    or: *Boji bana ye n' denw la.*

Excerpts from a *kòmò* association song performed by Seydou Camara, June 1978, for the author. Transcribed and translated by Sekuba Camara and the author.

16. *Dankunga, subagai ye nyogon benn'a ro.*
    Dankun rokolon te.

This is part of a smiths' song often performed at festivals or when smiths gather to dance. It is about crossroads and sorcerers and the powers of smiths, because, as sorcerers themselves, they can detect and counteract these malevolent activities. Performed by Seydou Camara in June 1978; transcribed and translated by Sekuba Camara and the author.

17. *Nana ma man di fo ko-jugu-lon.* See Bird and Kendall 1980.

18. Interview with Sekuba Camara, June 1978. It is not clear to me whether all *somaw* braided their hair, or just those who were smiths.

19. *Numu Satigi turu kèlè fenjugu turu.*
    Soma min man'a ye,
    Kalokalo soma min man'a ye,
    A muri be caya.

Song performed by Seydou Camara, June 1978; transcribed and translated by Sekuba Camara and the author.

20. The verb used to signify all that is *ka foronto.* The etymology was provided by Sekuba Camara, June 1978.

21. Dieterlen 1951:181–184 and Labouret 1934:120.

22. Interview with Seydou Camara, June 1978.

23. Interview with Sedu Traore, August 1973.

24. Sedu Traore made this statement in August 1973, after the ground had not been dry for months. He noted that fact, saying it was the work of smiths, undertaken after the marabouts had tried and failed to bring rain. He further pointed out that marabouts would normally demand a large payment for their services before making the attempt. From August on, after I had known Sedu for five months and had worked closely with him as an apprentice for four, he began to compare the position of smiths and that of the marabouts in the context of smiths' roles and with emphasis on the relative ethics and abilities of the two groups. He noted that the marabouts tended toward duplicity and, at times, dishonesty, by misrepresenting their capabilities and seeking to add to their personal fortunes. Most smiths would say such things, because marabouts are the chief competitors in many of their activities.

25. An introduction to the literature about African divination can be found in Bascom 1969, Evans-Pritchard 1937, Gebauer 1964, Maclean 1971, and Turner 1967.

26. Bird 1974:12–19, lines 302–507, provides a vivid view of several Mande divination techniques.

27. Interview with Sekuba Camara, June 1978.

28. Monteil 1924:103–104.

29. See Laye 1971a:20–26, 28. Laye 1971b:122 describes the snake as advancing rapidly, making various gestures with its head and mouth, returning to its original position, and repeating the process. These motions would then be interpreted in dreams during the night.

30. Charles Bird, personal communication, September 1973, and interviews with Bourama Soumaoro (Satigi's son), February 1973; Kalilou Tera, July 1977; Sekuba Camara, June 1978.

31. See Rodney 1970:11, 237–238 and Murdock 1959:71.

32. Laing 1825:245–246.

33. Imperato 1977a:203–206 and Harley 1941a. Ouologuem 1968:169–171 refers to the use of trained serpents and to techniques of training poisonous serpents to kill specific people through a conditioning program that involves stimuli of pain and smell.

34. This usage carries over into the western hemisphere. Marie Leveau, one of the better known *hoodoo* doctors to practice in New Orleans, was allegedly called to her profession by a large rattlesnake that came and spoke to her, then remained with her throughout her career, as did the small black snake of Laye's father. See Hurston 1935:240–243.

35. Interview with Seydou Camara, January 1973.

36. The names of these figures remain problematic. Seydou Camara provided me with the meanings and names of figures used in cowry and stone divination in January 1973. Sedu Traore and Charles Bird provided those for *cenda* in August and April 1973, respectively. In the latter divination technique, *kumardise* is the name given to upside down triangles, suggesting ancestors and death. In stone divination the same name, this time attached to a triangle which faces up, connotes the idea of man, and, as it was explained to me, does not carry the meanings associated with either of the *cenda* triangles. Considerable research is needed to clarify the meanings of divination figure names. Clearly, they are, like all vital symbols, subject to variation and transformation, and we should expect to find meanings changing from region to region, community to community, and person to person.

37. Laing 1825:298.

38. Bird 1974:117.

39. Brett-Smith 1984:141.

40. Bird 1974:117.

41. Interview with Sekuba Camara, June 1978. He also said that foreseeing in water is called *ka yelike jila;* throwing cowries, *nkoloni fili;* and rubbing sandals, simply *sambarakòròw,* "old sandals."

42. This technique is called *duga,* "the vulture." It is worth noting that as much variation occurs in the use of soothsaying techniques as in the use of terminology for concepts such as sorcery. Often different techniques have the same names.

43. Sekuba Camara called this kind of divination *nkonsigi.*

44. Objects quite similar in appearance are known widely in west Africa, among the Senufo, for example, and the Toma and Bete. The basic form remains the same; specific ingredients can be shifted to change the object's function. Invariably, however, their function revolves around the harnessing of energy. Paulme 1962:166–167 discusses another type of divination object, a sculpted clay head called *gle.* The expert practitioner who owns the sculpture also carries an animal tail bundle. Imperato 1977a:36–37, 57–58 cites another type of Mande device, called *sirikun,* which is made from an animal horn, hair, and hide. It too can be used for divination, but it is also said to be able, when so directed by a ritual expert, to inflict all manner of unpleasantries on people, according to its specific design and ingredients.

45. Interview with Sedu Traore, September 1973. Most of the medicines Sedu uses are not included in either Dalziel 1937 or Traore 1965, suggesting that much research remains to be carried out and that traditional west African herbal-based medicines are numerous indeed. As befits the principles of *dalilu* knowledge, I was not privy to the names of many medicines or their ingredients. In some instances I provide an etymology for the names of diseases and cures. In numerous instances, however, etymologies were not known by either the people I interviewed or my research assistants.

46. Raffenel 1856:417.

47. See Herbert 1975. Herbert was most helpful in discussing the topic with me and in providing me with an advance copy of the text. See also Imperato 1968:868–873 and 1977a:162–175.

48. See Laing 1825:339–340.
49. See Imperato 1968:869–870.
50. Park 1799:276–277.
51. Ibid.
52. Laing 1825:371.
53. Gray and Dochard 1825:140.
54. Travélé 1913:22, 136, 140 defines amulet as *farila*, *sebe*, *tafo*, and *basi*, while defining *basi* as "remède, fetiche," and *boli* as "idole, gris-gris." Bazin 1965 [1906]: 59, 80, 520 defines *basi* as "remède (moins employé que *foura*)" and "gris-gris, remède superstitieux," *boli* as "gris-gris, fetiche" and *sebe* as "amulette (suspendue au cou dans un sacket)." The Commission Technique du Bambara de l'education de base 1968:2, 23 defines *basi* as "fetiche" and *seben* as "gris-gris." For additional thoughts on *boli* and *basi* see Delafosse 1923:379–380, 382–383.
55. Henry 1910:63–67 insists that "tax" is a proper translation, but the argument is based on his feeling that the Bamana are slaves to their superstitions. Bazin 1965 [1906]:513 describes *saraka* as "alms giving" and "consecration by the laying on of hands."
56. As to the exact nature of these personal powers, we find ourselves again in a dilemma of terminology. The forces that inhabit and animate human beings receive a variety of names and a multitude of interpretations among the Mande. Brett-Smith 1984:139 uses the term *nganinya*, which she defines as "individual will." Cissé 1973:157 interprets the concept (which he spells *naniya*) as faith, the resolute inner belief from which people think and act. One's "vital force," *nyama*, can also be seen as the power implanted in amulets. Sedu Traore said the power was a part of the blacksmiths' patrimony, *fatyen*.
57. For examples of the *kòmò* signs, see Dieterlen and Cissé 1972:81–176, and especially the shapes of the signs such as that for *ja*, the soul of one's recessive sex, on p. 112.
58. Laing 1825:236, 238. See also Park 1815:38–39.
59. See Daget and Konipo 1951 and Holas 1950. Herbert 1973 and 1984 addresses copper amulets on a broad west African scale. Arkell 1937:152–155 discusses spiral brass amulets used in the eastern Sudan and Egypt.
60. *Cenyon* can also mean "colleague" and, in the plural form, "people who collect together," that is, are each other's equals. Interviews with Magan Fane, August and September 1973.
61. Jobson 1968 [1623]:63.
62. Park 1799:38–43, 187, 206, 235–236.
63. Gray and Dochard 1825:317.
64. Interviews with Magan Fane, August and September 1973.
65. Interviews with Sedu Traore, 1973. I observed a number of such devices in blacksmiths' forges, but only Sedu would allow me to photograph his.
66. Not all smiths wear these amulets, which occur in various types. One is pure white; another has long, thin red and blue triangular shapes that point toward the bead's center, and is quite large. In Ségou I met a smith wearing this large version with two portions missing. Upon my inquiry, he informed me that the bead had popped on two occasions when individuals had attempted to poison him. Interview with Kodari Fane, May 1973.
67. Hopkins 1972:99.
68. Ibid.
69. Sedu Traore made this point emphatically to me during an interview in September 1973.
70. My data derive from a series of interviews with Sedu Traore from April to September 1973. On one occasion I transported Sedu and a young lady back to her family's village, where she and Sedu proceeded to argue behind closed doors for the ter-

mination of the lady's relationship with a future husband. Sedu was successful, and received two chickens for his trouble.

71. Pascal James Imperato, personal communication, December 1971.

72. See Laing 1825:297–298, Dieterlen 1951:114, and Pâques 1954:58.

73. See Monteil 1924:294. In the end this action did little to detour the young rogue, who, in fact, acted brilliantly within the cultural frame of social-political dialogue between *badenya* and *fadenya*.

74. The view I reflect in this section is that maintained by the practitioners themselves. For a view from the vantage point of Western medicine, see Imperato 1977a: 186–187, 189–190.

75. I interviewed nineteen smiths on this topic. Fifteen were Kantes from the same town and one was a master smith from the region of Ségou. I must note that I worked in Mali for over seven months before any smith was willing even to mention the topic. Among the nonsmiths with whom I discussed the operation and its cultural frame were Abdulaye Sylla (February 1973), Abdulaye Sissoko (April, August, and October 1973), Dugutigi Traore (a nonpracticing smith of the Sarracole ancestry from Nioro, April 1973), Chiekna Sangare (June and September 1973), Kalilou Tera and Sekuba Camara (June and July 1978). The information published on Bamana and other Mande societies' circumcision and excision practices is most useful. Jobson 1968 [1623]:139–147 witnessed circumcision in 1620 on the Gambia River, and noted that it was associated among the Mandingo with a tremendous celebration and that the individual he saw undergo the operation did so with great calm and dignity. Park 1799:265–266 observed circumcision's association with subsequent marriage and prolific child production, and described the ceremonial aftermath of the surgery. Among the more modern authors, the following include discussions of the operation and its meanings: Chéron 1933; Cissé 1971, especially pp. 149–151, where the souls *ni* and *ja* are considered; Dieterlen 1951:57–61 (the *ni* and *ja* or *dya*), 64–65 (*wanzo*), 180–188 (circumcision and excision); Fadiga 1934; Henry 1910:124–198; Labouret 1934:77–87; Monteil 1924:234, 240–248; Pâques 1954:91–93; Tauxier 1927:390–410; Traore 1965:276–277, 483–484; Zahan 1960:85. Dieterlen describes the force she calls *wanzo* as a negative, destructive, and "evil" type of energy lodged in every young man's foreskin and every young woman's clitoris as a result of a mythical event involving the creator woman known as Musokoroni. She says it represents disorder and, therefore, prevents people from establishing harmonious marriages. Thus, social stability and procreation demand that it be removed.

76. Interestingly, Dieterlen 1951:188 indicates that the female members of blacksmith families who excise in the region of Ségou protect themselves from what she calls the *wanzo* emitted during the surgery with bracelets and charms and a black salve that they smear on their eyes.

77. See Dieterlen 1951:181–184, who provides the following gloss for the Bamana name: "head of the knife, mother of the circumcision."

78. Zahan 1960:127.

79. His words were: *A bè ja nyè kè!*

80. See Tegnaeus 1950:1–53, especially pp. 43–48.

81. Bird 1974:introduction.

IV. THE BLACKSMITHS' SCULPTURE

Parts of the section on *kòmò* masks appeared in my *Secret Sculptures of Komo: Art and Power in Bamana (Bambara) Initiation Associations*. Working Papers in the Traditional Arts, 4. Philadelphia: Institute for the Study of Human Issues, 1979.

1. Zahan 1963:127.

2. Mary Jo Arnoldi, personal communication, 1981.

3. Goldwater 1960, Kjersmeier 1935–1938, and Lem 1948.

4. James T. Brink, personal communication, July 1981.

5. *A dila cogo ca nyè, a baara ka ce na.* One might also hear: "The way it's sculpted is good," *Bo cogo a ca nyi.* For more information about this category of sculpture, see Arnoldi 1977 and 1983 and Imperato 1972a.

6. For additional information about *kore* symbolism and the sculpture, see Henry 1908 and 1910:121–126 and Zahan 1960:121–370.

7. See Fernandez 1969 and 1973.

8. Ezra 1981.

9. For examples see Arnoldi 1977 and 1983.

10. Interviews with Sidi Ballo, June and July 1978, and with Sedu Traore and his family, July 1978.

11. Interview with Sedu Traore, July 1978.

12. A related type of praise in the Mande languages is to call people "children" of their profession, such as "children of blacksmithing," *numudenw.*

13. Interviews with Dramane Dunbiya and Magan Fane, August 1973.

14. James T. Brink, personal communication, November 1980.

15. Kalilou Tera, personal communications, June and July 1978.

16. Interview with Sidi Ballo, June 1978.

17. Travélé 1913:208 and Bazin 1965 [1906]:390.

18. Commission Technique du Bambara de l'education de base 1968:16.

19. Ibid., 20.

20. Bazin 1965 [1906]:458. He says that *mani nyège* means "to sculpt a statue" and that *nyègèba* means "sculptor, painter, dyer, embroiderer," a synonym of *nyègèlikela.*

21. John Lewis, personal communication, May 1980.

22. Perhaps the finest example of this is the iron figure of a woman in the collection of Paul and Ruth Tishman (Ill. 64). See McNaughton 1981:28.

23. Kalilou Tera, personal communication, August 1977.

24. Charles Bird, personal communication, August 1976.

25. *Jaga jòn bèe n'i la kunun-kan.* Bird 1974:11, line 282.

26. McNaughton 1979b:23.

27. *Ka bada fereka,*
    Musa wulen kanin jina y'o nyinabo la.
Excerpt from a blacksmiths' song performed by Seydou Camara, June 1978. Transcribed and translated by Sekuba Camara and the author.

28. *A y'a woloma, woloma, yii!* This line is from a lengthy narrative performed by Seydou Camara in June 1978 for the author. It tells of his own personal history. Transcribed and translated by Sekuba Camara and the author.

29. *An ka sira jèya de! Mori ka sira jèya tè.*

30. Interview with Sedu Traore, August 1973.

31. Ibid.

32. The judgment was made on the basis of shape, dot decoration, and the pattern of rust present on the piece. It was made initially by Bourama Soumaoro in April 1973 and corroborated by Magan Fane in July 1973. Oral tradition surrounds things such as spears with a magic aura, just as it does great heroes, all of course in the name of enlarging the symbolism of grandeur that animates those heroes in the epics and songs. Innes 1974:121, note 598, recounts a legend that states that the great fighter and strategist Fakoli (whom he calls Faa Koli) had a special spear which, when driven into the body of some unhappy foe, produced nine dangerous bloody wounds. For data on the sacred use of spears within the *jo (djo)* of Bougouni, see Pâques 1964:79–80.

33. Pascal James Imperato, personal communication, March 1974, provided me with the names used for these lamps in the Bamana regions where I did not work.

34. Haselberger 1965:445.

35. See Desplagnes 1907:fig. 165.

36. Anita J. Glaze, personal communication, March 1974.

37. Delafosse 1912:pl. XLI. The legend beneath the plates locates Donko in the Circle of Gaoua. The author made his illustration under very poor lighting conditions, but it is clear that this "kind of burial vault" contained at least twelve wooden figures, a spear head, pots, a calabash dance rattle, and the lamp.

38. René Bravmann, personal communication, October 1980.

39. Judith Perani, personal communication, April 1974.

40. This lamp to the god Shango appears on the cover of the *Kroeber Anthropological Society Papers* 36 (1967). William Bascom, who documented the lamp, also observed similar lamps, up to three feet tall, used by worshippers of Ogun, god of iron, at Ila, where they were carried from one *orisha* shrine to another as part of the annual Ogun cermonies. William Bascom, personal communication, March 1972. For the Ifa lamp, see Beier 1959:56, 58.

41. von Luschan 1919:429, 679.

42. I interviewed this Fane smith in August 1973.

43. I saw the lamp in the shop of one of Bamako's reputable art dealers. He was not sure of its region of origin.

44. The technique involves passing red-hot iron between the tips of a pair of smith's tongs while twisting the metal with another pair of tongs.

45. Interview with Bourama Soumaoro, February 1973.

46. Interview with Ba Sinale Konate, June 1978.

47. *Se y'a ta ye, jamana y'a ta ye, nisòngo be sara a ye, mugu y'a ta ye, marafa y'a ta ye, mògò y'a ta ye, bagan y'a ta ye.* Interview with Sidi Ballo, June 1978.

48. Interview with Mama Konate, March 1973.

49. Interview with Ba Sinale Konate, June 1978.

50. Kalilou Tera, personal communication, August 1977.

51. The shaft of one lamp was likened to the *dangala (dankala)*, a type of poisonous snake. The other was likened to the *saje*, a class of snakes that are pale in color.

52. Interview with Sedu Traore, September 1973.

53. Kalilou Tera, personal communication, July 1977.

54. Zahan 1950:136.

55. Imperato and Shamir 1970:40.

56. Dieterlen and Cissé 1972:123.

57. Ibid., 127.

58. Ibid., 170.

59. Ibid., 159.

60. Ibid., 134.

61. Ibid., 117.

62. Ibid., 156.

63. Ibid., 153.

64. Pascal James Imperato, personal communication, March 1974.

65. Cissé 1971:149–151.

66. Pâques 1964:68.

67. Kalilou Tera, personal communication, July 1977.

68. Pascal James Imperato, personal communication, March 1974.

69. See McNaughton 1975:introduction.

70. Cole 1972:fig. 51.

71. Thompson 1971b:II/1–3.

72. von Luschan 1919:Taf. 108.

73. See Herskovits 1967:I, pl. 13.

74. Griaule and Dieterlen 1965.

75. Laude 1973:fig. 40, 41, 67.

76. See the field notes by Charles Bird in McNaughton 1975, as well as Imperato 1978:23–24 and Desplagnes 1907:pl. LXXXV.

77. Arnaud 1921:fig. 3.
78. See Cole 1972:86.
79. Imperato 1983:45. He also says they are called *sono*, a name normally associated with the more westerly regions of the Mande diaspora.
80. Ezra 1983:40 and 1986:9 and Pâques 1956:375. Imperato 1983:45 notes that similar iron sculptures were manufactured near Bamako for tourists in the 1960s and 1970s.
81. Ezra 1986:9.
82. Goldwater 1960:17.
83. Imperato 1983:39–40, 41.
84. Interview with Dramane Dunbiya, April 1973.
85. Ibid.
86. Interview with Magan Fane, August 1973.
87. Goody 1971 describes the reasons why horses became such effective symbols of military power in west Africa, by explaining the manners in which they enhanced the capabilities of those groups who used them.
88. See field notes in McNaughton 1975.
89. Interview with Sidi Ballo, June 1978.
90. Ezra 1986:30 and Cashion 1984:I, 159–162.
91. Imperato 1983:45.
92. Traore 1962:23.
93. Interview with twelve members of the Kante family of smiths, September 1973.
94. Interview with Dramane Dunbiya, April 1973.
95. Imperato 1983:27–31, 45.
96. Peter M. Weil, personal communication, August 1981. See also Weil 1973.
97. Ibid. See also da Mota 1960:630–631.
98. da Mota 1965:149, 150 refers to a text written in 1506 and 1508 by Duarte Pacheco Pereira, called "Esmeraldo de Situ Orbis" (Book 1, chapter 29), and to unspecified Portuguese texts.
99. These data about *sono* were compiled by da Mota and presented in the articles cited in notes 97 and 98 above. In addition, Lampreia 1962:entries 412–417 described and catalogued sixteen of the staffs. *Escultura Africana* illustrates two, one of which is topped with a camel. Bassani 1979 has summarized some of da Mota's findings and provided illustrations of a number of outstanding staffs.
100. Koroma 1939.
101. da Mota 1965:152.
102. I witnessed such behavior on more than one occasion. The reason for it involved both the protection of nonmembers from its power and the protection of *kòmò* secrecy. Now, with Islam present in most communities, the secrecy also becomes a kind of diplomatic behavior which enhances tranquil relations between strong religious forces.
103. In his lengthy section about *boliw*, Henry 1910:253–258 claims that human torsos were sometimes used as part of the ingredients, but he seems to have been as strongly offended by what he considered a particularly pagan combination of ingredients compiled, as he puts it, through sympathetic magic. His illustrations 148 and 152 most effectively capture the visual characteristics I describe. See also Monteil 1924:270, 273–278 and Dieterlen 1951:145.
104. Dieterlen 1951:92–93.
105. Interview with Magan Fane, August 1973.
106. I witnessed this event in the home of a *kòmòtigi* whose *jo* was located in the Circle of Bamako in February 1973. Alternate names that imply this power were recorded by Henry 1910:187–188 and Monteil 1924:271, but their etymologies are very uncertain and we must, therefore, consider them only tentatively applicable. Henry records the term *kòmò-kala*, which I would translate as "handle or staff of the

kòmò." The use of the term reflects the use of another, *nyamakala*, which identifies individuals as energy sources. Monteil recorded the term *tama gengen ba*, which he did not translate. *Gengen* could be *gwen*, "chase," repeated. This would make the phrase read "the large *tama* chaser," thereby likening the horn to a spear *(tama)* and reflecting the notion of chasing as it is used in the context of the *kòmò*.

107. The prices are those one would find in communities for new objects. In the relatively rare instances when one encounters *kòmò* horns for sale in the art shops of large towns, they reflect their special value by being exceptionally expensive.

108. Charles Bird, personal communication, May 1977.

109. Dieterlen and Cissé 1972:48 indicate that materials such as various types of leaves, powdered bones, and powdered minerals go into the making of *kòmò* masks as well, and the information certainly fits our sense of these masks as the most complex of *daliluw* compositions.

110. Interview with Sedu Traore, October 1973. He meant that the unfortunate individual would go insane.

111. Ibid.

112. The smith was Sedu Traore and he expected to construct the mask in spring 1974. He informed me of it in October 1973.

113. I qualify this statement because in one instance I know of, Sedu Traore was commissioned to construct a *kòmòkun* for an association branch in the Bèlèdougou region well to the north of his home. Sedu was not inclined to provide any more information on the subject and so it was not clear to me whether he intended to manufacture a very straightforward mask, leaving the complexities of personalized *daliluw* for another smith to carry out, or whether he actually intended to dance the mask himself at that branch.

114. Rubin 1974:11 and Bohannan 1953:84–85.

115. . . . *I bada koma siyaman ye,*
           I ma wara ye.

Excerpt from a song sung by *kòmò* masters during divination proceedings when they dance the mask, or simply for entertainment and festivals. This version was performed by Seydou Camara in June 1978. Transcribed and translated by Sekuba Camara and the author.

116. Travélé 1929:135 describes these costumes. See also Monteil 1924:271 and Henry 1910:148. Smiths and *kòmò* members between Bamako and Bougouni told me about the costume.

117. See Zahan 1974:pl. XXIV. He made the photograph at Douga during a daytime performance of the *jo*. He is one of a select group of Westerners who have actually seen the masks in situ; another is Hans Himmelheber, who made the celebrated photograph illustrated in Goldwater 1960. Henry 1910 made pictures of beautiful *nama* and *kònò* masks but apparently never saw a *kòmò* mask.

118. A notion of the range of style in *kòmò* masks can be acquired by consulting the following works: Dieterlen and Cissé 1972:pl. II, III; Goldwater 1960:11, ills. 21–23; and Zahan 1974:pl. XXIII, XXIV. Of these eight masks, one substitutes small antelope horns for large ones at the rear of the dome shape, diminishing the size of that extension. In two masks the dome is not emphasized and merely appears as a thick area behind the mouth. Two masks display teeth carved into that long mouth; the rest do not. Porcupine quills are attached to five of the eight; feathers appear only twice, once in association with quills. On one, the skull of a bird appears with a series of small clay lumps, the latter resembling miniature *boliw*. One of the masks illustrated by Dieterlen and Cissé is very unusual because it is not totally covered with sacrificial materials; although they are present, the mask seems designed to reveal the features carved on the wood. During my own work I encountered a *kòmò* mask which, like this, allowed the carved details to be clearly visible. Here, though, sacrificial matter had originally been thickly applied in two circular areas on either side of the dome

shape and the mask was much narrower and very much more elongated than that cited by Dieterlen and Cissé. The latter mask is also the only one which suggests in its appearance a single rather than an assemblage of animals.

119. Zahan 1960:252, 268.

120. *Fakoli kunba, Fakoli daba.*
This line is present in many versions of Fakoli's famous praise song, the *Janjon*. The song is widely known in its various versions across Mali today and is often performed as part of the Sunjata epic. For additional information about it, see Bird and Kendall 1980:20–21. One version of it is published in Innes 1974:260–323. The reader may also consult Diabaté 1970.

121. Zahan 1960:80.

122. Kalilou Tera, personal communication, 1977.

123. The bamboo horn was reported in use by Travélé 1929:134 in western Bamana country. Henry 1910:147 indicates that around Ségou the sound was produced by the largest flute that is a part of the *boli*, while other *jo* officials accompanied the dancer with bamboo flutes. Monteil's data (1924:271) are similar. He indicates that the same instruments were used by the dancing mask wearer and that the sounds could be interpreted by the *jo's* bard to the *kòmòtigi*, the results being considered divinatory pronouncements.

124. Charles Bird and Kalilou Tera, personal communication, July 1977.

125. Though many smiths provided and verified much of the information that follows about performance, Sekuba Camara worked with me extensively on it. I must thank him for helping me bring it into focus.

126. *Ee jina muso . . . n'bolo bila,*
N' ye doonin fò di nya ye.
Son tè mògò n'i kònò rò ce,
N' bolo bila n' ye kuma dinya ye.
This excerpt is from one of Seydou Camara's *kòmò* songs. Recorded, transcribed, and translated by Sekuba Camara and the author, June 1978.

127. *Sumoso kadogèlèn Hari n' a natuma to,*
K'a nalen ko laje.
Sumoso kòkòle Hari bada na tuma to.
Performed by Seydou Camara, June 1978. Transcribed and translated by Sekuba Camara and the author.

128. *Jòn kunandi i ma kun i ye*
Don bèe dugu sa jè ko tè kele di.
Mògò bi tògòma,
Kaban k'i sunuma dinya rò.
Don bèe dugu sa jè ko man kan.
Performed by Seydou Camara, June 1978. Transcribed and translated by Sekuba Camara and the author.

129. *N'be n'bolo su i nyè na.*
Kalilou Tera, personal communication, 1977.

130. Bird 1974: introduction provides a discussion of the importance of discovering the secrets of a person's power.

131. Performed by Seydou Camara, July 1978. Recorded, transcribed, and translated by Sekuba Camara and the author.

132. Monteil 1924:299.

133. Henry 1910:148 and Monteil 1924:298.

134. Thompson 1971a:379–380.

135. Interview with Yaya Traore, August 1978.

V. THE MANDE SMITHS AS MEN OF MEANS

1. See, for example, Zahan 1960:55–57, 74, 78, 306 or Imperato 1983:29–31, 34, 42–45, 47–49.
2. Brooks 1985:20–21, 46–49, 51–53, 77–78, 85, 176, and especially 132–136.
3. *Numukènin yiri dòn bali,*
   Ja bali.
   Numuden kulu tè sèlèdo sènè.
   Numukènin nègèdòn bali,
   Ja baliya.
   Numukè kulu tè sèlèdo sènè.
   Numukènin jala dòn bali,
   Ja baliya.
   Numuden kulu tè sèlèdo sènè.
Excerpt from a song sung at a bird masquerade performance in a small town west of Bamako on the Mande Plateau, June 1978. Transcribed and translated by Kalilou Tera and the author.
4. Bailleul 1981:147 and Kalilou Tera, personal communication, June 1978.
5. Kalilou Tera, personal communication, June 1978.
6. Bailleul 1981:170.
7. Bird and Kendall 1980:15–16.
8. *Sa ka yafa i'ma, balima saya,* or *fò ti mògò banna,* or *ah, Dankelen mògò, fò ti mògò banna,* or *ne bolo bè n'kò i fanaye.* All of these praise lines are from a song sung at the bird masquerade performance I attended on the Mande Plateau in June 1978. In the second praise line *mògò,* meaning "person," was used in the song to refer specifically but indirectly to the masquerade dancer. The same is true in the next praise line, where the word "person" follows the phrase "savage and solitary beast." Sometimes this is done in response to interdictions against speaking the name of a masked dancer and sometimes it is done simply as a matter of style. Translations and explanations of these praise lines were provided by Kalilou Tera, June 1978.
9. See chapter III for an earlier reference to this performance, during which the song excerpts presented in the previous footnote were recorded.
10. Bailleul 1981:39. Kalilou Tera provided the etymology, in June 1978.
11. Bailleul 1981:159–160. Bird and Kendall 1980:16, 18 discuss this concept and, in footnote 3, pp. 23–24, demonstrate the potential relationship between the words for "means" and "eye."
12. Bird and Kendall 1980:17–21.
13. See chapter I.
14. Tegnaeus 1950:47 discusses beliefs about Bamana and Maninka smiths. He also discusses similar beliefs among the Bozo, Somono, and Sorko (p. 43), and farther afield in Burkina Faso, the Bobo (pp. 42–43), Lobi (p. 41), Gurma (p. 40), Mossi (pp. 37–39), and Dogon (pp. 16–20).
15. Hutton 1961:xiii, in the foreword to his first edition, says some 5,000 publications dealt with caste in India as of 1946.
16. Dumont 1970:21.
17. Dumont 1970:46–61, 212.
18. Hutton 1961:180 and Ketkar 1909:121.
19. Srinivas 1965 [1952]:26.
20. Stevenson 1954:46.
21. Dumont 1970:201.
22. Vaughan 1970:59 discusses this phenomenon. See also Cline 1937:114–140 for the classic summary of these kinds of data, especially his charts, pp. 128–140.
23. Berreman 1963:198.
24. Ibid.

25. Ibid.
26. Vaughan 1970:62.
27. Wright forthcoming.
28. Vaughan 1970:61–62, 80–81, 85, 89.
29. Wright forthcoming.
30. Ibid.
31. Gellner 1970:26.
32. Karp forthcoming.
33. Ibid.
34. Kendall 1982.
35. Barnes 1980:9–13.

Bibliography

Adandé, Alexandre. 1951. "Masques africaines." *Notes africaines* no. 51:78–80.

Aitchison, Leslie. 1960. *A History of Metals.* 2 vols. New York: Interscience Publishers.

Ajayi, J. F. A. de, and Michael Crowder, eds. 1972. *History of West Africa.* Vol. 1. New York: Columbia University Press.

al-Bakri, Abū. 1965 [1911–1913]. *Description de l'Afrique septentrionale.* Translated by Mac Guckin de Slane. Paris: A. Maisonneuve.

American Society for Metals. 1961. *Metals Handbook.* Metals Park: American Society for Metal.

Amselle, Jean Loup. 1972. "Histoire et structure sociale du Wasulu avant Samori." Paper presented at the Conference on Manding Studies, University of London, School of Oriental and African Studies.

Andree, Richard. 1914. "Seltene Ethnographica des städtischen Gewerbe-Museums zu Ulm." *Baessler-Archiv* 4:29–38.

Appia, Béatrice. 1943. "Masques de Guinée française et de Casamance." *Journal de la Société des Africanistes* 13:153–182.

———. 1944. "Notes sur la génie des eaux en Guinée." *Journal de la Société des Africanistes* 14:33–41.

———. 1965. "Les forgerons du Fouta-Djallon." *Journal de la Société des Africanistes* 35(2):317–352.

Archinard, Louis. 1882. "Fabrication de la poudre à tirer par les Malinkés du pays de Kita et du Fouladougou." *Revue d'Ethnographie* 1:526–527.

———. 1884. "La fabrication du fer dans le Soudan." *Revue d'Ethnographie* 3:249–255.

Arkell, Anthony John. 1937. "The Double Spiral Amulet." *Sudan Notes and Records* 20:152–155.

———. 1966. "The Iron Age in the Sudan." *Current Anthropology* 7(4):451–484.

Arnaud, Robert. 1921. "Notes sur les Montagnards Habé des cercles de Bandiagara et de Hombori (Soudan français)." *Revue d'Ethnographie et des Traditions populaires* 2:241–313.

Arnoldi, Mary Jo. 1977. *Bamana and Bozo Puppetry of the Segou Region Youth Societies.* West Lafayette: Purdue University.

———. 1983. "Puppet Theatre in the Segu Region in Mali." Ph.D. diss., Indiana University.

"Art from the Sahel." 1974. Exhibition checklist. New York: African-American Institute.

Arts primitifs dans les ateliers d'artistes. 1967. Paris: Musée de l'Homme.

Atkins, Guy, ed. 1972. *Manding Art and Civilisation.* London: Studio International.

Aubert, Alfred. 1939. "Coutume Bambara (cercle de Bougouni) (1932)." In *Coutumiers juridiques de l'A.O.F.* Paris: Larose, pp. 2–126.

Avery, Donald H., and Peter Schmidt. 1979. "A Metallurgical Study of the Iron Bloomery, Particularly as Practiced in Buhaya." *Journal of Metals* 31(10):14–20.

Awooner, Kofi. 1976. *The Breast of the Earth.* Garden City: Doubleday.

Ayensu, Edward S. 1978. *Medicinal Plants of West Africa.* Algonac, Mich.: Reference Publications.

Bailleul, Charles. 1981. *Petit Dictionnaire, Bambara-Français, Français-Bambara*. Amersham: Avesbury Publishing Co.

Balandier, Georges. 1948. "Danses de sortie d'excision à Boffa, Guinée Française." *Notes africaines* no. 38 : 11–12.

———. 1968. *Daily Life in the Kingdom of the Kongo*. Translated by Helen Weaver. New York: Pantheon Books.

Bambara from Saint-Louis. 1948. "La colonie bambara de Ndioloffen et de Khor à Saint-Louis." *Notes africaines* no. 40 : 18–20.

Bandi, Hans-Georg, and H. Breuil. 1961. *The Art of the Stone Age*. Translated by Ann E. Keep. London: Methuen.

Barnes, Sandra T. 1980. *Ogun: An Old God for a New Age*. Occasional Papers in Social Change, 3. Philadelphia: Institute for the Study of Human Issues.

Barth, Heinrich. 1857. *Travels and Discoveries in North and Central Africa 1849– 1855*. London: Longman, Brown, Green, Longmans & Roberts.

Bascom, William Russell. 1967. *African Arts*. Berkeley: Lowie Museum of Anthropology.

———. 1969. *Ifa Divination*. Ibadan: Ibadan University Press.

Bassani, Ezio. 1979. "Sono from Guinea Bissau." *African Arts* 12(4) : 44–47, 91.

Baumann, Hermann, and Diedrich Westermann. 1948. *Les peuples et les civilisations de l'Afrique, suivi des langues et de l'education*. Paris: Payot.

Bazin, Hippolyte. 1965 [1906]. *Dictionnaire Bambara-Français précédé d'un abrégé de grammaire Bambara*. Ridgewood. N.J.: Gregg Press.

Bedaux, Rogier M.A. 1972. "Tellem, reconnaissance archéologique d'une culture de l'Ouest Africain au moyen âge: recherches architectoniques." *Journal de la Société des Africanistes* 42(2) : 103–185.

———. 1974. "Tellem, reconnaissance archéologique d'une culture de l'Ouest Africain au moyen âge: les appuienuque." *Journal de la Société des Africanistes* 44 : 7–42.

———. 1977. *Tellem, een bijdrage tot de geschiedenis van de Republiek Mali*. Berg en Dal: Afrika Museum.

———. 1980. "The Geographic Distribution of Footed Bowls in the Upper and Middle Niger Region." In *West African Culture Dynamics: Archaeological and Historical Perspectives*. Edited by B. K. Swartz and Raymond E. Dumett. The Hague: Mouton, pp. 247–258.

Bedaux, Rogier M. A., T. S. Constandse-Westermann, L. Hacquebord, A. G. Lange, and J. D. van der Waals. 1979. "Recherches archéologiques dans le Delta Interieur de Niger." *Palaeohistoria* 20 : 91–220.

Beier, Ulli. 1959. *A Year of Sacred Festivals in One Yoruba Town*. Lagos: Nigeria Magazine.

Bellamy, Dr. 1886. "Notes ethnographiques recueillies dans le Haut-Sénégal." *Revue d'Ethnographie* 5 : 81–84.

Ben-Amos, Paula. 1976. "Men and Animals in Benin Art." *Man* 11(2) : 243–252.

Berreman, Gerald D. 1963. *Hindus of the Himalayas*. Berkeley: University of California Press.

Binger, Louis Gustave. 1892. *Du Niger au Golfe de Guinée par le pays de Kong et le Mossi*. 2 vols. Paris: Hachette.

Bird, Charles S. 1971. "Oral Art in the Mande." In *Papers on the Manding*. Edited by Carleton T. Hodge. Bloomington: Indiana University Press, pp. 15–26.

———. 1972. "Heroic Songs of the Mande Hunters." In *African Folklore*. Edited by Richard Dorson. Garden City: Doubleday, pp. 275–294.

———. 1976. "Poetry in the Mande: Its Form and Meaning." *Poetics* 5(2) : 89–100.

Bird, Charles S., ed. 1982. *The Dialects of Mandekan*. Bloomington: African Studies Program, Indiana University.

Bird, Charles S., with Mamadou Koita and Bourama Soumaoro. 1974. *The Songs of Seydou Camara, Vol. I, Kambili.* Bloomington: African Studies Program, Indiana University.

Bird, Charles S., and Martha B. Kendall. 1980. "The Mande Hero." In *Explorations in African Systems of Thought.* Edited by Ivan Karp and Charles S. Bird. Bloomington: Indiana University Press, pp. 13–26.

Bohannan, Paul. 1953. *The Tiv of Central Nigeria.* London: International African Institute.

———. 1963. *Social Anthropology.* New York: Holt, Rinehart and Winston.

Bouys, P. 1943. "Samory et les forgerons de Dabakala." *Notes africaines* no. 17: 11–12.

Bovill, E. W. 1968. *The Golden Trade of the Moors.* 2d ed. London: Oxford University Press.

Bovill, E. W., ed. 1964. *Missions to the Niger: The Letters of Major Alexander Gordon Laing, 1824–1826.* Cambridge: Cambridge University Press.

Brasseur, George. 1961. "Étude de géographie regionale: le village de Tenentou (Mali)." *Bulletin de l'I.F.A.N.*, ser. B, 23(3–4):607–675.

Brasseur, George, and G. LeMoal. 1963. *Cartes ethnodémographiques de l'Afrique Occidentale.* Feuilles 3, 4 (northern, southern, central and eastern Mali). Daker: I.F.A.N.

Brasseur, George, and G. Savonnet. 1960. *Carte ethnodémographiques de l'Afrique Occidentale.* Feuille 2 (western Mali). Dakar: I.F.A.N.

Brasseur-Marion, Paule. 1964. *Bibliographie générale du Mali (anciens Soudan français et Haut-Sénégal-Niger).* Dakar: I.F.A.N.

———. 1972. "Documentation concernant les Manding." Paper presented at the Conference on Manding Studies, University of London, School of Oriental and African Studies.

Bravmann, René A. 1973. *Open Frontiers: The Mobility of Art in Black Africa.* Seattle: University of Washington Press.

———. 1974. *Islam and Tribal Art in West Africa.* Cambridge: Cambridge University Press.

———. 1975. "Masking Tradition and Figurative Art among the Islamized Marka." In *African Images; Essays in African Iconology.* Edited by Daniel F. McCall and Edna G. Bay. New York: Africana Publishing Co., pp. 144–169.

Brett-Smith, Sarah Catharine. 1982. "Symbolic Blood: Cloths for Excised Women." *Res* 3(Spring):15–31.

———. 1983. "The Poisonous Child." *Res* 6(Autumn):47–64.

———. 1984. "Speech Made Visible: The Irregular as a System of Meaning." *Empirical Studies of the Arts* 2(2):127–147.

Brink, James T. 1978. "Communicating Ideology in Bamana Rural Theater Performance." *Research in African Literature* 9(3):382–394.

———. 1979. "Innovation of the Theatrical Frame in Bamana Drama Performance." *Central Issues in Anthropology* 1(1):1–13.

———. 1980. "Organizing Satirical Comedy in Kote-Tlon: Drama as a Communication Strategy among the Bamana of Mali." Ph.D. diss., Indiana University.

———. 1981. "Antelope Headdress (*Chi wara*)." In *For Spirits and Kings: African Art from the Paul and Ruth Tishman Collection.* Edited by Susan Vogel. New York: Metropolitan Museum of Art, pp. 24–25.

———. 1982. "Time Consciousness and Growing Up in Bamana Folk Drama." *Journal of American Folklore* 95(378):415–434.

Brooks, George E. 1985. *Western Africa to c/1860 A.D.: A Provisional Historical Schema Based on Climate Periods.* Working Papers Series, 1. Bloomington: African Studies Program, Indiana University.

Butt-Thompson, Fredrick William. 1929. *West African Secret Societies, Their Organisations, Officials and Teaching.* London: H.F. & G. Witherby.

Caillié, René. 1965 [1830]. *Journal d'un voyage à Temboctou et à Jenne dans l'Afrique centrale, précédé d'observations faites chez les Maures Braknas, les Nalous, et d'autres peuples; pendant les années 1824, 1825, 1826, 1827, 1828.* 3 vols. Paris: Editions anthropos.

Calame-Griaule, Geneviève. 1965. *Ethnologie et langue; la parole chez les Dogon.* Paris: Gallimard.

Calvocoressi, D. S., and Nicholas David. 1979. "A New Survey of Radiocarbon and Thermoluminescence Dates for West Africa." *Journal of African History* 20(1):1–29.

Calvocoressi, D. S., and R. N. York. 1971. "The State of Archaeological Research in Ghana." *The West African Journal of Archaeology* 1:87–103.

Camara, Sory. 1976. *Gens de la parole: essai sur la condition et le rôle des griots dans la société malinké.* The Hague: Mouton.

Campbell, J. Morrow. 1909–1910. "Native Iron Smelting in Haute Guinee (West Africa)." *Transactions of the Institution of Mining and Metallurgy* 19:458–462.

Capron, J. 1957. "Quelques notes sur la société du Do chez les populations Bwa du cercle de San." *Journal de la Société des Africanistes* 27(1):81–129.

Cashion, Gerald Anthony. 1984. "Hunters of the Mande: A Behavioral Code and Worldview Derived from a Study of Their Folklore." Ph.D. diss., Indiana University.

Chernoff, John Miller. 1979. *African Rhythm and African Sensibility: Aesthetics and Social Action in African Musical Idioms.* Chicago: University of Chicago Press.

Chéron, George. 1923. "Usages minianka (Soudan Français)." *Revue d'Ethnographie et des Traditions populaires* 4(14):139–148.

———. 1931a. "Le Dyidé." *Journal de la Société des Africanistes* 1(2):285–289.

———. 1931b. "Les Tyeblenke." *Journal de la Société Africanistes* 1(2):281–283.

———. 1933 "La circoncision et l'excision chez les Malinké." *Journal de la Société des Africanistes* 3(2):297–303.

Chevrier, M. A. 1906. "Note relative aux coutumes des adeptes de la société secrète des Soymos, indigenes fétichistes du littoral de la Guinée." *L'Anthropologie* 17:359–376.

Chittick, H. N. 1971. "The Coast of East Africa." In *The African Iron Age.* Edited by Peter L. Shinnie. Oxford: Clarendon Press, pp. 108–141.

Cissé, Diango. 1970. *Structures des Malinké de Kita.* Bamako: Éditions Populaires.

Cissé, Youssouf. 1964. "Notes sur les sociétés de chasseurs Malinké." *Journal de la Société des Africanistes* 34(2):175–226.

———. 1973. "Signes graphiques, representations, concepts et texts relatifs à la personne chez les Malinké et les Bambara du Mali." In *La notion de la personne en Afrique noire.* Edited by Germaine Dieterlen. Paris: Éditions du Centre National de la Recherche Scientifique, pp. 131–179.

Claerhout, Adriaan. 1976. "Two Kuba Wrought-Iron Statuettes." *African Arts* 9(4):60–64, 92.

Clark, J. D. 1967. "A Record of Early Agriculture and Metallurgy in Africa from Archaeological Sources." In *Reconstructing African Cultural History.* Edited by Creighton Gabel and Norman R. Bennett. Boston: Boston University Press, pp. 3–24.

Clement, Pierre. 1948. "Le forgeron en Afrique noire, quelque attitudes du groupe à son egard." *La Revue de Geographie humaine et d'Ethnologie* 1(2):35–58.

Cline, Walter Buchanan. 1937. *Mining and Metallurgy in Negro Africa.* Menasha, Wis.: George Banta Publishing Co.

Coghlan, Herbert Henery. 1956. *Notes on Prehistoric and Early Iron in the Old World.* Oxford: Oxford University Press.

Cole, Herbert M. 1972. "Ibo Art and Leadership." In *African Art and Leadership.* Edited by Douglas Fraser and Herbert Cole. Madison: University of Wisconsin Press, pp. 79–98.

Cole, Herbert M., and Doran H. Ross. 1977. *The Arts of Ghana.* Los Angeles: Museum of Cultural History, University of California.

Commission Technique du Bambara de l'education de base. 1968. *Lexique Bambara.* Bamako: Ministère de l'Education nationale.

Cornet, Joseph. 1973. *Art from Zaire, 100 Masterworks from the National Collection.* New York: The African-American Institute.

Coste-D'Arnobat, Charles Pierre. 1789. *Voyage au pays de Bambouk, suivi d'observations intéressantes sur les castes indiennes, sur la Hollande et sur l'Angleterre.* Paris: Deferde et Maisonneuve.

Curtin, Phillip. 1973. "The Lure of Bambuk Gold." *Journal of African History* 14(4):623–632.

Curtis, J. E., T. S. Wheeler, J. D. Muhly, and R. Maddin. 1979. "Neo-Assyrian Iron-Working Technology." *Proceedings of the American Philosophical Society* 123(6):369–390.

Daget, J., and M. Konipo. 1951. "La pince-amulette chez les Bozos." *Notes africaines* no. 51:80–81.

Dalby, David. 1967. "A Survey of the Indigenous Scripts of Liberia and Sierra Leone: Vai, Mende, Loma, Kpelle, and Bassa." *African Language Studies* 8:1–51.

———. 1968. "The Indigenous Scripts of West Africa and Surinam: Their Inspiration and Design." *African Language Studies* 9:156–197.

———. 1971. "Introduction: Distribution and Nomenclature of the Manding People and Their Language." In *Papers on the Manding.* Edited by Carleton T. Hodge. Bloomington: Indiana University Press, pp. 1–13.

———. 1972. "Who are the Manding?" In *Manding Art and Civilisation.* Edited by Guy Atkins. London: Studio International, p. 4.

Dalziel, John McEwen. 1937. *The Useful Plants of West Tropical Africa.* London: Crown Agents for Oversea Governments and Administrations.

Darbo, Seni. 1972. "A Griot's Self-Portrait: The Origins and Role of the Griot in Mandinka Society as Seen from Stories Told by Gambian Griots." Paper presented at the Conference on Manding Studies, University of London, School of Oriental and African Studies.

Dard, Jean. 1825. *Dictionnaire français-wolof et français-bambara.* Paris: L'Imprimerie royale.

Davies, Oliver. 1966. "Comment." *Current Anthropology* 7(4):471–472.

———. 1967. "Timber Construction and Wood-Carving in West Africa in the Second Millennium B.C." *Man* n.s. 2:115–118.

———. 1967. *West Africa Before the Europeans: Archaeology and Pre-History.* London: Methuen.

———. 1973. *Excavations at Ntereso, Gonja, Northern Ghana.* Pietermaritzburg: University of Natal Press.

de Almada, Alvares. 1964. "Tratado breve dos rios de Guiné do Cabo Verde." In *Monumenta Missionaria Africana: Africa ocidental, 1570–1600.* Ser. 2, vol. 3. Edited by Antonio Brasio. Lisbon: Agência-Geral do Ultramar, pp. 229–378.

de Heusch, Luc. 1956. "Le symbolisme du forgeron en Afrique." *Reflets du Mond* 10:57–70.

Delafosse, Maurice. 1899. "Les Vai, leur langue et leur systeme d'ecriture." *L'Anthropologie* 10:129–156, 294–314.

———. 1912. *Haut-Sénégal-Niger.* Paris: Larose.

————. 1923. "Terminologie religieuse au Soudan." *L'Anthropologie* 33:371–383.

————. 1929. *La langue mandigue et ses dialectes (Malinké, Bambara, Dioula), Tome I: Introduction, grammaire, lexique français-mandingue.* Paris: Paul Geuthner.

————. 1955. *La langue mandingue et ses dialectes (Malinké, Bambara, Dioula), Tome II: Dictionnaire mandingue-français.* Paris: Paul Geuthner.

Delange, Jacqueline. 1962. "Le bansonyi du pays Baga." *Objets et Mondes* 2(1):3–12.

Desplagnes, Louis. 1903. "Étude sur les tumuli du Killi dans la region de Goundam." *L'Anthropologie* 14:151–172.

————. 1907. *Le plateau central nigérien.* Paris: Larose.

Diabaté, Massa Makan. 1970. *Kala Jata.* Bamako: Éditions Populaires.

Dieterlen, Germaine. 1948. "L'arme et l'outil chez les anciens Bambara." *Africa* 18(1):105–111.

————. 1951. *Essai sur la religion Bambara.* Paris: Presses Universitaires de France.

————. 1954. "Les rites symboliques du mariage chez les Bambara." *Zaire* 8(October):815–841.

————. 1955. "Mythe et organisation sociale au Soudan français." *Journal de la Société des Africanistes* 25(1-2):39–76.

————. 1957. "The Mande Creation Myth." *Africa* 27(2):124–139.

————. 1959. "Mythe et organisation sociale en Afrique occidentale (suite)." *Journal de la Société des Africanistes* 29(1):119–138.

————. 1965–1966. "Contribution à l'étude des forgerons en Afrique occidentale." *Annuaire de l'École practique des hautes Études* 73:1–28.

————. 1970. "La serrure et sa clef (Dogon, Mali)." In *Échanges et communications.* 2 vols. Edited by Jean Pouillon and Pierre Maranda. The Hague: Mouton, pp. 7–28.

Dieterlen, Germaine, and Youssouf Cissé. 1972. *Les fondements de la société d'initiation du Komo.* Paris: Mouton.

Dieterlen, Germaine, and Zacharie Ligers. 1959. "Un objet rituel bozo: le *Maniyalo.*" *Journal de la Société des Africanistes* 28(1–2):33–42.

————. 1959. "Note sur un talisman Bambara." *Notes africaines* no. 83:89–91.

Diop, Majhemout. 1971. *Histoire des classes sociales dans l'Afrique de l'ouest; I: Mali.* Paris: F. Maspero.

Donne, John. 1972. "Bogolanfini: A Mud-Painted Cloth." Paper presented at the Conference on Manding Studies, University of London, School of Oriental and African Studies.

————. 1973. "Bogolanfini: A Mud-Painted Cloth from Mali." *Man* n.s. 8:104–107.

Douglas, Mary Tew. 1966. *Purity and Danger.* London: Routledge & Kegan Paul.

Doumbia, Paul Emile Namoussa. 1936. "Étude du clan des forgerons." *Bulletin du Comité d'Études historiques et scientifiques de l'Afrique Occidentale Française* 19(2–3):334–360.

Drewal, Henry John. 1977. *Traditional Art of the Nigerian Peoples: The Milton D. Ratner Family Collection.* Washington, D.C.: Museum of African Art.

Drewal, Margaret Thompson. 1977. "Projections from the Top in Yoruba Art." *African Arts* 11(1):43–49, 91.

Dumont, Louis. 1970. *Homo Hierarchicus, An Essay on the Caste System.* Translated by Mark Sainsbury. Chicago: University of Chicago Press.

Dupire, Marguerite. 1962. *Peuls nomades.* Paris: Institut d'ethnologie.

————. 1970. *Organisation sociale des Peul.* Paris: Plon.

Durand, Oswald. 1932. "Les industries locales au Fouta." *Bulletin du Comité d'Études historiques et scientifiques d'Afrique Occidentale Française* 15(1):42–71.

Échard, N. 1965. "Note sur les forgerons de l'Ader (Pays Hausa, République du Niger)." *Journal de la Société des Africanistes* 35(2):353–372.

Eliade, Mircea. 1972. *The Forge and the Crucible.* Translated by Stephen Corrin. New York: Harper and Row.

Escultura Africana. 1960. Lisbon: Junta de Investigações do Ultramar.

Evans-Pritchard, Edward Evan. 1937. *Witchcraft, Oracles and Magic among the Azande.* Oxford: Clarendon Press.

Ezra, Kate. 1981. "Mother and Child" and "Female Figure." In *For Spirits and Kings: African Art from the Paul and Ruth Tishman Collection.* Edited by Susan Vogel. New York: Metropolitan Museum of Art, pp. 26–28.

———. 1983. "Figural Sculpture of the Bamana of Mali." Ph.D. diss., Northwestern University.

———. 1986. *A Human Ideal in African Art: Bamana Figurative Sculpture.* Washington, D.C.: National Museum of African Art, Smithsonian Institution Press.

Fadiga, Bouillagui. 1934. "Une circoncision chez les Markas du Soudan." *Bulletin du Comité d'Études historiques et scientifiques de l'Afrique Occidentale Française* 17(4):564–577.

Fagan, Brian. 1969. "Radiocarbon Dates for Sub-Saharan Africa." *Journal of African History* 10(1):149–169.

Fage, J. D. 1978. *An Atlas of African History.* 2d ed. New York: African Publishing Co.

Fagg, Angela. 1972. "A Preliminary Report on an Occupation Site in the Nok Valley, Nigeria: Samun Dukiya, AF/70/1." *West African Journal of Archaeology* 2:75–79.

Fagg, Bernard. "Recent Work in West Africa: New Light on the Nok Culture." *World Archaeology* 1(1):41–50.

Fernandez, James W. 1969. "Principles of Opposition and Vitality in Fang Aesthetics." *Journal of Aesthetics and Art Criticism* 25(1):53–64.

———. 1973. "The Exposition and Imposition of Order: Artistic Expression in Fang Culture." In *The Traditional Artist in African Societies.* Edited by Warren L. d'Azevedo. Bloomington: Indiana University Press, pp. 194–220.

———. 1979. "The Mission of the Metaphor in Expressive Cultures." *Current Anthropology* 15(2):119–145.

Filipowaik, Wladyslaw. 1985. "Iron Working in the Old Kingdom of Mali." In *African Iron Working: Ancient and Traditional.* Edited by Randi Haaland and Peter Shinnie. Norway: Norwegian University Press, pp. 36–49.

Fivaz, Derek, and Patricia E. Scott. 1977. *African Languages: A Genetic and Decimalised Classification for Bibliographic and General Reference.* Boston: G. K. Hall.

Flam, Jack. 1970. "Some Aspects of Style Symbolism in Sudanese Sculpture." *Journal de la Société des Africanistes* 40(2):137–150.

Flight, Colin. 1973. "A Survey of Recent Results in the Radiocarbon Chronology of Northern and Western Africa." *Journal of African History* 14(4):531–554.

Foltz, William J. 1965. *From French West Africa to the Mali Federation.* New Haven: Yale University Press.

———. 1969. "Social Structure and Political Behavior of the Senegalese Elite." *Behavior Science Notes* 4(2):145–163.

Forbes, R. H. 1933. "The Black Man's Industries." *Geographical Review* 23:230–247.

Forbes, Robert James. 1950. *Metallurgy in Antiquity.* Leiden: E. J. Brill.

Francis-Boeuf, Claude. 1937. "L'industrie autochtone du fer en Afrique Occidentale Française." *Bulletin du Comité d'Études historiques et scientifiques de l'Afrique Occidentale Française* 20(4):403–464.

Franklin, Alan D., Jacqueline S. Olin, and Theodore A. Wertime. 1978. *The Search for Ancient Tin.* Washington, D.C.: Smithsonian Institution Press.

Frobenius, Leo. 1913. *The Voice of Africa.* 2 vols. Translated by Rudolf Blind. London: Hutchinson.

————. 1921–1931. *Atlas Africanus.* Munich: C. H. Beck.

————. 1933. *Kulturgeschichte Afrikas.* Zurich: Phaidon.

Fuchs, P. "Les figurines en metal d'Ouagadougou." *Notes africaines* no. 87:76–82.

Galhano, Fernando. 1971. *Esculturas e objectos decorados da Guiné Portuguesa no Musu de Etnologia do Ultramar.* Lisbon: Junta de Investigações do Ultramar.

Galliéni, Joseph Simon. 1885. *Mission d'exploration du Haut-Niger: Voyage au Soudan français (Haut-Niger et pays de Ségou), 1879–1881.* Paris: Hachette.

Ganay, Solange de. 1940. "Rôle protecteur de certaines peintures rupestres du Soudan français." *Journal de la Société des Africanistes* 10(1–2):87–98.

————. 1947. "Un jardin d'essai et son autel chez les Bambara." *Journal de la Société des Africanistes* 17:57–63.

————. 1949. "Aspects de mythologie et de symbolique Bambara." *Journal de Psychologie normale et pathologie* 41(2):181–201.

————. 1949. "On a Form of Cicatrization among the Bambara." *Man* 49:53–55.

Gardi, Bernhard. 1985. *Ein Markt wie Mopti: Handwerkerkasten und traditionelle Techniken in Mali.* Basel: Ethnologisches Seminar der Universität und Museum für Völkerkunde.

Gardi, Rene. 1969. *African Crafts and Craftsmen.* Translated by Sigrid MacRae. New York: Van Nostrand Reinhold Co.

Gebauer, Paul. 1964. *Spider Divination in the Cameroons.* Milwaukee: Milwaukee Public Museum.

Geertz, Clifford. 1973. *The Interpretation of Cultures.* New York: Basic Books.

————. 1976. "Art as a Cultural System." *Modern Language Notes* 91(6):1473–1499.

Gellner, Ernest. 1970. "Concepts and Society." In *Rationality.* Edited by Bryan R. Wilson. New York: Harper Torchbooks, pp. 18–49.

Gennep, M. A. van. 1911. "Études d'ethnographie algérienne. II. Les soufflets algériens." *Revue d'Ethnographie et de Sociologie* 2:270–276.

Glaze, Anita J. 1975. "Women Power and Art in a Senufo Village." *African Arts* 8(3):24–29, 64–68.

————. 1981a. *Art and Death in a Senufo Village.* Bloomington: Indiana University Press.

————. 1981b. "Staff for a Champion Cultivator." In *For Spirits and Kings: African Art from the Paul and Ruth Tishman Collection.* Edited by Susan Vogel. New York: Metropolitan Museum of Art, pp. 48–49.

Gluck, Julius F. 1966. "African Architecture." In *The Many Faces of Primitive Art.* Edited by Douglas Fraser. Englewood Cliffs, N.J.: Prentice-Hall, pp. 224–243.

Goldwater, Robert J. 1960. *Bambara Sculpture from the Western Sudan.* New York: Museum of Primitive Art.

————. 1964. *Senufo Sculpture from West Africa.* New York: Museum of Primitive Art.

Goody, Jack. 1971. *Technology, Tradition, and the State in Africa.* Oxford: Clarendon Press.

Goucher, Candice L. 1981. "Iron Is Iron 'Til It Is Rust: Trade and Ecology in the Decline of West African Iron-Smelting." *Journal of African History* 22(2):179–189.

Gray, William, and Staff Surgeon Dochard. 1825. *Travels in Western Africa in the Years 1818–1821.* London: J. Murray.

Green, Kathryn L. Forthcoming. "Dyula." In *Muslim Peoples: A World Ethnographic Survey.* 2d ed. Edited by Richard V. Weekes.

Greenberg, Joseph Harold. 1966. *The Languages of Africa.* 2d ed. Bloomington: Indiana University Press.

Griaule, Marcel. 1938. *Masques Dogon.* Paris: Institut d'ethnologie.

————. 1948. *Dieu d'eau; entretiens avec Ogotemmêli.* Paris: Éditions du Chêne.

————. 1952. "Reflexions sur des symboles soudanais." *Cahiers internationaux de Sociologie* 13:8–30.

Griaule, Marcel, and Germaine Dieterlen. 1951. *Signes graphiques soudanais.* Paris: Hermann.

————. 1965. *Le renard pâle.* Paris: Institut d'ethnologie.

Grove, Alfred Thomas. 1967. *Africa South of the Sahara.* Oxford: Oxford University Press.

Guébhard, Paul. 1911. "Notes contributives à l'étude de la religion, des moeurs et des coutumes des Bobo du cercle de Koury (Soudan français)." *Revue d'Ethnographie et de Sociologie* 2:125–188.

Guilhem, Marcel, and S. Toé. 1963. *Précis d'histoire du Mali.* Paris: Ligel.

Hall, H. U. 1920. "Fetish Figures of Equatorial Africa." *Museum Journal* (Philadelphia) 11(1):27–55.

————. 1924. "A Congo Fetish and Divining Image from the Coast Region." *Museum Journal* (Philadelphia) 15(1):58–69.

Hamy, E. T. 1882. "Note sur les figures et les inscriptions gravées dans la roche à El Hadj Mimoun, près Figuig." *Revue d'Ethnographie* 1:129–137.

Harley, George Way. 1941a. *Native African Medicine, with Special Reference to Its Practice in the Mano Tribe of Liberia.* Cambridge: Harvard University Press.

————. 1941b. *Notes on the Poro in Liberia.* Cambridge: Peabody Museum.

————. 1950. *Masks as Agents of Social Control in Northeast Liberia.* Cambridge: Peabody Museum.

Harris, Marvin. 1968. *The Rise of Anthropological Theory.* New York: Crowell.

Haselberger, Herta. 1965. "Bemerkungen zum Kunsthandwerk im Podo (Republik Mali)." *Baessler-Archiv* n.F 13:433–499.

Hau, K. 1973. "Pre-Islamic Writing in West Africa." *Bulletin de l'I.F.A.N.* 35(1):1–45.

Hauenstein, Alfred. 1978. "Le serpent dans les rites, cultes et coutumes de certaines ethnies de Côte d'Ivoire." *Anthropos* 73(3/4):525–560.

Haywood, Austin Hubert Wightwick. 1962. *Through Timbuctu and Across the Great Sahara.* London: Seeley, Service.

Hecquard, Louis Hyacinthe. 1855. *Voyage sur la côte et dans l'intérieur de l'Afrique occidentale.* Paris: Benard.

Henry, Joseph. 1908. "Le culte des esprits chez les Bambara." *Anthropos* 3:702–717.

————. 1910. *L'âme d'un peuple africain: les Bambara, leur vie psychique, éthique, sociale, religieuse.* Münster: Aschendorff.

Herbert, Eugenia E. 1973. "Aspects of the Use of Copper in Pre-Colonial West Africa." *Journal of African History* 14(2):179–194.

————. 1975. "Smallpox Inoculation in Africa." *Journal of African History* 16(4):539–559.

————. 1984. *Red Gold of Africa: Copper in Precolonial History and Culture.* Madison: University of Wisconsin Press.

Herskovits, Melville J. 1967. *Dahomey, an Ancient West African Kingdom.* 2 vols. Evanston: Northwestern University Press.

Hodge, Carleton T., ed. 1971. *Papers on the Manding.* Bloomington: Indiana University Press.

Hodges, Henry. 1971. *Artifacts; An Introduction to Early Materials and Technology.* London: John Baker.

Holas, Bohumil. 1948. "Le masque Komo de Korodou." *Notes africaines* no. 38:24–25.

————. 1950. "Pince-amulettes des Guerye." *Notes africaines* no. 48:123–125.

————. 1966. *Les Senufo, y compris les Maninka.* 2d ed. Paris: Presses Universitaires de France.

Holsoe, S. 1972. "The Manding in Western Liberia: An Overview." Paper presented at the Conference on Manding Studies, University of London, School of Oriental and African Studies.

Holý, Ladislav. 1968. *Social Stratification in Tribal Africa*. Prague: Academia.

Hopkins, Nicholas S. 1971. "Maninka Social Organization." In *Papers on the Manding*. Edited by Carleton T. Hodge. Bloomington: Indiana University Press, pp. 99–128.

————. 1972. *Popular Government in an African Town: Kita, Mali*. Chicago: University of Chicago Press.

Hottot, R. 1956. "Teke Fetishes." *Journal of the Royal Anthropological Institute* 86(1):25–36.

Huard, Paul. 1969. "Introduction et diffusion du fer au Tchad." *Journal of African History* 8(3):377–404.

Huet, Michel. 1978. *The Dance, Art, and Ritual of Africa*. New York: Pantheon Books.

Huizinga, Johan, Rogier M. A. Bedaux, and J. D. van der Waals. 1979. "Anthropological Research in Mali." In *National Geographic Society Research Reports*. Washington, D.C.: National Geographic Society, pp. 281–307.

Hurston, Zora Neale. 1935. *Mules and Men*. Philadelphia: J. B. Lippincott.

Hutton, J. H. 1961. *Caste in India*. 3d ed. London: Oxford University Press.

Ibn Batuta. 1335. *Tuḥfat al-nuẓẓār fī gharāʾib al-amṣār*. Translated by C. Defremery and B. R. Sanguinetti as *Voyage d'Ibn Batoutah*. 1922–1949. 4 vols. Paris: Imprimerie Nationale. English version translated by H. A. R. Gibb, *The Travels of Ibn Battuta, A.D. 1325–1354*. 1958–1971. 3 vols. Cambridge: Cambridge University Press.

Ibn, Faḍl Allāh al-Umarī. 1337. *Masālik el Abṣār fī mamālik el amṣār*. Translated by Gaudfroy-Demombynes as *Masālik el Abṣār fī mamālik el amṣār, I. L'Afrique moins l'Egypte*. 1927. Paris: Paul Geuthner. An excerpt from this translation ("Le royaume de Mali et ses dependences") can be found in *Notes africaines* no. 82(1959):59.

Imperato, Pascal James. 1968. "The Practice of Variolation among the Songhai of Mali." *Transactions of the Royal Society of Tropical Medicine and Hygiene* 62:869–873.

————. 1970. "The Dance of the Tyi Wara." *African Arts* 4(1):8–13, 71–80.

————. 1971a. "Contemporary Adopted Dances of the Dogon." *African Arts* 5(1):28–33, 68–72.

————. 1971b. "Twins among the Bambara and Malinke of Mali." *Journal of Tropical Medicine and Hygiene* 74(7):154–159.

————. 1972a. "Contemporary Masked Dances and Masquerades of the Bamana (Bambara) Age Sets from the Cercle of Bamako, Mali." Paper presented at the Conference on Manding Studies, University of London, School of Oriental and African Studies.

————. 1972b. "Door Locks of the Bamana of Mali." *African Arts* 5(3):52–56.

————. 1974a. "Bamana and Maninka Covers and Blankets." *African Arts* 7(3):56–67, 91.

————. 1974b. *The Cultural Heritage of Africa*. Chanute, Kans.: Safari Museum Press.

————. 1975. "Bamana and Maninka Twin Figures." *African Arts* 8(4):52–60, 83–84.

————. 1975. *A Wind in Africa: A Story of Modern Medicine in Mali*. St. Louis: Warren H. Green.

————. 1977a. *African Folk Medicine: Practices and Beliefs of the Bambara and Other Peoples*. Baltimore: York Press.

————. 1977b. *Historical Dictionary of Mali*. Metuchen, N.J.: The Scarecrow Press.

————. 1978. *Dogon Cliff Dwellers: The Art of Mali's Mountain People.* New York: L. Kahan Gallery.
————. 1979. "Letter to the Editor." *African Arts* 12(4):6–7.
————. 1980. "Bambara and Malinke Ton Masquerades." *African Arts* 12(4):47–55, 82–85, 87.
————. 1983. *Buffoons, Queens and Wooden Horsemen: The Dyo and Gouan Societies of the Bambara of Mali.* New York: Kilima House.
Imperato, Pascal James, and Marli Shamir. 1970. "Bokolanfini: Mud Cloth of the Bamana of Mali." *African Arts* 3(4):32–41, 80.
Innes, Gordon, ed. 1974. *Sunjata: Three Mandinka Versions.* London: School of Oriental and African Studies.
Interaction: The Art Styles of the Benue River and East Nigeria. 1974. West Lafayette: Purdue University.
Jackson, Michael. 1977. *The Kuranko: Dimensions of Social Reality in a West African Society.* New York: St. Martin's Press.
Janzen, John M., and Wyatt MacGaffey. 1974. *An Anthology of Kongo Religion.* Lawrence: University of Kansas Press.
Jobson, Richard. 1968 [1623]. *The Golden Trade, or A Discovery of the River Gambra, and the Golden Trade of the Aethiopians.* London: Dawsons of Pall Mall.
Johnson, John William. 1978. "The Epic of Sun-Jata: An Attempt to Define the Model for African Epic Poetry." Ph.D. diss., Indiana University.
————. 1986. *The Epic of Son-Jara: A West African Tradition.* Bloomington: Indiana University Press.
Johnson, Marion. 1972. "Manding Weaving." Paper presented at the Conference on Manding Studies, University of London, School of Oriental and African Studies.
Jones, William I. 1976. *Planning and Economic Policy: Socialist Mali and Her Neighbors.* Washington, D.C.: Three Continents Press.
Karp, Ivan. Forthcoming. "Laughter at Marriage: Subversion in Performance." In *Transformations of African Marriage.* Edited by David Parkin and David Nyamaweya. London: International African Institute.
Kendall, Martha. 1982. "Getting to Know You." In *Semantic Anthropology.* Edited by David Parkin. London: Academic Press., pp. 197–209.
Kense, Francois J. 1983. *Traditional African Iron Working.* African Occasional Papers, 1. Calgary: Department of Archaeology, University of Calgary.
Kerharo, Joseph. 1950. *Plantes médicinales et toxiques de la Côte d'Ivoire–Haute-Volta.* Paris: Vigot Frères.
Kerharo, Joseph, and A. Bouquet. 1950. *Sorciers, féticheurs et guérisseurs de la Côte d'Ivoire–Haute-Volta: les hommes, les croyances, les pratiques; pharmacopée et thérapeutique.* Paris: Vigot Frères.
Ketkar, Shridhar V. 1909. *The History of Caste in India: Evidence of the Laws of Manu on the Social Conditions in India during the Third Century A.D., Interpreted and Examined, with an Appendix on Radical Defects of Ethnology, vol. I.* Ithaca: Taylor & Carpenter.
Kjersmeier, Carl. 1935–1938. *Centres de style de la sculpture nègre africaine.* Translated by France Gleizal. 4 vols. Paris: A. Morance.
Klemp, Egon, ed. 1970. *Africa on Maps Dating from the Twelfth to the Eighteenth Century.* Translated by Margaret Stone and Jeffrey C. Stone. New York: McGraw-Hill.
Klusemann, Kurt. 1924. "Die Entwicklung der Eisengewinnung in Afrika und Europa." *Mitteilungen der Anthropologische Gesellshaft in Wein* 54:120–140.
Knight, Roderick. 1972. "Mandinka Drumming." *African Arts* 7(4):24–35.
Koroma, V. H. 1939. "The Bronze Statuettes of Ro-Ponka, Kafu Bolom." *Sierra Leone Studies* no. 22:25–28.

Kyerematen, A. A. Y. 1964. *Panoply of Ghana*. London: Longmans.

Labouret, Henri. 1934. *Les Manding et leur langue*. Paris: Larose.

———. 1939. "La parenté à plaisanteries en Afrique occidentale." *Africa* 12(3): 244–253.

Laing, Alexander Gordon. 1825. *Travels in the Timannee, Kooranko, and Soolima Countries, in Western Africa*. London: John Murray.

Lajoux, Jean Dominique. 1963. *The Rock Paintings of Tassili*. Translated by G. D. Liversage. London: Thames and Hudson.

Lambert, Nicole. 1961. "Le site néolithique de Medinet Sbat dans l'Ifozoueten (Mauritanie)." *Bulletin de l'I.F.A.N.*, ser. B, 23(3–4):423–455.

———. 1969. "Exploitation minière et métallurgie protohistorique de cuivre en Sahara occidental." Paper presented at the African Studies Association Meeting, Montreal.

———. 1970. "Medinet Sbat et la protohistoire de Mauritanie occidentale." *Antiquités africaines* 4:15–62.

Lambert, Nicole, and G. Souville. 1970. "Influences oriental dans la nécropole megalithique du Tayadirt (Maroc)." *Antiquités africaines* 4:63–74.

Lampreia, José D. 1962. *Catálogo-inventário da Secção de Etnografia do Museu da Guiné Portuguesa*. Lisbon: Junta de Investigações do Ultramar.

Langer, Susanne K. 1957. *Problems of Art: Ten Philosophical Lectures*. New York: Charles Scribner's Sons.

Laude, Jean. 1964. *Iron Sculpture of the Dogon*. New York: Galérie Kamer.

———. 1973. *African Art of the Dogon: The Myths of the Cliff Dwellers*. New York: Viking Press.

Launay, R. 1972. "Manding 'Clans' and 'Castes'." Paper presented at the Conference on Manding Studies, University of London, School of Oriental and African Studies.

Lawal, Babatunda. 1970. "Yoruba Sango Sculpture in Historical Retrospect." Ph.D. diss., Indiana University.

———. 1975. "Yoruba-Sango Ram Symbolism: From Ancient Sahara or Dynastic Egypt?" In *African Images: Essays in African Iconology*. Edited by Daniel F. McCall and Edna G. Bay. New York: Africana Publishing Co., pp. 225–251.

Laye, Camara. 1971a. *A Dark Child*. Translated by James Kirkup and Ernest Jones. New York: Farrar, Straus and Giroux.

———. 1971b. *A Dream of Africa*. Translated by James Kirkup. New York: Collier.

Leach, Edmund. 1960. "Introduction: What Should We Mean by Caste." In *Aspects of Caste in South India, Ceylon, and Northwest Pakistan*. Edited by Edmund Leach. Cambridge: Cambridge University Press, pp. 1–10.

Lebeuf, Annie M.D., and Viviana Pâques. 1970. *Archéologie maliene*. Paris: Musée de l'Homme.

Lebeuf, L. P. 1943. "Une boite à antimoine." *Notes africaines* no. 10:8.

Legassick, M. 1966. "Firearms, Horses and Samorian Army Organization 1870–1898." *Journal of African History* 7(1):95–115.

Leith-Ross, Sylvia. 1970. *Nigerian Pottery*. Lagos: Ibadan University Press.

Lem, F. H. 1948. *Sculptures soudanaises*. Paris: Arts et métiers graphiques.

Lestrange, M. de. 1950. "Génies de l'eau et de la brousse en Guinée française." *Études guinéenes* 4:1–24.

Levtzion, Nehemia. 1972. "The Differential Impact of Islam among the Soninke and the Manding." Paper presented at the Conference on Manding Studies, University of London, School of Oriental and African Studies.

———. 1973. *Ancient Ghana and Mali*. London: Methuen.

Lewis, John. 1979. "Descendence and Crops: Two Poles of Production in a Malian Peasant Village." Ph.D. diss., Yale University.

Leynaud, Emile. 1966. "Fraternités d'âge et sociétés de culture dans la Haute-Vallée du Niger." *Cahiers d'Études Africaines* 6(21):41–68.

Lhote, Henri. 1952. "La connaissance du fer en Afrique occidentale." *Encyclopédie Mensuella d'Outre-Mer* 2:269–273.

———. 1959. *The Search for the Tassili Frescoes*. Translated by Alan Houghton Brodrick. London: Hutchinson.

Lima, Augustu Guilhermo Mesquitela. 1977. "Le fer en Angola." *Cahiers d'Études Africaines* 17(2–3):345–353.

Little, Kenneth L. 1949. "The Role of the Secret Society in Cultural Specialization." *American Anthropologist* 51(2):199–212.

———. 1967. *The Mende of Sierra Leone: A West African People in Transition*. Rev. ed. London: Routledge & Kegan Paul.

Luschan, Felix von. 1909. "Eisentechnik in Afrika." *Zeitschrift für Ethnologie* 41:22–59.

———. 1919. *Die Altertümer von Benin*. Berlin and Leipzig: Vereinigung wissenshaftlicher Verleger.

Maclean, Una. 1971. *Magical Medicine: A Nigerian Case-Study*. Middlesex: Penguin Books.

Maddin, Robert, James D. Muhly, and Tamara S. Wheeler. 1977. "How the Iron Age Began." *Scientific American* 237(4):122–131.

Made of Iron. 1966. Houston: Art Department, University of St. Thomas.

Maesen, Albert. 1940. "De Plastiek im de Kultuur van de Senufo van de Ivoorkunst." Ph.D. diss., University of Ghent.

Makarius, Laura. 1968. "The Blacksmith's Taboos: From the Man of Iron to the Man of Blood." *Diogenes* 62(Summer):25–48.

Malzy, Pierre. 1943. "Un cas de phosphorescence humain." *Notes africaines* no. 18:1–2.

———. 1943. "Phosphorescence humaine." *Notes africaines* no. 19:11–12.

Mandel, Jean-Jacques, and Armelle Brenier-Estrine. 1977. "Clay Toys of Mopti." *African Arts* 10(2):8–13.

Maquet, Jacques. 1970. "Rwanda Castes." In *Social Stratification in Africa*. Edited by Arthur Tuden and Leonard Plotnicov. New York: The Free Press, pp. 93–124.

Maret, P. de, F. van Noten, and D. Cahen. 1977. "Radiocarbon Dates from West Central Africa: A Synthesis." *Journal of African History* 18(4):481–505.

Margarido, A., and F. Germain-Wasserman. 1972. "On the Myth and Practice of the Blacksmith in Africa." *Diogenes* 78(Summer):87–122.

Marty, Paul. 1920–1921. *Études sur l'Islam et les tribus du Soudan*. 4 vols. Paris: Leroux.

Mauny, Raymond. 1952. "Essai sur l'histoire des métaux en Afrique occidentale." *Bulletin de l'I.F.A.N.*, ser. B, 14(2):545–595.

———. 1961. *Tableau geographique de l'Ouest africain au Moyen Age*. Dakar: I.F.A.N.

———. 1970. *Le siècles obscurs de l'Afrique noire; histoire et archéologie*. Paris: Fayard.

McCulloch, Merran. 1950. *The Peoples of Sierra Leone*. London: International African Institute.

McIntosh, Roderick J., and Susan Keech McIntosh. 1979. "Terracotta Statuettes in Mali." *African Arts* 12(2):51–53, 91.

McIntosh, Susan Keech, and Roderick J. McIntosh. 1980. "Jenne-Jeno: An Ancient African City." *Archaeology* 33(1):8–14.

McNaughton, Patrick R. 1970. "The Throwing Knife in African History." *African Arts* 3(2):54–60, 89.

———. 1975. *Iron Art of the Blacksmith in the Western Sudan*. West Lafayette: Purdue University.

———. 1979a. "Bamana Blacksmiths." *African Arts* 12(2):65–71, 92.

———. 1979b. *Secret Sculptures of Komo: Art and Power in Bamana (Bambara) Initiation Associations.* Philadelphia: Institute for the Study of Human Issues.

———. 1981. "Staff with Female Figure." In *For Spirits and Kings: African Art from the Paul and Ruth Tishman Collection.* Edited by Susan Vogel. New York: Metropolitan Museum of Art, pp. 28–29.

———. 1982a. "Language, Art, Secrecy and Power: The Semantics of Dalilu." *Anthropological Linguistics* 24(4):487–505.

———. 1982b. "The Shirts that Mande Hunters Wear." *African Arts* 15(3):54–58, 91.

Meillassoux, Claude. 1968. *Urbanization of an African Community; Voluntary Associations in Bamako.* Seattle: University of Washington Press.

———. 1973. "Note sur l'étymologie de *nyamakala*." *Notes africaines.* no. 89:79.

Miner, Horace. 1953. *The Primitive City of Timbuctoo.* Princeton: Princeton University Press.

Moal, G. le. 1960. "Les habitations semi-souterraines en Afrique d'ouest." *Journal de la Société des Africanistes* 30(2):193–203.

Molin, Paul Marie. 1955. *Dictionnaire bambara-français et français-bambara.* Issy-les-Moulineaux: Les Presses Missionnaires.

———. 1960. *Recueil de proverbes bambaras et malinkés.* Issy-les-Moulineaux: Les Presses Missionnaires.

Mollien, Gaspard T. 1820. *Travels in Africa, to the Sources of the Senegal and Gambia in 1818.* London: Sir R. Phillips.

Monod, Theodore. 1938. *Contributions à l'étude du Sahara occidental. Fascicule I: Gravures, peintures et inscriptions rupestres.* Paris: Librairie Larose.

———. 1943. "Phosphorescence humaine." *Notes africaines* no. 19:11–12.

Monteil, Charles. 1915. *Les Khassonke.* Paris: Ernest Leroux.

———. 1924. *Les Bambara du Ségou et du Kaarta.* Paris: Larose.

———. 1929. "Les empires du Mali (étude d'histoire et de sociologie soudanaises)." *Bulletin du Comité d'Études historiques et scientifiques de l'Afrique Occidentale Française.* 12(3–4):291–447.

———. 1932. *Une cité soudanaise: Djenne, métropole du delta central du Niger.* Paris: Société d'Éditions Geographiques, Maritimes et Coloniales.

Moore, Francis. 1738. *Travels into the Inland Parts of Africa.* London: Edward Cave.

Moser, Rex. 1974. "Foregrounding in the 'Sunjata,' the Mande Epic." Ph.D. diss., Indiana University.

Mota, Teixeira da. 1960. "Descoberta de bronzes antigos na Guiné Portuguesa." *Boletim Cultural da Guiné Portuguesa* 15:625–632.

———. 1965. "Bronzes antigos da Guiné." *Actas do Congresso Internasional de Etnografia* 4:149–154.

Munson, Patrick J. 1980. "Archaeology and the Prehistoric Origins of the Ghana Empire." *Journal of African History* 21(4):457–466.

Murdock, George Peter. 1959. *Africa: Its People and Their Culture History.* New York: McGraw-Hill.

N'Diaye, Bokar. 1970a. *Les castes au Mali.* Bamako: Éditions Populaires.

———. 1970b. *Groups ethniques au Mali.* Bamako: Éditions Populaires.

Niane, Djibril Tamsir. 1965. *Sundiata, an Epic of Old Mali.* Translated by G. D. Pickett. London: Longmans.

Oliver, Roland, and Brian M. Fagan. 1975. *Africa in the Iron Age.* Cambridge: Cambridge University Press.

Ortoli, J. 1936. "Une race de pêcheurs: les Bozo." *Bulletin des Recherches soudanaises* 4 (October):152–178.

———. 1939. "Coutume Bambara (Cercle de Bamako) (1935)." In *Coutumier juridique de l'A.O.F., II (Soudan).* Paris: Larose.

Ouologuem, Yambo. 1968. *Bound to Violence.* Translated by Ralph Manheim. London: Educational Books.

Pageard, Robert. 1959. "Note sur les Kagoro et la chefferie de Soro." *Journal de la Société des Africanistes* 29(2):261–272.

———. 1962. "Travestis et marionnettes de la région de Ségou." *Notes africaines* no. 93:17–20.

Palau Marti, Montserrat. 1957. *Les Dogons*. Paris: Presses Universitaires de France.

Pâques, Viviana. 1954. *Les Bambara*. Paris: Presses Universitaires de France.

———. 1956. "Les 'Samake.'" *Bulletin de l'I.F.A.N.*, ser. B, 18(3–4):369–390.

———. 1964. "Les bouffons sacrés de Bougouni." *Journal de la Société des Africanistes* 34(1):63–110.

Park, Mungo. 1799. *Travels in the Interior Districts of Africa*. London: W. Bulmer.

———. 1815. *The Journal of a Mission to the Interior of Africa in the Year 1805*. London: John Murray.

Paulme, Denise. 1940. *Organisation sociale des Dogon (Soudan français)*. Paris: Domat-Montchrestien.

———. 1939. "Parenté à plaisanteries et alliance par le sang en Afrique occidentale." *Africa* 12(4):433–444.

———. 1957. "Des riziculteurs africains: les Baga (Guinée française)." *Les Cahiers d'Outre-Mer* 10(39):257–278.

———. 1962. *Une société de Côte d'Ivoire hier et aujourd'hui: les Bété*. Paris: Mouton.

Pereira, Duarte Pacheco. 1956. *Esmeraldo du Situ Orbis. Côte occidentale d'Afrique du Sud Marocain au Gabon (1506–1508)*. Translated by Raymond Mauny. Bissau: Centro de Estudos da Guiné Portuguesa.

Person, Yves. 1967. "Un cas de diffusion: les forgerons de Samori et la fonte à la cire perdue." *Revue française d'Histoire d'Outre-Mer* 54:219–226.

Phillipson, D. W. 1975. "The Chronology of the Iron Age in Bantu Africa." *Journal of African History* 14(3):321–342.

Plass, Margaret. 1959. *7 Metals of Africa*. Philadelphia: University of Pennsylvania Museum.

Pleiner, Radomir. 1980. "Early Iron Metallurgy in Europe." In *The Coming of the Age of Iron*. Edited by Theodore A. Wertime and James D. Muhly. New Haven: Yale University Press, pp. 375–416.

Plotnicov, Leonard, and Arthur Tuden, eds. 1970. *Essays in Comparative Social Stratification*. Pittsburgh: University of Pittsburgh Press.

Posnansky, Merrick. 1968. "Bantu Genesis—Archaeological Reflexions." *Journal of African History* 9(1):1–11.

———. 1977. "Review Article, Brass Casting and Its Antecedents in West Africa." *Journal of African History* 18(2):287–300.

Posnansky, Merrick, and Roderick J. McIntosh. 1976. "New Radiocarbon Dates for Northern and Western Africa." *Journal of African History* 17(2):161–195.

Proschan, Frank. 1979. *Les traditions du masque et de la marionnette dans la République de la Guinée/Puppetry and Masked Dance Traditions of the Republic of Guinea*. Washington, D.C.: The Smithsonian Institution.

Prost, André. 1939. "L'industrie de fer en Afrique noire occidental." *Afrique française renseignements coloniaux* 3:82–85.

Proteaux, Maurice. 1918–1919. "Notes sur certains rites magico-religeux de la haute Côte d'Ivoire." *L'Anthropologie* 29:37–52.

———. 1925. "Divertissements de Kong." *Bulletin du Comité d'Études historiques et scientifiques de l'Afrique Occidentale Français* 8(4):606–850.

Prussin, Labelle. 1970. "Sudanese Architecture and the Manding." *African Arts* 3(4):13–18, 64, 67.

———. 1973a. "The Architecture of Djenne: African Synthesis and Transformation." Ph.D. diss., Yale University.

———. 1973b. "Review Article, African Terra Cotta South of the Sahara." *African Arts* 6(3):66–68.

————. 1977. "Pillars, Projections and Paradigms." *Architecture* 7(1):65–81.

Quimby, L. "The Psychology of Magic among the Dyula." Paper presented at the Conference on Manding Studies, University of London, School of Oriental and African Studies.

Quinn, Charlotte A. 1972. *Mandingo Kingdoms of the Senegambia.* Evanston: Northwestern University Press.

Raffenel, Anne. 1856. *Nouveau voyage dans le pays des Nègres, suivi d'études sur la colonie du Sénégal et de documents historiques, géographiques et scientifiques.* Paris: Napoleon Chaix.

Raulin, Henri. 1967. *La dynamique des techniques agraires en Afrique tropicale du nord.* Paris: Éditions du Centre National de la Recherche Scientifique.

Reynolds, Barrie. 1968. *The Material Culture of the Peoples of the Gwembe Valley.* New York: Praeger.

Richter, Dolores. 1980. *Art, Economics and Change: The Kulebele of Northern Ivory Coast.* La Jolla: Psych/Graphic Publishers.

Rodney, Walter. 1970. *A History of the Upper Guinea Coast, 1545–1800.* Oxford: Clarendon Press.

Rubin, Arnold. 1974. *African Accumulative Sculpture.* New York: Pace Gallery.

Saikou, Balde. 1935. "Les forgerons du Fouta Djallon." *L'Education Afrique* 24: 125–162.

Saint-Père, J. H. 1925. *Les Sarakolle du Guidimakha.* Paris: Larose.

Savary, Claude. 1967. *Notes à propos du symbolisme de l'art dahoméen.* Geneva: Musée et Institute d'Ethnographie.

Schmidt, Peter R. 1978. *Historical Archaeology: A Structural Approach in an African Culture.* Westport, Conn.: Greenwood Press.

Schmidt, Peter, and Donald H. Avery. 1978. "Complex Iron Smelting and Prehistoric Culture in Tanzania." *Science* 201(4361):1085–1089.

Schoff, Wilfred H. 1912. *The Periplus of the Erythraean Sea.* London: Longmans.

Schweinfurth, Georg August. 1875. *Artes Africanae.* Leipzig: F. A. Brockhaus.

The Secret Museum of Mankind. n.d. New York: Manhattan House.

Shaw, Thurstan. 1968. "Radiocarbon Dates in Nigeria." *The Journal of the Historical Society of Nigeria* 4(3):460–461.

————. 1969. "On Radiocarbon Chronology of the Iron Age in Sub-Saharan Africa." *Current Anthropology* 10(2–3):226–229.

————. 1970. *Igbo-Ukwu.* 2 vols. Evanston: Northwestern University Press.

————. 1978. *Nigeria: Its Archaeology and Early History.* London: Thames and Hudson.

Shinnie, Peter L. 1971. "The Sudan." In *The African Iron Age.* Edited by Peter L. Shinnie. Oxford: Clarendon Press, pp. 89–107.

————., ed. 1971. *The African Iron Age.* Oxford: Clarendon Press.

Sidibé, Mamby. 1929. "Les sorciers mangeurs d'hommes au Soudan Français." *Outre-Mer* 1:22–31.

————. 1930. "Nouvelles notes sur la chasse au Birgo (Cercle de Kita, Soudan Français)." *Bulletin du Comité d'Études historiques et scientifiques de l'Afrique Occidentale Français* 13(1):48–67.

————. 1959. "Les gens de caste ou *nyamakala* au Soudan français." *Notes africaines* no. 81:13–17.

Sieber, Roy. 1961. *The Sculpture of Northern Nigeria.* New York: Museum of Primitive Art.

————. 1972. *African Textiles and Decorative Arts.* New York: Museum of Modern Art.

————. 1972. "Kwahu Terracottas, Oral Traditions, and Ghanaian History." In *African Art and Leadership.* Edited by Douglas Fraser and Herbert M. Cole. Madison: University of Wisconsin Press, pp. 173–183.

————. 1973. "Art and History in Ghana." In *Primitive Art and Society.* Edited by Anthony Forge. New York: Oxford University Press, pp. 70–96.

Sieber, Roy, and Arnold Rubin. 1968. *Sculpture of Black Africa: The Paul Tishman Collection.* Los Angeles: Los Angeles County Museum of Art.

Sigrid, Paul. 1970. *Afrikanische Puppen.* Berlin: Baessler-Archiv.

Simmons, William S. 1967. "The Supernatural World of the Badyaranke of Tonghia (Senegal)." *Journal de la Société des Africanistes* 37(1):41–72.

————. 1971. *Eyes of the Night: Witchcraft among a Senegalese People.* Boston: Little, Brown.

Soderberg, Bertil. 1968. "The Sistrum: A Musicological Study." *Ethnos* 33:90–133.

Soper, Robert C. "New Radiocarbon Dates for Eastern and Southern Africa." *Journal of African History* 15(2):175–192.

Soumaoro, Bourama, Charles S. Bird, Gerald Cashion, and Mamadou Kante. 1976. *Seyidu Kamara Da Donikiliw: Kambili.* Bloomington: African Studies Program, Indiana University.

Southall, Aidan W. 1970. "Stratification in Africa." In *Essays in Comparative Social Stratification.* Edited by Leonard Plotnicov and Arthur Tuden. Pittsburgh: University of Pittsburgh Press, pp. 231–272.

Srinivas, Mysore N. 1965 [1952], *Religion and Society among the Coorgs of South India.* New York: Asia Publishing House.

————. 1962. *Caste in Modern India and Other Essays.* New York: Asia Publishing House.

Stevenson, H. N. C. 1954. "Status Evaluation in the Hindu Caste System." *Journal of the Royal Anthropological Institute* 84(1–2):45–65.

Stone, George Cameron. 1961 [1934]. *A Glossary of the Construction, Decoration and Use of Arms and Armor in All Countries in All Times, Together with Some Closely Related Subjects.* New York: Jack Brussel.

Sutton, J. E. G. 1971. "The Interior of East Africa." In *The African Iron Age.* Edited by Peter L. Shinnie. Oxford: Clarendon Press, pp. 154–159.

————. 1972. "New Radiocarbon Dates for Eastern and Southern Africa." *Journal of African History* 13(1):1–24.

Szumowski, G. 1957. "Pseudotumulus des environs de Bamako." *Notes africaines* no. 75:66–73.

————. 1958. "Pseudotumulus des environs de Bamako (suite)." *Notes africaines* no. 77:1–11.

Talley, Geannine E. 1977. "The Blacksmith: A Study in Technology, Myths and Folklore." Ph.D. diss., University of California at Los Angeles.

Tautain, L. 1884. "Notes sur les castes chez les Mandingues, et en particulier chez les Banmanas." *Revue d'Ethnographie* 3:343–352.

Tauxier, Louis. 1921. *Le noir de Bondoukou.* Paris: Éditions Ernest Leroux.

————. 1927. *La religion Bambara.* Paris: Paul Geuthner.

————. 1942. *Histoire des Bambara.* Paris: Paul Geuthner.

Tegnaeus, Harry. 1950. *Le héros civilisateur.* Stockholm: Studia Ethnographica Upsaliensia.

Tellem; 10 jaar onderzoek in West Afrika. 1975. Utrecht: Instituut voor Antropobiologie von de Rijksuniversiteit.

Thomas, Louis Vincent. 1959. *Les Diola; essai d'analyse fonctionelle sur une population de Basse-Casamance.* Mâcon: Imprimerie Protat Frères.

Thomassey, Paul, and Raymond Mauny. 1951. "Campagne de fouilles à Koumbi Saleh." *Bulletin de l'I.F.A.N.* 13(2):438–462.

————. 1956. "Campagne de fouilles à Koumbi Saleh (Ghana?)." *Bulletin de l'I.F.A.N.* 18(1–2):117–140.

Thompson, Robert Farris. 1969. "Abatan: A Master Potter of the Egbado Yoruba." In *Tradition and Creativity in Tribal Art.* Edited by Daniel Biebuyck. Berkeley: University of California Press, pp. 120–182.

———. 1971a. "Aesthetics in Traditional Africa." In *Art and Aesthetics in Primitive Societies.* Edited by Carol Jopling. New York: E. P. Dutton, pp. 374–381.

———. 1971b. *Black Gods and Kings.* Los Angeles: Museum of Cultural History, University of California.

———. 1973. "Yoruba Artistic Criticism." In *The Traditional Artist in African Societies.* Edited by Warren d'Azevedo. Bloomington: Indiana University Press, pp. 19–61.

———. 1974. *African Art in Motion.* Los Angeles: University of California Press.

Traore, Dominique. 1965. *Comment le noir se soigne-t-il? Ou médecine et magie africaines.* Paris: Présence Africaine.

Traore, Issa B. 1961. *Un héros: Koumi-Diosse.* Bamako: Éditions Populaires.

Traore, Mamadou. 1943. Untitled article. *Notes africaines* no. 18:10.

Travélé, Moussa. 1913. *Petit dictionnaire français-bambara et bambara-français.* Paris: Paul Geuthner.

———. 1928. "Note sur les coutumes des chasseurs bambara et malinké du cercle de Bamako (Soudan Français)." *Revue d'Ethnographie et des Traditions populaires* 9(34–36):207–212.

———. 1929. "Le Komo ou Koma." *Outre-Mer* 1:127–150.

———. 1931. "Usages relatifs aux jumeaux en pays Bambara." *Outre-Mer* 3(1): 99–102.

Trigger, Bruce G. 1969. "The Myth of Meroe and the African Iron Age." *African Historical Studies* 2(1):23–50.

Trimingham, J. Spencer. 1961. *Islam in West Africa.* Oxford: Clarendon Press.

———. 1962. *A History of Islam in West Africa.* London: Oxford University Press.

Turner, Victor. 1967. *A Forest of Symbols.* Ithaca: Cornell University Press.

Tylecote, Roland F. 1975. "The Origin of Iron Smelting in Africa." *West African Journal of Archaeology* 5:1–9.

———. 1970. "Iron Working at Meroe, Sudan." *Bulletin of the History of Metallurgy* 4:62–72.

———. 1976. *A History of Metallurgy.* London: Metals Society.

Tymowski, Michael. 1967. "Le Niger, voie de communication des grands états du Soudain occidental jusqu'à la fin du XVIᵉ siècle." *Africana Bulletin* no.6: 73–95.

Underwood, Leon. 1964. *Masks of West Africa.* London: Alec Tiranti.

van der Merwe, Nikolaas J. 1969. *The Carbon-14 Dating of Iron.* Chicago: University of Chicago Press.

———. 1980. "The Advent of Iron in Africa." In *The Coming of the Age of Iron.* Edited by Theodore A. Wertime and James D. Muhly. New Haven: Yale University Press, pp. 463–506.

van der Merwe, Nikolaas J., and Minze Stuiver. "Dating Iron by the Carbon-14 Method." *Current Anthropology* 9(1):48–53.

Vansina, Jan. 1968. "The Use of Ethnographic Data as Sources for History." In *Emerging Themes of African History.* Edited by T. O. Ranger. Dar es Salaam: East African Publishing House, pp. 97–124.

———. 1969. "The Bells of Kings." *Journal of African History* 10(2):187–197.

———. 1979. *Children of Woot.* Madison: University of Wisconsin Press.

Vaughan, James H., Jr. 1970. "Caste Systems in the Western Sudan." In *Social Stratification in Africa.* Edited by Arthur Tuden. New York: Free Press, pp. 59–92.

———. 1973. "əŋkyagu as Artists in Marghi Society." In *The Traditional Artist in African Societies.* Edited by Warren d'Azevedo. Bloomington: Indiana University Press, pp. 162–193.

Vlach, John M. 1973. *Phillip Simmons: Afro-American Blacksmith.* Bloomington: Folklore Students Association Preprint Series, Indiana University.

Vogel, Susan, ed. 1981. *For Spirits and Kings: African Art from the Paul and Ruth Tishman Collection.* New York: Metropolitan Museum of Art.

Wainwright, G. A. 1945. "Iron in the Napatan and Meroitic Ages." *Sudan Notes and Records* 26:4–35.

Weil, Peter M. 1971. "The Masked Figure and Social Control: The Mandinka Case." *Africa* 41(4):279–293.

———. 1972. "Mande Age Grade Systems: Social Persistence and Cultural Flexibility in History." Paper presented at the Conference on Manding Studies, University of London, School of Oriental and African Studies.

———. 1973. "The *Chono:* Symbol and Process in Authority Distribution in Mandinka Political Entities of Senegambia." Paper presented at the Southwestern Anthropological Association Meeting, San Francisco.

———. 1976. "Agrarian Slavery to Capital Farming in a West African Society." Paper presented at the 75th Annual Meeting of the American Anthropological Association, Washington, D.C.

Welmers, William. 1958. "The Mande Languages." *Georgetown University Monograph Series* 11:9–24.

———. 1971. "Niger-Congo, Mande." In *Current Trends in Linguistics, Vol. 7 (Linguistics in Sub-Saharan Africa).* Edited by T. A. Sebeok. The Hague: Mouton, pp. 113–140.

Wertime, Theodore A. 1980. "The Pyrotechnologic Background." In *The Coming of the Age of Iron.* Edited by Theodore A. Wertime and James A. Muhly. New Haven: Yale University Press, pp. 1–24.

Wertime, Theodore A., and James D. Muhly, eds. 1980. *The Coming of the Age of Iron.* New Haven: Yale University Press.

Wilks, Ivor. 1961. *The Northern Factor in Ashanti History.* Legon: Institute of African Studies.

Willett, Frank. 1971a. *African Art, an Introduction.* London: Oxford University Press.

———. 1971b. "A Survey of Recent Results in the Radiocarbon Chronology of Western and Northern Africa." *Journal of African History* 12(3):339–370.

Williams, Denis. 1969. "African Iron and the Classical World." In *Africa in Classical Antiquity.* Edited by L. Thompson and J. Ferguson. Ibadan: Ibadan University Press, pp. 62–81.

———. 1974. *Icon and Image: A Study of Sacred and Secular Forms of African Classical Art.* New York: New York University Press.

Wilson, Monica. 1951. *Good Company: A Study of Nyakyusa Age-Villages.* London: International African Institute.

Wright, Bonnie L. Forthcoming. "The Power of Articulation." In *The Creativity of Power.* Edited by William Arens and Ivan Karp.

Zahan, Dominique. 1950. "Pictographic Writing in the Western Sudan." *Man* 50:136–138.

———. 1960. *Sociétés d'initiation Bambara: Le N'Domo, Le Koré.* Paris: Mouton.

———. 1963. *La dialectique du verbe, chez les Bambara.* Paris: Mouton.

———. 1972. "Modèle et l'objet d'art chez les Bambara (Mali)." Paper presented at the Conference on Manding Studies, University of London, School of Oriental and African Studies.

———. 1974. *The Bambara.* Leiden: E. J. Brill.

———. 1980. *Antilopes du soleil: arts et rites agraires d'Afrique noire.* Vienna: A. Schendl.

Zeltner, Francois de. 1910a. "La confrérie du N'Tomo en Afrique occidentale." *Bulletin et Mémoires de la Société d'Anthropologie,* ser.6, 1(June 16):322–323.

———. 1910b. "Le culte du Nama au Soudan." *Bulletin et Mémoires de la Société d'Anthropologie,* ser.6, 1(July 21):361–362.

Index

Abstraction: in sculpture, 102, 104, 105, 106, 108, 122–123; in other blacksmiths' activities, 103

Aesthetics, 38, 39, 106–107, 143. *See also* Sculpture: aesthetic considerations

Agriculture, 2, 4, 33–34, 40, 41, 50, 104, 120, 147

Ambiguity of smiths' profession, 9, 10, 11, 13, 130, 156. *See also* Blacksmiths: ambivalence toward; Blacksmiths: as sorcerers

Amulets: covers, 6, 16, 58, 202n16; makers, 6, 7, 16, 17; uses, 13, 14, 16, 58, 60–64 *passim*, 131; and *nyama*, 16, 59, 60; knotted string, 43; types, 58–64, 68, 207n66; antidotes, 63

Appia, Béatrice, 20

Archinard, Louis, 35

Arnoldi, Mary Jo, 101

Articulation, 25, 26–27, 28, 37–39, 42, 43, 106, 126, 129, 143, 144, 146, 149, 155; of social and spiritual space, 40, 50, 51, 64, 66, 72

Aubert, Alfred, 7–8

Badenya, 14, 64, 156

Badyaranke, 128

Ballo, Sidi: his bird masquerade, 47, 103, 106, 107–108, 154, 163; on iron lamps, 118; on iron figures, 125

Bamako, 10, 25, 35, 44, 45, 46, 56, 62, 64, 65, 70, 114, 118, 123–126 *passim*, 132, 144, 204n20, 210n43, 211n80&106, 212n116, 214n3

Banamba, 31

Baninko, 201n6 (preface)

Bani River, 122, 124, 127

Bards, 3, 20, 62, 159, 201n1(I); efficacy of their speech, 7; and *nyama*, 16

Basi, 59, 112, 124

Bazin, Hippolyte, 108, 207n54&55, 209n20

Beafada (Biafada), 128

Bèlèdougou, 31, 55, 65, 126, 203n9, 212n113

Bellamy, Dr., plant collector, 8

Bellows, 23, 24; rhythms, 24–25, 36

Benin (kingdom), 115, 121

Berreman, Gerald, 157, 160

Binger, Louis-Gustave, 57

Bird, Charles, 15, 55, 125, 137, 153, 155

Bird masquerade, 47, 106

Blacksmiths, 148; knowledge, 3, 7, 8, 12, 16, 20–21, 41, 42–43, 44, 49–50, 51, 52, 56, 57, 61, 63, 64–65, 66, 68–72 *passim*, 150, 151; ambivalence toward, 3, 4, 7–10, 11, 13, 14, 15, 18, 19–20; as sorcerers, 3, 8, 102, 133, 136–145 *passim*, 148, 151; and *nyama*, 3, 12, 16, 17, 18, 19, 20–21, 59, 64, 151, 152, 159; as advisers, intermediaries, mediators, 7, 8, 9, 40, 64–66, 148; female clan members, 7, 22; as doctors, 8, 56–58, 148; and bush spirits, 8, 18, 20, 102; as rulers, 9; joking relationships, 10; trade monopolies, 12, 148; dramatic and aggressive behavior, 15, 136, 142–143; and bush, 17, 18, 22; legendary, 19, 52, 127, 146; apprenticeship, 22, 23, 27, 28, 30, 39; in communities, 22; masters, 23, 25, 30–31, 32; specializations, 32, 36, 50, 51, 56, 58, 64, 66, 101–102; gun-making, 36; trade secrets, 41; and *daliluw*, 43, 44; and occult poisons, 44; inherited skills and knowledge, 43, 50–51, 56–57, 150, 151, 161, 162; as diviners, 52–56 *passim*; and amulets, 58–64, 207n66; neutrality of, 64; as circumcisors, 66–71 *passim*; and *kòmò*, 130; as entrepreneurs, 148; as articulators, facilitators, transformers, 149, 150–151, 154, 156, 162, 163, 164

Boat makers, 27, 34

Bobo, 115, 214n14

Boliw, 59, 131, 132, 138, 211n103

Bondoukou, 46

Bouglé, Celestin, 156–157, 160

Bougouni, 31, 45, 118, 122, 123, 124, 142, 144, 204n20, 209n32, 212n116

Bozo, 57, 61, 115, 122, 127, 129, 214n14

Braco, 129

Bravmann, René, 46, 115

Brett-Smith, Sarah, 55, 207n56

Brink, James T., 103, 107

Brooks, George, 148

Bush, 17, 19, 20, 26, 71, 133, 134, 137

Camara, Seydou, 50, 53–56 *passim*, 109, 110

Campbell, Morrow, 23

Casamance, 128

Caste: application to *nyamakalaw*, 8–9, 156–161 *passim*; Indian system, 8, 9, 156–158, 160

Circumcision, 19, 103, 113–114, 130, 208n75

Cissé, Youssouf, 15, 17, 119, 120, 207n56

Ci wara, 39
Clarity (*jayan*), 108, 143, 144
Competition, 14, 17, 19, 69

de Mota, Teixeira, 128, 129
Daget, Jacques, 61
Daliluw, 103, 111; defined, 42; uses, 43, 56, 68, 69, 71, 113, 114, 121, 124, 131; gift, 43, 59; owners, 43, 47; dangers, 44; types, 44, 113; fire-spitting, 44–46; invisibility, 47, 48
Dankelen, 135, 154
Dankòròba, 154
Decoration, 27, 37, 38. *See also* Sculpture: decoration
Delafosse, Maurice, 15, 115
Desplagnes, Louis, 31, 115
Dibi, 143, 144
Dieterlen, Germaine, 17, 50, 70, 119, 208n75 &76
Dioila, 115
Divination: practitioners, 6, 7, 13, 47, 48, 51–56 *passim;* beliefs about, 51–52, 56, 110; types of, 51–56 *passim*, 206n36 &42&44; and *nyama*, 51, 54; and *kòmò*, 132, 137, 141
Djalonke (Jallonke), 52
Dochard, Staff Surgeon, 32, 62–63
Dogon, 31, 37, 115, 121–122, 214n14
Donko, 115, 210n37
Douga, 212n117
Dumont, Louis, 156, 157
Dunbiya, Dramane, 25, 29, 107, 124, 127
Durand, Oswald, 8
Dyara, Fa Sine, 52
Dyula, 35, 36

Edo, 121
Elders, 18, 40, 66, 67, 68, 113, 115, 126, 130, 135
Endogamy, 3, 4, 41, 157, 158, 159
Epic poetry, 1, 6, 13, 14, 103, 137, 155
Ezra, Kate, 123

Fadenya, 14, 69, 156
Fakoli, 109
Fane, Magan: on occult objects, 61, 62, 132; on circumcision, 69, 70; on carving, 102; aesthetics, 107; on iron-art, 112–115 *passim*
Farim, 129
Farmers, 1, 2, 4, 10, 22, 32, 33, 38
Faseke, Bala, 62
Father childness, 14, 69, 156
Fetish, 18. *See also* Power objects
Filth: as translation of *nyama*, 8, 18
Finaw (*funew*), 7
Fire powder, 45
Fire-spitting, 44–46, 142, 144
Forges, 23, 24, 28, 30

Forging: tools, 28, 29, 30; techniques, 29; hammering rhythms, 30
Fouta Djallon, 8, 128
Fula, 5, 8, 10, 56, 61, 112, 128

Gambia River, 32, 58, 62, 122, 127, 128, 208n75
Garankew, 6
Gellner, Ernest, 160
Ghana Empire, 201n2(I)
Glaze, Anita J., 115
Goldwater, Robert, 123–124
Goucher, Candice L., 23
Gray, William, 32, 58, 62, 125
Griaule, Marcel, 17, 122
Gundow, 41, 61, 141
Guns and gun-making, 35–37, 38, 112, 204n20
Gurma, 214n14
Gwan, 105, 109

Harley, George, 53
Harmony, social and spiritual, 14, 17, 53, 55, 64–66, 151
Haselberger, Herta, 115
Hausa, 120
Henry, Joseph: description of *nyama*, 15, 17, 18; observations about bush spirits, 18; payments for amulets, 59, 207n55; *boliw*, 131, 132, 211n103, 213n123; on *kòmò*, 136, 137, 142, 211n106
Herbert, Eugenia, 57
Heroes, 13, 14, 49, 51, 71, 153, 155, 156
Hopkins, Nicholas, 40, 64, 203n1
Hunters, 2, 5, 17, 35; fraternities, 1, 5, 143; and *nyama*, 16, 133; and the bush, 17, 58; equipment, 35, 112; and blacksmiths, 71–72; and women, 125
Hutton, J. H., 157

Ideology, 149, 152–156, 159, 160–164
Igbo, 121, 122
Imperato, Pascal, 39, 53, 57, 119; on iron objects, 118, 120, 122, 124, 127; on hunters' hats, 126
Inherited powers and attributes, 3, 7, 43, 150, 161, 162. *See also* Blacksmiths: inherited skills and knowledge
Initiation associations, 13, 19, 101, 106, 109, 124. *See also Ci wara; Gwan; Jo; Kòmò; Kònò; Kore; Ntomo*
Iron: sources of, 31; imported, 31; traditionally smelted, 60, 114
Iron lamps: distribution, 114–115; types of, 115, 116; figural aspects, 116; uses of, 118–119; symbolism of, 119–120
Iron smelting, 3, 16, 18, 20–21, 31, 60, 126, 148. *See also* Blacksmithing techniques: smelting; *Nyama* and iron smelting
Iron smelting furnaces, 20–21, 23, 31–32;

types, 31; air tubes (tuyeres), 32; charcoal, 32

Iron working: bellows work, 23–26, 36; forging, 28–31, 116, 123; quenching, 29–30; smelting, 31–32; gun-making, 35–37; use of flux, 36; products, 29, 30, 32, 33, 35, 39

ja, 103
Jago (jako), 107, 108
Jayan, 108, 143, 144
Jealousy, 12, 14, 64, 65, 69, 155
Jeliw. See Bards
Jinèw. See Spirits: bush
Jiridòn. See Science of the trees
Jo, 124
Jobson, Richard, 32, 62, 208n75
Johnson, John William, 17, 18
Joking relationships, 10–11
Jow. See Initiation associations

Kaarta, 2, 3, 8, 9, 125
Kabu, 128
Kala (word), 8, 18
Kante, Sumanguru, 60–63 *passim*, 126, 153, 161
Karp, Ivan, 160–161
Kayes, 20, 31, 45
Kendall, Martha, 153, 155, 161
Ketkar, Shridhar, 157
Khasonke, 8, 114
Kilisi. See Secret speech
Kita, 64
Knowledge: and power, 12, 13, 41, 42–51 *passim*, 58–64 *passim*, 71, 72, 103, 109, 110, 112, 113, 114, 121, 124–125, 126, 127, 130–142 *passim*, 144, 150, 155
Kolokani, 64
Kòmò, 13, 19, 48, 59, 68, 119, 149. *See also* Initiation associations
Kòmò horns (*kòmò buruw*), 131, 132–133, 212n107
Kòmò masks (*kòmòkunw*), 19, 46, 47, 154; functions, 129, 130, 131, 137, 139, 140–143; ambiguity, 130, 134; and *nyama*, 132, 134, 135; construction, 133, 212n109; and bush spirits, 134, 135, 139–140; age, 134–135; costumes, 135–136; symbolism, 136–138; performing, 137, 138, 139–140; aesthetics, 143–144
Konate, Ba Sinale, 117, 118
Konate, Mama, 118
Konipo, M., 61
Kònò, 105
Kore, 104, 105, 109
Kòròtiw, 44, 49, 69, 111
Koulikoro, 62–63
Kouloubali, Mamari Biton, 66
Kule, 5, 18, 101, 202n14
Kuranku, 52

Labouret, Henri, 10, 15, 17, 43, 50

Laing, Alexander Gordon, 52–53, 54, 57, 58, 61, 66
Laye, Camara, 52
Leaders, 2, 13, 16, 40, 41, 66, 123, 127, 128, 130
Leather workers, 3, 6, 16, 34, 159
Ligbi, 46

Maesen, Albert, 46
Mali Empire, 1, 2, 62, 109, 127–130 *passim*
Mandinga, 201n3 (preface)
Mandingo, 32, 115, 201n3 (preface), 208n75
Mandinka, 122, 127
Marabouts, 6, 51, 52, 60, 110, 132, 205n24
Marghi, 158
Markala, 10, 101, 106, 201n10, 203n1
Masiri, 107, 108, 118, 143
"Masters of medicine," 47
"Masters of secret things," 47
"Masters of the leaves," 47
"Means," 154, 155, 156, 162, 163
Meat vendors, 5
Medicine, traditional, 6, 7, 8, 13, 45, 47, 56–58
Meillassoux, Claude, 203n53
Monteil, Charles: remarks about slaves, 2–3; description of *nyamakalaw*, 8; view of blacksmiths, 8; description of *nyama*, 15, 17; on people's perceptions of smiths, 20; description of blacksmith myth, 52; on Mamari Kouloubali, 66; on *boliw*, 132; on *kòmò*, 136, 142, 212n106, 213n123
Moore, Francis, 32
Mopti, 115
Moriw, 6
Mother childness, 14, 64, 156
Musa, Red, 110
Muslims, 62, 64, 66
Muso Koroni, 127
Myths, 19, 62, 109, 125, 127, 130, 146

Nama, 68
N'Diaye, Bokar, 5, 8, 18, 19
Ndomajiri, 19, 127, 146
Nègè, 60
Nganaw. See Heroes
Niany, blacksmith, 8
Niger River, 62, 115, 122
Nobles, 1, 4
Ntomo, 19, 109, 146, 163. *See also* Initiation associations; Ndomajiri
Numuw. See Blacksmiths
Nupe, 115
Nya gwan, 130
Nyama, 41, 71, 103, 112; and specialized professional clans, 3; and words, 7, 16, 43; defined, 15; and sorcery, 15; beliefs about, 15–19, 120; and iron working, 16, 148; and iron smelting, 16, 20–21, 60; and political power, 16; and the bush, 16, 17; as a

Nyama (*continued*)
    rationale for behavior, 16, 17, 64; as an ex-
    planation for the organization of the world,
    16; as a system of cause and effect, 17; and
    bush spirits, 18; as meaning feces, trash,
    18; neutrality of, 42; and circumcision,
    69–70; and *kòmò* masks, 131
Nyama (word), 8
Nyamakala. See Specialized professional
    clans
Nyamakala (word), 8, 18, 152, 203n53
Nya. See "Means"
Nyègèn, 108

Obscurity (*dibi*), 143–144
Occult energy. *See Nyama.*

Pajadinca, 128
Pâques, Viviana, 5, 120, 123
Park, Mungo, 31, 57–58, 61, 62, 125
Pharmacopoeia, traditional, 42
Phosphorescence, 45
Podo, 115
Poisons, occult, 44, 49, 69, 111, 126, 136
Pottery, 7, 22, 34
Power objects, 59, 62, 63, 113, 124, 126,
    130–145 *passim*
Praise sayers, 7
Prouteaux, Maurice, 46
Pyroengraving, 27, 105, 108

Quenching, 29–30

Raffenel, Anne, 8, 56
Revenge, 12, 14
Ritual, 43, 59, 112, 118, 127, 140, 148
Ro-Ponka, 129

Sacrifice, 54, 55, 59, 60, 112, 114, 124, 126,
    127, 133, 134, 135, 138, 143, 144, 203n6
Samory, 35, 36, 113
San, 25, 123
Saraka, 59. *See also* Sacrifice
Science of the trees, 42, 47, 48; relation to
    Western biology, 42; ingredients, 42
Sculpture: as blacksmiths' prerogative, 101;
    made by non-smiths, 101; types of, 101,
    103–107 *passim*, 109–112 *passim*, 131,
    132; style characteristics, 102–107 *passim*;
    style and Mande ideology, 102–110; aes-
    thetic considerations, 102, 105, 106, 107–
    109, 112–113, 117–118, 121, 126–127,
    138, 143–144; decoration, 107–109, 113,
    115, 117–118, 122, 123, 127, 143, 144;
    makers' personal variations, 105. *See also*
    Wood carvers: who are not *nyamakalaw;*
    Articulation; Decoration
Sèbènw, 58, 59. *See also* Amulets

Secrecy, 14, 41, 47, 51, 62, 111, 121, 126,
    130, 134, 141, 148, 150
Secret speech, 43, 48, 55, 56, 59, 69, 113
Ségou (state), 2, 3, 5, 62, 66, 125, 126,
    203n2
Ségou (town and area), 10, 15, 29, 44, 70,
    101, 106, 114, 115, 116, 136, 142, 203n2,
    207n66, 208n75&76, 213n123
Ségou Koro, 201n10
Senou, 9, 28, 202n14
Senufo, 46, 115, 206n44
Sidibé, Mamby, 40
Siw, 3, 113
Slave association, 3
Slaves, 1–4 *passim*
Smallpox variolation, 57
Snakes, 17, 52–53, 56
Social status, 7, 8, 9
Social structure: tripartite, 1; prohibitions
    and sanctions, 4, 130
Sogonikun, 104, 111
Soldiers, 2, 16, 61, 125, 126
Somaw, 49
Somono, 5, 214n14
Songhai, 10
Songs: masquerade performance, 20, 152;
    kòmò, 48, 129, 135, 139–142 *passim;*
    blacksmiths', 49, 50; circumcision, 68;
    hunters', 109, 110
Soninke, 6, 114, 128
Soolima Nation, 52, 54, 61
Sorcerers: blacksmiths as, 8; character, 12;
    nyamakalaw as, 12; and the bush, 17;
    killed by *kòmò*, 19; their knives, 38; types,
    46–50
Sorcery, 11–15; potential danger, 3; anti-so-
    cial, 8, 11, 12, 14, 48, 49, 58, 64, 69, 72,
    114, 131, 140, 141, 144, 152; Western per-
    ceptions, 11, 149; neutrality, 11–12; po-
    tential danger, 12; general population's
    reluctance to practice, 12; Mande view,
    12–13; and researchers, 12–13; in epic po-
    etry, 13; as part of daily life, 13, 14; and
    drama, 13, 14; and secrecy, 13; and politi-
    cal leadership, 12, 13, 16, 66, 127, 130; as-
    sociated with *fadenya*, 14; as means for
    controlling *nyama*, 15; and hunters, 16;
    joined with technology in blacksmiths'
    work, 20; as a focal point for smiths' cre-
    dentials as mediators, 41; products, 59;
    and *kòmò*, 131, 132; battles, 141–142. *See
    also* Blacksmiths: as sorcerers; *Nyama:* and
    political power
Sorko, 115, 122, 214n14
Soumaouro, Bourama, 117
Sounsan, 52
Space, conceptualized, 17
Spears, 112; supernatural, 48; symbolism of,

113; ceremonial use of, 113–114; as occult protection, 113

Specialized professional clans, 1, 103; identifying characteristics, 3; endogamy, 3; apprenticeship, 3, 12; and "father childness," 14; ambivalence toward, 3, 4, 7–10, 14, 15; importance of their services, 4, 5; as separate races, 3, 20; other citizens' perceptions, 3, 4; payment for services, 4; income supplements, 4; members, 5–7; variation of membership by region, 5; spiritual power, 3, 16; their professional monopolies, 12. *See also* Blacksmiths: ambivalence toward; Blacksmiths: as sorcerers; Ambiguity of smiths' profession; Inherited powers and attributes

Spirits: ancestor, 8, 55, 120, 123, 127, 203n6; bush, 8, 16, 17, 18, 20, 52, 110, 112, 134, 141, 144, 148, 152, 154; power, 18, 20. *See also* Blacksmiths: and spirits; *Kòmò* masks

spit, 43, 59, 113, 132

Srinivas, M. N., 157

Staffs: distribution, 121–122, 127–129; formal features, 122–123; uses, 123–129 *passim*; symbolism, 125–126

Stevenson, H. N. C., 157

Subagaw, 48

Sumanguru, Satigi, 50, 52

Sumosa Yiraba, 142

Sunjata, 61, 62, 63, 109, 113, 125, 126, 129, 130, 136, 153, 161

Supernatural, 11, 15, 48, 68–69, 71, 112, 113, 124, 130, 147, 148, 151

Symbolism, 113, 119–120, 125–126, 130, 136

Technical expertise, 3, 20, 24, 26–37, 160

Technology, 20, 28–32, 35–37, 147, 148, 151, 154, 160

Tegnaeus, Harry, 156

Tennentou, 123

Tera, Kalilou, 25, 107, 114, 119, 120, 137, 144, 153, 154

Thompson, Robert Farris, 144

Tònw. See also Youth associations

Tools: blacksmiths', 24, 26–31; farmers', 33–34, 39; earth-moving, 34; cooking, 34; boat builders', 34; woodworkers' (*kule*), 34; leather workers', 34; weavers', 34; hunters', 35–37; gun-making, 36. *See also* Iron forging: tools; Wood carving: tools

Trade secrets, 41, 61, 141. *See also* Secrecy

Traore, Cekoro, 37

Traore, Issa Baba, 126

Traore, Sedu, 29, 60, 112, 119, 155; chief's attitude toward, 9; his Fula friends, 10;

and secrecy, 13; aggressive behavior, 15; his town, 22; his lack of apprentices, 22–23; his family, 23, 37; his bellows rhythms, 24–25; carving a stool, 26; helps a young carver, 28; vacation after harvest, 33; technique for making bullets, 35–36; his ideas about form, 38, 107; on the science of the trees, 42; on knowledge, 42; on *daliluw*, 43, 45, 60; views on smiths, 44, 110; on rainmaking, 50–51, 205n24; and divination, 54–55; his herbal medicine, 56–57; and amulets, 59, 63, 64, 202n16; on *nyama*, 59; on circumcision, 69, 70, 71, 103, 163; on the human soul, 71, 103; on bird masquerade, 106, 108; on aesthetic criticism, 106–108; on marabouts, 110; on *kòmò*, 129, 138, 145

Traore, Yaya, 144

Travélé, Moussa, 108, 207n54

Vaughan, James, 158, 159

von Luschan, Felix, 115

Wasoulou, 31, 55, 110, 117, 134, 139, 140, 203n9

Weavers, 34

Weil, Peter M., 127, 128

Wilderness. *See* Bush

Wilson, Monica, 11

"Wise person," 47

Witch. *See* Sorcerers

Wolof, 10, 158–161 *passim*

Women: in blacksmith clans, 7, 22, 130

Wood carvers: who are not *nyamakalaw*, 5–6; blacksmiths as primary, 7

Wood carving: tools, 23, 26, 27; products, 26, 27, 28, 34, 35, 37; techniques, 26–28, 35; obtaining wood, 26; decoration, 27

Words, 6; efficacy of, 7, 16, 43

Wright, Bonnie, 158, 159, 160

Writing, traditional, 55, 58, 59, 69, 119

Wuli, 58, 62

Yoruba, 51, 57, 115, 121, 144

Youth, 101, 163, 164

Youth associations, 101, 104, 106, 107, 118, 149, 163

Zahan, Dominique: interpretation of *nyamakala* membership, 5, 101; description of *nyama*, 15, 18; etymology for *nyamakala*, 18, 203n53; discussion of *ntomo* hostility toward smiths, 19; and *Ci wara*, 39; on circumcision, 70–71; and traditional scripts, 119; on *kòmò*, 136, 137